Teaching in
Black and White

Teaching in Black and White

The Sisters of St. Joseph in the American South

Barbara E. Mattick

The Catholic University of America Press

Washington, D.C.

There is neither Jew nor Greek, there is neither slave nor free person, there is not male and female; for you are all one in Christ Jesus.

—Galatians 3:26–28

CONTENTS

ILLUSTRATIONS

PREFACE

According to Southern historian Elizabeth Fox-Genovese, the American ideal of domesticity was common throughout the country, but was especially strong in the South. An examination of the work of Catholic nuns in St. Augustine, Florida, provides a vehicle for evaluating the validity of these paradigms regarding a Southern Catholic community in the middle of the nineteenth century. Writing about the Sisters of St. Joseph in Florida and Georgia has also offered an opportunity to tell more fully the story of these remarkable women and to evaluate their significance in Catholic, women's, and African American history as played out in Florida and Georgia. It also contributes to a broader understanding of the educational development in Florida and reforms in Florida and the South during the Reconstruction and Progressive eras.

Until the 1980s, the only works about the Sisters of St. Joseph were written by their own members, two as master's theses about the sisters' schools. Michael Gannon's works, *Rebel Bishop* (1964), a biography of Augustin Verot, and *The Cross in the Sand* (1965), a history of the Catholic Church in Florida from 1513 to 1870, provide a great amount of detail, but give traditional top-down interpretations. Jane Quinn's *The Story of a Nun: Jeanie Gordon Brown* (1978) also provides much valuable detail about the history of the Sisters of St. Joseph of St. Augustine, but it primarily focuses on a single member of the congregation and does not place her story in the broader historical context. Since the 1980s, a large body of scholarly research on women religious has been produced, spurred by the creation of the Conference on the History of Women Religious in 1989, which has resulted in many valuable essays and publications. Few of them, however, deal with Catholicism in the South as the major focus. During this same period, work on black history has come into its own.

The history of education in the South is another area where this book provides a broader understanding. The Sisters of Mercy's St. Mary's Academy/Sisters of St. Joseph's St. Joseph's Academy appears to have been typical of other convent schools for girls, but entries from *Pascua Florida*, the students' publication, add greatly to the previous theses about the Sisters of St. Joseph's schools by providing a better understanding from the students' point of view.

The introduction of this book provides several aspects of the historical context of the Sisters of St. Joseph's arrival in Florida from their home in a remote, but historically and religiously significant, part of France in 1866. Equally important, especially for those who are not familiar with Roman Catholicism, specifically the lives of women religious, is a short overview of women religious beginning in the Middle Ages: how there came to be sisters as well as nuns, the effect of the decisions made at the Council of Trent upon them, and how they reflected Catholic culture and, oddly enough, their own contribution to the ideals concerning the proper roles of women in the United States, particularly in the American South centuries later.

As an international institution, the Catholic Church provided a network for women religious; but were Catholic sisters able to utilize it in the same way Protestant women used church groups and woman's clubs? Chapter 1 is about the Sisters of Mercy who preceded the Sisters of St. Joseph to St. Augustine. Chapter 2, on the early Sisters of St. Joseph who arrived in St. Augustine in 1866, shows how these women from different orders, indeed, participated in an international network of women religious.

The heart of the book is Chapter 3, which explores the postbellum rivalry between the Catholic French sisters and the teachers and missionaries of the Protestant American Missionary Association (AMA). Most of the chapter's information comes from the approximately 335 letters the Sisters of St. Joseph wrote back to their motherhouse in Le Puy, France. Copies of fewer than half of the letters from the first couple years (1866–67), the 1880s, and early 1900s were held at the Archives of the Sisters of St. Joseph in St. Augustine. As I began my research, many of those letters had been translated and typed, and Sister Thomas Joseph McGoldrick, the archivist of the archives, gave me access to them. There were, however, few letters from the 1870s.

In March 2004, I spent two weeks in Le Puy, France, at the Sisters of St. Joseph's motherhouse to do further research. Assisted by Sister Jacqueline Pirot, a Sister of St. Joseph from Aurillac, France, I was able to locate and make copies of letters that were missing from the collection in St. Augustine. Not until the 2008 publication of Sister Thomas Joseph's book *Beyond the Call* was any of the correspondence by the French Sisters of St. Joseph accessible to the public. Sister Thomas Joseph passed away in March 2022.

After the sisters in Le Puy received letters from Florida, they numbered them and copied them into large ledger books. The handwriting is consistent, but very small and sometimes hard to read. They, of course, were written in French; even letters originally written in English were translated into French before being entered into the book. There were nearly 200 copied letters, plus a few loose original letters. Translating the French letters was extremely labor-intensive, but they provide a rare look into the day-to-day lives of these remarkable women, revealing their inner thoughts, struggles, and hopes and even their senses of humor, as they experienced the American South.

Of particular value are the sisters' comments about the black people they came to teach. Coming from a remote part of France, they had never seen black people before, and their comments are refreshingly candid. Their references to the Protestant missionaries with whom they competed to save black souls were also quite frank and demonstrate how keen the rivalry was between the two groups. Most of the letters retrieved from Le Puy were written between 1870 and 1875, the period of their most intense competition.

Complementing the letters from the sisters are those of the missionaries of the American Missionary Association (AMA) who went to Florida during the Civil War to teach the freedmen. Dr. Joe Richardson graciously lent me copies of letters he acquired during his extensive research on the AMA. Heretofore, the efforts to evangelize the freedmen after the Civil War have been known only from the Protestant viewpoint, with only slight references to Catholic opposition. *Teaching in Black and White* brings the two stories together and addresses such questions as: What was the nature of the sisters' work with freedmen? Did their efforts result in failure, as many, including Bishop Verot, thought, or were there lasting influences that superseded the fact that relatively few African Americans remained Catholic or converted to Catholicism? Were there any differences in the way the sisters taught black people and poor white people? How did their work compare to that of the AMA?

The next four chapters focus on major events that dominated the last part of the pioneer years of the Sisters of St. Joseph. Chapter 4 tells of the Sisters of St. Joseph of St. Augustine's heroic care of victims during Florida yellow fever epidemics in 1877 and 1888. Their service did much to earn the respect of Florida's non-Catholics. Chapter 5 focuses on the sisters' work with white students, usually girls, in their academies, especially St. Joseph's Academy in St. Augustine, as well as their short stint of teaching Apaches held at the Castillo de San Marcos in St. Augustine. Chapter 6 describes the circumstances that precipitated the end of the French Mission from Le Puy, France, to St. Augustine, and the growth of Irish influences in Florida's Catholic Church that followed. Chapter 7 brings the sisters' story into the twentieth century and includes the wave of anti-Catholicism in Florida's legislature during the 1910s.

Chapter 8 may appear to be a departure from the rest of the book, for it describes the work of a few of the Sisters of St. Joseph in Florida who were sent from the motherhouse in St. Augustine in 1867 to serve as missionaries in Savannah, Georgia. Two of these sisters were among the initial group that came from France in 1866. Their work in Georgia followed a different pattern. In 1870, Bishop Verot, who had been the bishop of Savannah with jurisdiction over most of Florida, became the bishop of the newly created Diocese of St. Augustine, giving up his former authority over Georgia. A new bishop of Savannah, Ignatius Persico, was named as the prelate for the state of Georgia. Within two months, Persico separated the sisters in Savannah from their St. Augustine motherhouse and changed their name to the Order of the Sisters of St. Joseph of Georgia. These sisters have a story of their own, apart from the story of the sisters in St. Augustine.

In my initial research on the Sisters of St. Joseph of Georgia, I could find only secondary sources. Because the sisters had been cut off from the motherhouse in Le Puy, there was no correspondence with superiors in Le Puy as there had been concerning the sisters in St. Augustine, nor were there any at the Archives of the Diocese of Savannah or at the Mary Willis Library in Washington, Georgia. There were, however, letters and other materials about them at the Archives of the Carondelet

Sisters of St. Joseph (CSJ) in Carondelet (St. Louis), Missouri. The Sisters of Georgia amalgamated with this larger branch of the Sisters of St. Joseph in 1922.

Earlier versions of parts of this book have been published previously. Some of the material concerning domesticity vis-à-vis the early Catholic education of girls by women religious is in the introduction, and material in Chapter 1, which covers the work of the Sisters of Mercy, was originally included in a chapter entitled, "Ministries in Black and White: The Catholic Nuns of St. Augustine, 1859–1869," published as part of Bruce L. Clayton and John A. Salmond, eds., "*Lives Full of Struggle and Triumph*": *Southern Women, Their Institutions, and Their Communities* (Gainesville: University Press of Florida, 2003), 109–25. The material about the work of the Sisters of St. Joseph of St. Augustine during two yellow fever epidemics, found in Chapter 4, comes from my essay "Facing the Yellow Jack: The Northeast Florida Yellow Fever Epidemics of 1877 and 1888," *El Escribano: The St. Augustine Journal of History* (2005): 63–83. An edited version of Chapter 7 about anti-Catholicism appeared as "Challenging Racism and Anti-Catholicism: The Sisters of St. Joseph and Catholic Education in Early Twentieth-Century Florida," *American Catholic Studies: Journal of the American Catholic Historical Society* 132, no. 1 (2021): 29–49.

ACKNOWLEDGMENTS

I could never have completed my book without the encouragement and support of many people. Dr. Elna Green, my professor
for the history of the American South, introduced me to wom-
en's history, a new field since I began my academic career back
in the 1960s. Dr. Maxine Jones's classes on African American
history also opened to me whole new perspectives on American
history. While writing a seminar paper on the 1888 yellow fever
epidemic in Jacksonville, Florida, for Dr. Joe Richardson's seminar on Social History, I discovered the Sisters of St. Joseph of
St. Augustine, who nursed yellow fever patients in Jacksonville.
I found the sisters to be intriguing; thus began over ten years of
satisfying research on their work. I am indebted to Dr. Edward
Keuchel, who generously gave me his entire research file on Sister Mary Ann Hoare.

Central to this study was the support I received from Sister
Thomas Joseph McGoldrick, SSJ, the archivist for the Sisters
of St. Joseph of St. Augustine. She very graciously opened the
archives to me, sharing with me the remarkable letters the sisters wrote back to their motherhouse in Le Puy, France, in the
early years of their ministry in Florida. The letters are a treasure
that Sister Thomas Joseph published in *Beyond the Call*, making
them available to the public. I am pleased to have been able to
contribute to the gathering of copies of letters that were missing
from the collection in St. Augustine. In March 2004, with support from Florida State University, I traveled to the Sisters of

St. Joseph's archives at the motherhouse in Le Puy, France, where the entire Order of the Sisters of St. Joseph was founded in 1650. There, I was able to add to my research files and to complete the collection of letters at the sisters' archives in St. Augustine. Critical to the research in France was Sister Jacqueline Perot, a Sister of St. Joseph from Aurillac, France, who gave nearly two weeks of her time to assist me with my research at the motherhouse. Her brother even met me at the airport in Paris and saw that I got on the correct train to Le Puy. Sadly, Sister Jacqueline died from the Covid-19 virus in 2020. I am also grateful for a J. Leitch Wright Jr. Travel Award and a Morris Endowment Summer Research Award that funded trips to Savannah and St. Augustine. Thanks also go to the late Dr. Joe Richardson, who provided copies of letters of the American Missionary Association teachers and ministers who came to Florida. Their letters, paired with those of the Sisters of St. Joseph, provide a vehicle to compare the two groups' work at a very personal level.

Early on in my research, I contacted Dr. Elizabeth Fox-Genovese at Emory University, now deceased. She told me of the History of Women Religious Conference, a triennial gathering for the presentation of papers on the history of women in religious orders. I am grateful to the conference for allowing me to present three papers, at the 2004, 2007, and 2019 triennial meetings. Special encouragement came from Dr. Diane Batts Morrow, Dr. Carol Coburn, and Sisters Pat Byrne and Karen Kennelly.

Besides Sister Thomas Joseph, several other librarians, archivists, and historians provided valuable assistance: Gillian Brown, archivist for the Diocese of Savannah; Flo Turcotte and Bruce Chappell at the P. K. Yonge Library at the University of Florida, Gainesville; Sisters of the Blessed Sacrament, who graciously provided copies of letters between Mother Katharine Drexel and Bishop John Moore; Charles Tingley, librarian at the St. Augustine Historical Society; Susan Parker, former colleague at the Florida Department of State and then executive director of the St. Augustine Historical Society; David Nolan, historian in St. Augustine; and the wonderful staff at the State Library of Florida who obtained all those interlibrary loan requests for me. Two of the original sisters who came from Le Puy to St. Augustine were sent to establish a mission in Savannah and ended their days in Georgia. The story of the Sisters of St. Joseph who worked in the South is not complete without an account of their work. In 2016, I traveled to the Archives of the Sisters of St. Joseph of Carondelet, located in St. Louis, Missouri. Sister Jane Behlmann, CSJ, CA, and Catherine Lucy, CA, graciously shared the records and photographs of the Sisters of St. Joseph of Georgia, a branch that sprang from the Sisters in St. Augustine. My thanks also go to Lynn Brady, who created the map, and to Joy Luczynski, who provided valuable technical assistance in creating the index.

Most of my research was completed while working full time for the Florida Department of State's Division of Historical Resources, Bureau of Historic Preservation. I am grateful to Frederick Gaske, the director of the division and my "boss," and for my colleagues at the bureau for being so supportive of my efforts.

Then, in 2012, I received an email from Dr. Trevor Lipscombe, director of the Catholic University of America Press, asking if I would be interested in publishing my work with the press. Dr. Lipscombe has been a strong support, patiently teaching me, a non-Catholic, the intricacies of Catholic culture and Canon Law. I found that my being an Anglican in the ecclesiastical *via media* served me well, allowing me to find my way amid accounts of the relations between the Catholics and Protestants I studied.

My thanks and love abound to my long-suffering husband, Stan, who prayed me through when it just seemed too tough to keep going, and to the Lord, who answered those prayers so faithfully.

ABBREVIATIONS

AMA   American Missionary Association
AME   African American Episcopal
ARC   Amistad Research Center
ASSJLP   Archives of the Sisters of St. Joseph, Le Puy
ASSJSA   Archives of the Sisters of St. Joseph of St. Augustine, St. Augustine
CAB   Colored Auxiliary Bureau
CSJ   Carondelet Sisters of St. Joseph
CSJA   Carondelet Sisters of St. Joseph Archives
CSSR   Redemptorist Fathers
CSV   Clerics of St. Viator
FSC   Brothers of the Christian Schools
JASA   Jacksonville Auxiliary Sanitary Association
OP   Order of Preachers (Dominicans)
OSB   Order of St. Benedict
RSM   Religious Sisters of Mercy
SAER   St. Augustine Evening Record
SJ   Society of Jesus (Jesuits)
SSJ   Sisters of St. Joseph
SSJGA   Sisters of St. Joseph of Georgia
SSJSA   Sisters of St. Joseph of St. Augustine
WPA   Works Progress Administration

Teaching in
Black and White

Introduction

⇌

In September 1866, shortly after the end of the Civil War, at the behest of the Catholic bishop over Florida, Augustin Verot, eight Catholic Sisters of St. Joseph from Le Puy, France, went to St. Augustine to teach the newly freed slaves in Florida. Verot was a native of Le Puy and was well aware of the Sisters of St. Joseph's work, particularly in education. He had come to the United States in 1830 to teach at the Sulpician College of St. Mary's in Baltimore, Maryland, so was also well acquainted with life in America, including the institution of slavery. Arriving in the "Ancient City" of St. Augustine, the French sisters were assisted by Sisters of Mercy, whom Verot had asked to come from the North shortly before the Civil War to teach white Catholic girls. The French sisters' mission was to protect the former slaves from the "heretical" teachings of Protestant missionaries who were already at work in Florida and to educate the blacks to be able to live in a free society as good Catholics. This book tells the story of the efforts of the Sisters of St. Joseph in Florida and Georgia and provides some analyses of their work through the lenses of the history of blacks, women, Florida, and Catholicism in the South, from the mid-nineteenth century to 1922.

Although since the 1980s there has been a growing interest in evaluating the impact of the Catholic Church on American history, relatively little has been written on the Catholic Church in the South, especially after the Civil War, and women's history has been dominated by analyses of Protestant women from the Northeast.[1] This Northeastern view emphasizes the development of networks and bonds between women in urban settings through voluntary associations, mother's clubs, and charitable works. Activities in such groups as the Women's Christian Temperance Union ultimately led to political involvement of women and social change. As women's historian Elizabeth Fox-Genovese pointed out, however, the antebellum South was overwhelmingly rural, and there was little opportunity for the development of such networks. The lives of most women in the rural South were defined in and by their specific households. Another women's historian, Jean Friedman, says that Southern women were also slow to embrace change because of the constraints imposed on them by a strongly evangelical Protestantism that pervaded the South as opposed to the generally more liberal Protestantism of the Northeast.[2]

Catholicism, however, was indeed present in the South and played a role in shaping the lives of women in the region, especially in communities where there was a Catholic church. This book explores the Catholic Church's influence, particularly through the impact of Catholic sisters (also called women religious), particularly those who arrived to establish schools in Florida in the middle of the nineteenth century. A brief overview of the centuries-old history of women religious and their religious culture, particularly in France, is necessary to understand the work of these sisters and their responses to what they encountered in the course of pursuing their missions.

Since the twelfth century, the Roman Catholic Church has

1. For an excellent collection of essays about Southern Catholicism before the Civil War, see Randall M. Miller and Jon L. Wakelyn, eds., *Catholics in the Old South: Essays on Church and Culture* (Macon, Ga.: Mercer University Press, 1983).

2. Elizabeth Fox-Genovese, *Within the Plantation Household: Black and White Women of the Old South* (Chapel Hill: University of North Carolina Press, 1988), 78, 81; Jean Friedman, *The Enclosed Garden: Woman and Community in the Evangelical South, 1830–1900* (Chapel Hill: University of North Carolina Press, 1985).

provided an avenue for single women to have ministries devoted to prayer, education, and service to the needy. Only single women who, as a result of widowhood or because they had never married, were eligible for vocations as nuns. During the Middle Ages, these women were seen as "brides of Christ" and assumed that status by professing the vows of poverty, chastity, and obedience. The vows were permanent, and only the pope could grant dispensations from them. For a brief time, some women were able to work outside the convents, the establishments where they lived in community with other nuns. Because their chastity was essential to their roles as "brides of Christ," Boniface VIII, who was the pope from 1294 to 1303, required that nuns be separated out and protected from the world in their convents. This "enclosure" in cloisters meant that they could not have contact with the laity, precluding any work among the poor and needy. Their primary duty was the worship of God, exercised through a strict regimen of prayer, fasting, and other forms of self-denial.

The Council of Trent convened several sessions between 1545 and 1563 to address the church's internal problems and to defend or clarify Catholic doctrine. Of the Protestant Reformation and its aftermath, the Counter-Reformation, historian Elizabeth Rapley, suggests that the church "responded by a hardening of its positions: a greater respect for the sacrament of the Eucharist, an enhanced devotion to the Virgin [Mary] and the saints, a more hierarchical and clerical ecclesiology, and a renewed emphasis on the superiority of the clerical over the lay state." The Council also maintained that faith was not enough for salvation—the performance of good deeds also was necessary—and that Protestantism's "in faith alone" belief was heretical. In "Canons Concerning Justification," Canon 9 says, "If anyone says that the sinner is justified by faith alone, meaning that nothing else is required to cooperate in order to obtain the grace of justification, and that it is not in any way necessary that he be prepared and disposed by actions of his own will, let him be anathema."[3]

By the seventeenth century, however, the Catholic Church espoused two tenets common to Protestantism. The first was a higher estimation of the value of the spirituality of the laity, an idea spurred by Catholic bishop Francis de Sales in his 1608 work *Introduction to the Devout Life*, in which he argued one did not have to be a vowed religious to be devoted to God, but could live a devout life as a lay person.[4] The second was the principle that in order to be saved, one must have one's own conscious and informed acceptance of Jesus as one's Savior.

The Council of Trent also reinforced the restrictions on women religious that had grown lax since Pope Boniface VIII had imposed enclosure on nuns. Once again, nuns were confined to convents to prevent their interaction with the outside world. Congregations that had taught girls in their convents continued to do so, but under the new rules, when outside of the classrooms, the students were restricted from contact with the nuns.[5]

In 1607, the Compagnie de Notre-Dame became the first officially recognized female teaching congregation in France. It was located mostly in southern France, where Huguenots (French Protestants) were most concentrated. The order was unusual in that its purpose was not only to worship God but also to educate girls. Its creation was motivated by a desire to counter the educational opportunities the Protestants were offering. The Filles de Notre Dame, as they were called, were modeled after the Jesuits, a masculine teaching order, but they also consciously

---

3. Elizabeth Rapley, *The Dévotes: Women and Church in Seventeenth-Century France* (Montreal and Kingston: McGill-Queen's University Press, 1990), 11; Carol Coburn and Martha Smith, *Spirited Lives: How Nuns Shaped Catholic Culture and American Life, 1836–1920* (Chapel Hill: University of North Carolina Press, 1999), 17; H. J. Schroeder, OP, "Canons Concerning Justification," in *Canons and Decrees of the Council of Trent* (Rockford, Ill.: TAN, 1978), 42–46.

4. Francis de Sales, *Introduction to the Devout Life*, trans., ed. John K. Ryan (New York: Image Doubleday, 1989), 43–44.

5. Schroeder, *Canons and Decrees of Trent*, 220–21.

adopted the curriculum established by the Reformers. As explained by the mother superior over the school, "'So that the girls will be attracted away from the tainted heretic schools and into this institution, we shall teach them reading, writing and various kinds of needlework—in short, all the accomplishments suitable for well-brought-up young maids.'"[6]

Another women's order, the Compagnie de Sainte-Ursule (Ursulines), originated in Italy in the 1580s but came to France in 1597, primarily as catechizers for girls. By 1700, ten to twelve thousand Ursulines had established about 320 communities throughout France. They provided free day schools for young girls and later opened boarding schools for wealthier paying students, a pattern of Catholic educational outreach that lasted for centuries.[7]

Some women wanted to establish orders that carried on the traditional tasks expected of women religious, prayer and contemplation, but also performed charitable works and taught. Francis de Sales's *Introduction to the Devout Life* inspired laywomen, including Jane Frances de Chantal, a baroness he had been advising, to found the Visitandines (Visitation Sisters) in 1610. They did not follow the strict ascetic practices of the enclosed convents or take solemn (canonically binding) vows. Prayer and contemplation were part of their daily regime, but significantly, visits to the sick and the poor were also among their duties. The issue of this "mitigated" enclosure was unacceptable to the local French archbishop, however, and despite de Sales's arguments concerning the abilities of women and the propriety of such work for them, in 1616 the Visitation Sisters were forced to remove themselves from the world and accept full enclosure. In the 1620s, Vincent de Paul sought to avoid a similar fate by

6. Rapley, *Dévotes*, 46.

7. See Querciolo Mazzonis, *Spirituality, Gender, and the Self in Renaissance Italy: Angela Merici and the Company of St. Ursula (1474–1540)* (Washington, D.C.: The Catholic University of America Press, 2007).

insisting that his Daughters of Charity not become women religious but remain lay women so as to elude the ecclesiastical and legal restrictions imposed on nuns. Daughters of Charity, therefore, made no public vows and wore regular clothing rather than habits. They formed a lay group, a confraternity, not a congregation of nuns. Such groups established schools and served in orphanages, hospitals, and refuges.[8]

Europe in the seventeenth century was in great turmoil, ravaged by wars, famines, and epidemics. Those who had opposed the women's work among the needy finally accepted the unconventional "nuns" simply because they needed their services. "Uncloistered" women such as the Daughters of Charity proliferated; in France alone, ninety such congregations were founded between 1600 and 1720. Among them were the Sisters of St. Joseph, founded in Le Puy about 1650 under the leadership of Jesuit priest Pierre Médaille. Their primary purpose was to provide Christian education to children, but they were also "to work for their salvation and to devote themselves to all the exercises of which they were capable for the service of the neighbor." A second directive expresses the range of their calling even more emphatically. They were to practice "all the holy spiritual and corporal works of mercy of which women are capable." The Sisters of St. Joseph soon spread throughout France. Although they, like other Catholics, were persecuted and suppressed during the French Revolution, they reconstituted in the early nineteenth century and were a major teaching order again by midcentury.[9]

The parameters established for women religious during the sixteenth and seventeenth centuries remained in force in

8. Rapley, *Dévotes*, 35–40; Coburn and Smith, *Spirited Lives*, 18–20.

9. For a detailed discussion of the early Sisters of St. Joseph, see Patricia Byrne, CSJ, "French Roots of a Women's Movement: The Sisters of St. Joseph, 1650–1836" (Ph.D. diss., Boston College, 1985); Marguerite Vacher, *Des "régulières" dans le siècle: Les soeurs de Saint-Joseph du Père Médaille aux XVII et XVIII siècles* (Clermont-Ferrand: Soeurs de Saint-Joseph de Clermont-Ferrand et Éditions Adosa, 1991), 69, 89–90.

the nineteenth century. In 1882, Sister Austin Carroll, a Sister of Mercy, translated *The Religious: A Treatise on the Vows and Virtues of the Religious State*, written by French theologian Jean-Baptiste Saint-Jure in 1658. The publisher considered the book to be the "greatest work of France's greatest theologian" and hoped it would "cause a greater diligence and assiduity in the care of religious perfection."[10] Quoting writings of the early church fathers, the work gives detailed insight into the intended purpose of vows and congregational rules in the lives of men and women religious: to facilitate their quest for perfection.

One entered the religious life by taking public vows; such vows were what set a religious apart from everyone else. In the nineteenth century, women and men religious publicly took vows of poverty, chastity, and obedience. Some orders or congregations took additional vows; Sisters of Mercy, for example, also took a vow of service. These vows could be perpetual or temporary, solemn or simple. Both solemn and simple vows were taken for life, usually after a temporary period. Solemn vows canonically forbade a religious to act contrary to them. For example, a solemn vow of chastity made it impossible for a religious to be canonically married, and a solemn vow of poverty made it impossible for a religious to inherit. Simple vows were in force only in the ecclesiastical/spiritual sense.[11] The distinction between solemn and simple vows was a defining factor in classifying women religious. Women who were cloistered and who lived out a vocation of worship and contemplation away from the rest of the world took solemn vows and were technically "nuns" and members of "orders." Women who practiced a modified contemplative life and worked "in the world" took simple vows and were technically "sisters" and members of "congregations." In common

---

10. J.-B. Saint-Jure, *The Religious: A Treatise on the Vows and Virtues of the Religious State* (New York: P. O'Shea, 1882), ix.

11. Hector Papi, SJ, *Religious Profession: A Commentary on a Chapter of the New Code of Canon Law* (New York: P. J. Kenedy and Sons, 1918), 6–7.

parlance, however, sisters were often referred to as nuns and as members of orders.

Saint-Jure considered the vow of obedience to be the "principal and most excellent of all." The vow requires obedience to one's direct superior, but superiors do not have absolute power. Each order or congregation has a rule that defines the purposes and regulations of the organization. Members of the order or congregation voluntarily accept this rule and are bound to obey it. Superiors are also bound by the rule in that they cannot order one under their authority to do something that is contrary to their order's rule. The rule of each order (often incorporated into their order's constitution), not canon law, provides the meaning and structure for each religious body and is sacrosanct. Saint-Jure's 240-page discussion of the virtues of obedience makes it clear, however, that he considered prompt, unquestioning, and cheerful obedience to be the most spiritually efficacious kind, a sure sign of self-annihilation, giving oneself up to God totally. He did allow, however, that there were some circumstances that were beyond the rule of obedience, giving examples, of such: "a command to go to preach the Gospel to the infidels, in countries where there would be danger of death or captivity; to fast for a long time, not to eat meat for a month, and similar things to which the rule *does not* oblige."[12] The book, intended to be read by religious, provides a clear view of the expectations demanded and the ideals to be sought by women religious in the nineteenth century. To a large degree, it explains the actions and responses of the Sisters of Mercy and Sisters of St. Joseph as they carried on their missions in Florida and Georgia in the second half of the nineteenth century and early twentieth century.

Another important aspect in understanding nineteenth-century Catholicism is the change that occurred in popular piety. The roots of these changes lie in official policies adopted

12. Saint-Jure, *Religious*, 376.

after the Council of Trent in the sixteenth and seventeenth centuries to purify the common practices of the laity. The official pietistic practices adopted by the Council of Trent, such as the necessity for ordained priests, devotion to Mary and the Sacred Heart, and praying for intercession by the saints, to name a few, remained in force in the nineteenth century. They were augmented when, in an effort to standardize Catholic practice and to unify the church under the See of Rome, Pius IX, who was the pope from 1846 to 1878, encouraged a renewal of popular piety practiced by the masses. Such devotion would strengthen the hierarchy of the church from Rome on down to the local parish.[13]

Although Catholic and Protestant ideas of domesticity in the nineteenth century were very similar in that both focused on a strong home as being essential to the welfare of society, the differences between them are best seen by comparing their pietistic practices. Protestants held that the home should be the center of devotions; pious families would gather around a family altar for daily devotions led by the father. Family Bibles held a prominent place in such homes, and personal Bible reading was considered the key to personal spiritual growth. An individual's personal relationship with God, rather than a communal, sacramental relationship with the church, was most important. Sunday worship at church centered on the preaching of God's Word and instruction, and services often took place throughout the day.[14]

In contrast, Catholics emphasized the importance of membership in the church community. Preaching was secondary to observing the priest perform the sacrifice of the Mass,

13. Mark R. Francis, CSV, "Liturgy and Popular Piety in a Historical Perspective," in *Directory on Popular Piety and the Liturgy: Principles and Guidelines, A Commentary*, ed. Peter C. Phan (Collegeville, Minn.: Liturgical Press, 2005), 39–43; Colleen McDannell, *The Christian Home in Victorian America, 1840–1900* (Bloomington: Indiana University Press, 1986), 14–15. McDannell's study focuses on Irish Catholics in the North, but many of her findings apply to Southern Catholics in places where there were Catholic churches.

14. McDannell, *Christian Home in Victorian America*, 56, 72, 90–91.

something that could only be done by a priest at the church. Although Catholics were not forbidden to read the Bible, personal Bible study was not encouraged until the very late nineteenth century, for fear that it would be misinterpreted by the untrained laity. As education became more widespread in the United States, Bible reading was promoted to a greater extent. Before then, instead of Bible reading, the church encouraged the use of the rosary, or "praying the beads." Catholics also tended to use religious articles such as statues, holy pictures, and medals. These were not to be worshiped, as claimed by the Protestants, but were to remind Catholics of religious teachings.[15] In chapter 3's examination of the work of the Sisters of St. Joseph and their Protestant counterparts from the American Missionary Association, the contrast among these different approaches to pious religion stands out distinctly.

Although religious orders were well established in Europe for centuries, the first nuns did not come to the United States until the 1790s. The Ursuline Sisters were, indeed, in New Orleans in 1727, but this was before Louisiana became part of the United States by way of the Louisiana Purchase in 1803.[16] The country as a whole at that time was "avowedly Protestant" and did not trust Catholics, considering them to be superstitious idolaters. During much of the colonial period, most of the British colonies outlawed Catholicism and prohibited Catholics from holding public office. The largest number of Catholics lived in Maryland, where by 1765 there were about 20,000 of them.

Roman Catholics, though few in number, were some of the strongest supporters of the Patriots during the American

15. McDannell, *Christian Home in Victorian America*, 65, 70, 85–89, 93; Francis, "Liturgy and Popular Piety," 39–40. See also Ann Taves, *The Household of Faith: Roman Catholic Devotions in Mid-Nineteenth-Century America* (Notre Dame, Ind.: University of Notre Dame Press, 1986).

16. See Emily Clark, *Masterless Mistresses: The New Orleans Ursulines and the Development of a New World Society, 1727–1834* (Chapel Hill: University of North Carolina Press, 2007), for discussion of the Ursulines' work in French colonial New Orleans and during the city's antebellum American period.

Revolution. John Carroll, a prominent Catholic from Maryland, was part of a diplomatic mission with other Patriots to try to persuade Quebec, Canada, to join in the Revolution. He was a valuable member of the committee because he spoke French fluently. Although his diplomatic efforts failed, Carroll was influential in the early establishment of the United States. Catholics comprised the largest religious contingent in the Continental Army. By 1780, Catholic volunteers from throughout the colonies made up one-third of the soldiers and contributed greatly toward supplying provisions and services. Catholic officers also contributed to the effort; several from Philadelphia were a major factor in the success of America's fledgling navy. During the war, the other colonies became much more tolerant toward Catholicism. This was partly because of the loyalty and contributions "the Papists" were making toward the war effort and partly because the Patriots needed to maintain good relations with their crucial Catholic allies, France and Spain. Tolerance remained in effect after the Patriots won the Revolution, and the new United States allowed Catholics the freedom to practice their religion as guaranteed in the First Amendment of the United States Constitution in 1789.[17] After the American victory, Pope Pius VI appointed John Carroll, who was a Jesuit priest born in Maryland, the bishop of Baltimore in 1789; he was the first Roman Catholic prelate in the United States. When other dioceses were established, the pope appointed Carroll to be the first archbishop of the United States. As such, he laid a strong foundation of the Roman Catholic Church in America.

With the great influx of immigrants from Ireland and Germany between 1829 and 1859, the number of Catholics increased rapidly, and European sisters were recruited by the American Catholic Church to operate schools, hospitals, orphanages,

17. Robert Emmett Curran, *Papist Devils: Catholics in British America, 1574–1783* (Washington, D.C.: The Catholic University of America Press, 2014), 246–74.

and other agencies to assist the needy immigrants; indeed, thirty-nine foundations, communities of sisters, were established in the antebellum period. Thomas P. McCarthy's *Guide to Catholic Sisterhoods in the United States*, which describes orders in existence in the mid-twentieth century, reveals that women who felt the call to such a life in the Catholic Church generally had to be between the ages of fifteen and thirty-six, of reasonable intelligence, in good health, and of high character to be accepted into a religious order. According to the *Catholic Encyclopedia*, 1911 edition, one aspiring to be a religious generally had to be at least sixteen years old and to have completed one year in the novitiate. Those conditions probably are not much different from those applied a hundred years before. In most cases today, a person must be at least eighteen years old to enter a novitiate.[18]

Most of the Catholic immigrants went to Northern cities, where American workers saw them as threats to jobs. Anti-Catholic sentiments soon exploded in parts of the North. Nuns and priests, many of them immigrants themselves, dedicated themselves to working with the new arrivals. They were subjected to physical and verbal attacks and were accused of fantastic sexual immorality, murder, and infanticide. Such attacks were justified in the eyes of their perpetrators because they considered the decision of nuns to live single lives of celibacy to be unnatural and their sworn obedience to their superiors, including the pope, to be anti-American. They even accused Catholics of plotting to take over the country for the pontiff. Unlike the North, however, the South was primarily rural, with comparatively few immigrants and even fewer Catholics. Thus, the anti-Catholic rage of the North was not prevalent in the prosperous antebellum South.[19]

18. Thomas P. McCarthy, CVS, *Guide to the Catholic Sisters in the United States* (Washington, D.C.: The Catholic University of America Press, 1952), passim; Arthur Vermeersch, "Religious Profession," in *The Catholic Encyclopedia*, vol. 12 (New York: Robert Appleton, 1911), accessed September 9, 2021, http://www.newadvent.org/cathen/12451b.htm.

19. Mary Ewens, OP, *The Role of the Nun in Nineteenth-Century America: Variations*

The unmarried lives of women religious, in particular, challenged American concepts of true womanhood or domesticity that was embodied by motherhood and submission to a husband. According to Alexis de Tocqueville in his 1840 commentary on American life, "In the United States the inexorable opinion of the public carefully circumscribes woman within the narrow circle of domestic interests and duties and forbids her to step beyond it."[20] The American ideology of domesticity arose from middle-class Protestants in the Northeast. It emphasized the essential role of the family in imparting cultural values and maintaining social order in times of disorder or change.

Women, indeed, owed it to society to fulfill the prescribed roles of wife and mother. In her article "The Cult of True Womanhood, 1820–1860," Barbara Welter described what was expected of women in antebellum America. The four primary virtues were piety or religious devotion, sexual purity, submissiveness, and domesticity. Religion was the province of women, for men were supposedly too occupied with the day-to-day life of business to be concerned with piety. Women, though, could pursue piety without neglecting their responsibilities of caring for the home. Sexual purity was not necessarily expected for men, but for women its "absence was unnatural and unfeminine." Without purity, a female could not be a true woman.[21]

Although social norms allowed for "single blessedness," considering a single life to be better than a "loveless or unhappy marriage," most women fulfilled these ideals of womanhood

on the International Theme (Thiensville, Wisc.: Caritas, 2014), 116; Randall M. Miller, "A Church in Cultural Captivity: Some Speculations on Catholic Identity in the Old South," in Miller and Wakelyn, *Catholics in the Old South*, 12; John Higham, *Strangers in the Land: Patterns in American Nativism, 1860–1925* (Westport, Conn.: Greenwood Press, 1981), 113.

20. Alexis de Tocqueville, *Democracy in America*, trans. Henry Reeve, unabridged vols. 1 and 2 (1835) (New York: Bantam Dell, 2004), 731. The Ursulines contributed to the rise of anti-Catholicism among American Protestants because their independence and the success of their shrewd business practices challenged men's preeminence and the Southern cult of domesticity; Clark, *Masterless Mistresses*, 264.

21. Barbara Welter, "The Cult of True Womanhood, 1820–1860," *American Quarterly* 18 (Summer 1966): 154; Fox-Genovese, *Within the Plantation Household*, 202.

in the state of marriage and from their homes. In their homes, women were expected to exercise piety, not only teaching their children, but also bringing wayward husbands "back to God." They were to make their homes places of comfort and cheer by nursing the sick, maintaining a well-ordered household, and gracing their surroundings with beauty. Girls, therefore, had to learn to be proficient in various kinds of needlework and drawing room skills, such as singing and playing an instrument. Academic education for women was fine as long as it did not interfere with the primary goal of becoming a good homemaker. The seminaries and academies for girls emphasized that their programs would not hinder the development of the skills of domesticity but would "enlarge and deepen" a girl's ability to fulfill her God-given role of wife and mother. Protestants feared that nuns encouraged the young girls they taught in parochial schools to follow their example in entering convents, thus eroding the stabilizing influence of wives and mothers. The establishment of Protestant schools for girls became a focus of concern for Protestant communities, for through education they believed they could combat the growth of convents and the entrenchment of Catholicism in America.[22]

Catholics, however, defended their convent schools by claiming that the nuns supported and fostered the very ideals of motherhood and domesticity espoused by Protestants. Furthermore, nuns fully realized that most young women were destined to be wives and mothers and insisted that they made no effort to coerce those who did not have a vocation for the religious life. Indeed, the Council of Trent strictly prohibited forced

22. Welter, "Cult of True Womanhood," 162–70, passim; Joseph G. Mannard, "Maternity … of the Spirit: Nuns and Domesticity in Antebellum America," presented at the Cushwa Center Conference on American Catholicism, October 4, 1985, in The American Catholic Religious Life: Selected Historical Essays, ed. Joseph M. White (New York: Garland, 1988), 131. Ironically, the Filles de Notre Dame established their schools in seventeenth-century France to the influence of Protestant schools and then patterned their schools after the Protestant model.

professions; those who compelled a young girl to enter a convent or who forcibly prevented her from entering one would be excommunicated.[23] Nuns encouraged all women to live for God. Rather than encouraging the girls in the academies to enter the convent, the main goal of the teaching nuns was to prepare their students to be proper wives in middle- and upper-class homes. Just as it was in the seventeenth century, Catholic curricula were similar to those offered at Northern Protestant seminaries for girls. Nuns, therefore, supported rather than thwarted the enculturation of young girls with the ideals of domesticity.

23. Vermeersch, "Religious Profession."

Chapter 1

Preparing the Way

The Sisters of Mercy

Jean-Pierre Augustin Verot was consecrated vicar apostolic of
Florida and as titular bishop of Danaba in Baltimore, Maryland,
on April 25, 1858, and arrived in St. Augustine on June 1, 1858.
Although Florida had been a flourishing center of Catholicism
as a Spanish colony, by the time Verot assumed his new post,
it was a struggling mission field with only three or four priests.
Between 1821, the end of the Second Spanish Period, when Florida became part of the United States, and 1858, few bishops had
visited Florida. Verot's attentions to St. Augustine were, therefore, greatly appreciated by the Catholics there. The affection
with which he was regarded by the people of St. Augustine was
expressed in the announcement of his return from his recruitment trip that appeared in the local newspaper, the *St. Augustine
Examiner*: "We need not say how great is the joy of his spiritual children, who so well appreciate the winning qualities of this
worthy Prelate. It is with unfeigned pleasure we welcome and
record his safe return to the 'Ancient City' and the great success
he has attained in his tour in Europe."[1]

---

1. *St. Augustine Examiner*, October 29, 1859. Hereafter cited as *Examiner*.

The cheerful announcement of Verot's return reflected St. Augustine's close relationship with the Catholic Church despite the recent years of neglect. The Ancient City, settled by Catholic Spaniards nearly three hundred years before, remained a Catholic town. In 1860, St. Johns County, for which St. Augustine was the seat of government, had 2,000 Catholics in six churches, more than twice as many as the Methodists, who were the next-largest denomination.[2] The largest concentration of Catholics was in St. Augustine, with an estimated population of 952 white and 376 black Catholics.[3] The city was actually a Catholic enclave in Florida, for like most of the rest of the South in 1860, the state was rural, and most of its inhabitants were Protestant.[4] Florida received an influx of Protestants when the colony was transferred from Spain to the United States in 1821. Yet, despite the alarm of the Catholic bishop who wrote in June 1823 that St. Augustine was "overrun with Methodists and Presbyterians,"[5] the Ancient City remained a Catholic town, and Protestants remained in the minority. Furthermore, the Protestants who came into Florida were not overtly antagonistic to Catholics. The lack of hostility to Catholics in Florida and the South in general, as opposed to the hatred exhibited in the urban Northeast, was probably largely due to the rural character of the South and the small Catholic presence there.

The Catholics of St. Augustine, therefore, were overjoyed

2. U.S. Census, Miscellaneous Statistics, 1860. St. Johns County then included what is now Flagler County.

3. Michael V. Gannon, *Rebel Bishop: Augustin Verot, Florida's Civil War Prelate* (Milwaukee: Bruce, 1964), 25.

4. Michael V. Gannon, *The Cross in the Sand* (Gainesville: University Press of Florida, 1965), 152. In 1860, Florida had a population of 140,424. There were only a few cities and towns: the largest included Pensacola (pop. 2,876), Key West (pop. 2,832), Jacksonville (pop. 2,118), Tallahassee (pop. 1,932), and St. Augustine (pop. 1,914); Joseph C. G. Kennedy, *Population of the United States in 1860: Compiled from the Original Returns of the Eighth Census* (Washington, D.C.: Government Printing Office, 1864), 54.

5. George E. Buker, "The Americanization of St. Augustine, 1821–1865," in *The Oldest City: St. Augustine, Saga of Survival,* ed. Jean Parker Waterbury (St. Augustine: St. Augustine Historical Society, 1983), 158.

when the bishop returned with six priests, and "two Religious Ladies and several other persons to aid him in the Florida Mission." He also had five students at the Theological Seminary of Baltimore preparing for the work in Florida. Before the end of the year, Verot also recruited five Sisters of Mercy from Providence, Rhode Island, in the Diocese of Hartford, Connecticut, and five Brothers of the Christian Schools (Christian Brothers) from Canada.[6]

The Sisters of Mercy is a Roman Catholic order founded in Dublin, Ireland, by Catherine McCauley on December 12, 1830. Among the first sisters of the new order was Frances Warde. As Mother Mary Frances Xavier, she brought seven Sisters of Mercy to the United States to establish a convent in Pittsburgh in 1843. There, the sisters operated educational institutions, orphanages, and hospitals. By 1846, the sisters had founded additional Mercy convents in New York City and Chicago.[7] Bishop Bernard O'Reilly from Providence, Rhode Island, was greatly impressed with the Sisters of Mercy's work and in 1850 asked them to establish a house in Providence, the See of the Diocese of Hartford, to teach. Ursuline Sisters had gone to Boston in 1820, and the Daughters of Charity, founded by Elizabeth Seton, had been established there in 1831, but the sisters in Providence would be the first Sisters of Mercy in New England.

Because of strong anti-Catholic influences of the Know-Nothings in New England at this time, the sisters' decision to accede to Bishop O'Reilly's plea was not lightly made. According to Sisters of Mercy rules, no sister is forced to accept an

6. *Examiner*, October 29, 1859; Gannon, *Cross in the Sand*, 168; "Information on the Sisters of Mercy Who Were in St. Augustine Florida, (1859–1869)," typescript from the Archives of the Sisters of Mercy, Providence, Rhode Island, on file at the Archives of the Sisters of St. Joseph, St. Augustine, no. 301.2, hereafter cited as ASSJSA.

7. *Seventy-Five Years in the Passing with The Sisters of Mercy, Providence, Rhode Island, 1851–1926* (Providence: Providence Visitor Press, 1926), 31–40, 75; *A Little Sketch of the Work of the Sisters of Mercy in Providence, Rhode Island, from 1851 to 1893* (Providence: J. A. and R. A. Reid, Printers, 1893), 14.

assignment. Of those who offered themselves for Providence, in addition to Mother Xavier, four were chosen: Srs. M. Paula Lombard, M. Josephine Lombard (Sr. Paula's blood sister), M. Camillus O'Neil, and M. Joanna Fogarty. The sisters, dressed in "civilian" clothes rather than their habits, stole into Providence under cover of night on March 11, 1851, but because their first Mass in the city was held the next morning, March 12 is considered the foundation day for the Sisters of Mercy in Providence. The conditions were very poor, especially when compared with the comforts of the well-established motherhouse in Pittsburgh, and the atmosphere was very hostile. Know-Nothing rowdies regularly broke the convent windows, shouted at them during the night, and taunted the sisters when they were out in public.[8] Even so, within six months they had grown to twenty members and had full ministries underway, teaching children, visiting the sick, helping the poor, catechizing beginners in the Catholic faith, establishing sodalities, and instructing adults.[9] Their St. Xavier's Academy grew steadily, leading to the construction of a brick facility on Claverick Street in 1856.

In March 1855, as the Claverick Street building was still under construction, a Know- Nothing mob surrounded the convent, threatening to burn it down and kill all its inhabitants. At the risk of his life, Bishop O'Reilly defended the nuns by confronting the crowd, and after the mayor of Providence read the Riot Act, the crowd finally dispersed. For several nights after that, Catholic men stood guard around the convent, and there were no further incidents.[10]

The sisters continued with their ministries in Providence, and soon, at the requests of other bishops, houses were

8. Sister Mary Hermenia Muldrey, RSM, *Abounding in Mercy: Mother Austin Carroll* (New Orleans: Habersham, 1988), 35, 32–33.

9. *Seventy-Five Years*, 80.

10. Muldrey, *Abounding in Mercy*, 31. For a detailed account, see Kathleen Healy, RSM, ed., *Sisters of Mercy: Spirituality in America 1843–1900* (New York and Mahwah, N.J.: Paulist Press, 1992), 111–13.

established in other dioceses: Rochester, New York, in 1857; Manchester, New Hampshire, in 1858; and St. Augustine, Florida, in 1859. Mother Frances Xavier Warde had left Providence to establish the new house in Manchester. The new superior in Providence was Mother M. Josephine Lombard, one of the original Sisters of Mercy in Providence. In 1859, she sent five sisters to St. Augustine.[11]

The Sisters of Mercy who went to St. Augustine were led by a young mother superior, Mary Ligouri from Virginia, who was only twenty-five years old. By 1860, there was a total of nine other sisters at the newly established St. Mary's Convent in St. Augustine: Sr. Mary Agnes, age twenty-eight, from England; Sr. Mary Aloysius, age twenty-one, from Massachusetts; Sr. Mary Evangelist, age twenty-one, from Maryland; Sr. Mary Teresa, age thirty, also from Maryland; Sr. Mary Augustine, age thirty-five, from France; Sr. Mary Josephine, age forty, also from France; Sr. Mary Regina, age twenty-five, from Florida; Sr. Mary Ann, age twenty-four, from Ireland; and Sr. Mary Dora, age thirty-five, also from Ireland.[12] Sisters in the order all had religious names beginning with "Mary" and were sometimes referred to using only their second name. Sister Regina, from Florida, probably joined the convent after it was established in St. Augustine.

The 1860 census population schedule for Providence shows that Mother Ligouri and the others sent to the "Ancient City" had left a substantial institution. In addition to Mother Josephine Lombard, there were twenty-three other sisters, twenty-one of whom were born in Ireland; the other three were from New York, Connecticut, and Massachusetts. Seventy-seven girls, ages two to fourteen, boarded at the convent school, St. Xavier's

---

11. *Seventy-Five Years*, 91–96, 41–42.

12. U.S. Census, Population Schedules, St. Johns County, 1860. The census taker misspelled Mother Liguori's name, entering it as Legoria; Sister Aloysius's name, entering it as Aloisious; and Sister Regina's name, entering it as Ragina.

PREPARING THE WAY

Academy. Only twelve of the girls were over ten years old. In addition, twenty-four boys and ten girls, ages two to seventeen, attended the sisters' day school. At the Sisters of Mercy's Home for Orphans and Friendless Children, located next door to the convent, two black women were employed as servants.[13]

The teaching methods of the Sisters of Mercy were probably shaped by the teaching philosophies held by Mother Xavier Warde. She firmly believed in the power of joy and encouraged her sisters: "'Since God loves a cheerful giver, let us try to be cheerful *workers*, taking nothing away from the glory of His blessed service by half-heartedness in the discharge of our duties. We must be steeped in holy joy and eagerness to imitate our Divine Model in performing the lowly offices of labor and prayer, teaching and instructing.'" She disapproved of severe punishment, preferring instead the use of love and fear of disapproval from teachers or parents, and as punishment the loss of places of honor or the removal of merits. She sought to instill "honesty in thought, word, and deed ... truth and sincerity, exerting every effort to obviate falsehood and deceit."[14]

The sisters' schools ran from 9:00 a.m. to noon, then from 2:00 to 4:00 in the afternoon. The curriculum included catechism, arithmetic, history, geography, English grammar, spelling, and penmanship. Also emphasized were etiquette, including courtesy, and "correct positions for sitting, walking, and standing, practise in graceful carriage, bowing, repose of manner, and in the essentials of good breeding." Girls also received lessons in domestic arts, including knitting, darning, sewing, and cooking. Music and the "cultivation of good reading habits" were emphasized as extracurricular activities. The sisters also established sodalities, societies to inculcate good Catholic piety. In 1855, the cathedral

13. U.S. Census, Population Schedules, Providence, Rhode Island, 1860, Entry 587/909.

14. Sister Mary Loretto O'Connor, RSM, AM, *Merry Marks the Century* (Providence: Sisters of Mercy, 1951), 118, 121.

parochial school in Providence had three sodalities for the children: Children of Mary, Angel Guardian, and Infant Jesus.[15]

With such an auspicious background, the Sisters of Mercy arrived in St. Augustine in the fall of 1859 and settled into a small house on St. George's Street across from the cathedral. In December, shortly after the arrival of the sisters, the "Ladies of the Roman Catholic Church" held a fair. The newspaper reported that the proceeds from the event were to be "devoted to the education projects now in movement in this City. A very worthy object which should be cheerfully and faithfully sustained by our people, both Catholic and Protestant."[16] The sisters started St. Mary's Academy, a boarding school / day school for white girls, after the first of the year. According to the census, there were eight boarding students who ranged in age from twelve to sixteen years old, all from Florida. This was the first Catholic convent school in the state.[17] The 1860 Social Statistics Schedule shows there were two teaching sisters for fifty students in the female academy (including the boarding students) and two teaching sisters for seventy-five students in their free school.[18]

In addition to teaching academic subjects, the Sisters of Mercy also taught the Roman Catholic catechism. Although it was illegal for them to teach slaves basic academic subjects, they were allowed to give them, along with whites, religious instruction. Carroll writes that "special attention was given to the colored population, and Bishop Verot, who was devoted to the race, greatly valued the zeal of the sisters in instructing them. Their children learned to sing with spirit several hymns, and the Bishop delighted in hearing them execute their favorite, with more vigor than beauty, in staccato movement.

15. O'Connor, *Merry Marks the Century*, 121–22.

16. *Examiner*, December 31, 1859.

17. Karen Harvey, *St. Augustine and St. Johns County: A Pictorial History* (Virginia Beach, Va.: Donning, 1980), 117.

18. U.S. Census, 1860. Social Statistics for St. Johns County, Florida.

'I am a little Catholic,
And Christian is my name,
And I believe in the Holy Church
In every age the same.'"[19]

The schools for white boys, established by the Christian Brothers Verot brought from Canada in 1859, were important components of the Catholic education available in St. Augustine, the male counterparts of the Sisters of Mercy's schools for white girls. The Brothers of the Christian Schools was founded in Reims, France, in 1680. The order's establishment was in keeping with centuries of Catholic policy to teach the young and provide free schools for the poor. In France many *petites écoles* arose for the common people.[20]

The brothers arrived in St. Augustine on September 1, 1859, and moved into a two-story frame building, "a pretty little house" on the west side of Charlotte Street, south of Bridge Street, surrounded by a large garden. It was about five blocks south of the cathedral. By 1861, the number of boarders increased so much that the brothers added a wooden wing onto the house.[21] The 1860 federal census lists five brothers: Brothers Lucien, age forty (the head of the household, presumably the superior); Alexander, age thirty-four; Louis, age thirty-five; Stanislas, age twenty-two; and Quinton, age twenty-one. Boarding with the brothers were six boys, ages nine to fifteen; two were from South Carolina, three from Florida, and one from Maryland. The brothers had fifty students in their Male Academy (including

19. Sister Mary Theresa Austin Carroll, RSM, *Leaves from the Annals of the Sisters of Mercy in Four Volumes*, vol. IV, *Containing Sketches of the Order in South America, Central America, and the United States, by a Member of the Order of Mercy* (New York: P. O'Shea, 1895), 4:332; hereafter cited as Austin Carroll, *Leaves*.

20. Brother Joseph Paul, "Institute of the Brothers of the Christian Schools," *The Catholic Encyclopedia*, vol. 8 (New York: Robert Appleton, 1910), accessed April 23, 2022, http://www.newadvent.or/cathen/08056a.htm.

21. Justin Lucian, FSC, compiler, *The Brothers of the Christian Schools in St. Augustine, Florida, 1859–1863* (Memphis, Tenn.: Christian Brothers University. For Private Circulation, 2003), unpaged [28–29, 32, 35].

the six boarders) and sixty-five in their free school for white boys. The curriculum in the brothers' schools included calligraphy and drawing, arithmetic, and geography. Etiquette for classes called for little speaking and a maintenance of good order.[22]

The education of their white youth was one of the major concerns of the citizens of St. Augustine. In reviewing recent internal improvements of the city, the editors of the *Examiner* rejoiced over the awakening of an interest in education and proclaimed, "San Augustine is in a fair way to be celebrated for the plenteousness and excellence of her school privileges, not on a sickly and fluctuating basis, but we hope and believe possessing the very best elements of permanency."[23] A month later, however, the editors gave an unexpected strong warning against the establishment of church related schools:

The moment our schools erect fortifications of *sect* and *ism* around them, that moment, we honestly believe, they strike the first blow at their own ruin. The school room is not the place to teach religious dogmas; these legitimately belong to the Sunday-schools and the consecrated teachers of religion; the development of the intellect, the training and storing the mind with knowledge, accompanied and hallowed by those mild influences and examples which inculcate practical piety, are the department of the presiding spirits in the school-room. The *worth of a school for youth*, does not hinge upon the question [illegible] Methodist or Episcopal or Roman Catholic. It hinges upon *this* rather—Is it a source of *light*? is the young mind wisely and successfully trained there? Are those principles formed in it which it will do to guide our life by in after years? Are children taught to revere the majority of broad moral right? Are they fitted for true noble manhood and womanhood? We are opposed in every sense and on every ground to sectarian schools.[24]

22. U.S. Census, 1860, Population Schedule for St. Johns County, Florida, entry 418 and Social Statistics for St. Johns County; Lucian, *Brothers of the Christian Schools*, 5.

23. *Examiner*, January 7, 1860.

24. *Examiner*, February 11, 1860.

Bishop Verot was discouraged by this public reaction, but pressed forward with the establishment of the schools and laid the foundations for a new convent building for the Sisters of Mercy in the fall of the year.[25] Sisters of Mercy chronicler Mother Austin Carroll described the new building:

On the lower floor were five rooms, and a large hall designed for a chapel. Another hall in the shape of an L projected from the rear to which it was joined by an immense arch supported by three square pillars. Parlors and domestic offices were on the ground-floor; on the second were class-rooms, dormitories, and Community room.... Everything was well adapted for the duties of the Sisterhood, and the schools were soon full.[26]

The sisters and students moved into the new facility in August 1861.

In spite of the *Examiner*'s strong warnings against church-related schools, a little more than a year later, the same editor had almost euphoric praise for the four schools that had been established in St. Augustine by the Catholic Church—that is, St. Mary's Academy / day school and a free school for white girls and the Christian Brothers' academy / day school and free school for white boys:

Too much gratitude cannot be felt by the citizens of St. Augustine, to the Catholic Bishop and Priests, under whose auspices the schools connected with that Church have been established, and to the Sisters and Brothers who are engaged in instructing our youth. There is a great work to be done here amongst the Youth of that Church, and none other but the Bishops, Priests, and Teachers of their own faith can so readily reach the heart of the matter, and faithfully they seem to be executing the duty, with untiring energy they devote themselves to this labor of love, ... and a large Charity school is also connected with their Institution.[27]

25. Gannon, *Rebel Bishop*, 29; Austin Carroll, *Leaves*, 4:332.
26. Austin Carroll, *Leaves*, 4:332.
27. *Examiner*, April 6, 1861.

The citizens were particularly impressed with the improved behavior of all the students, but the girls and the sisters who taught them won the highest praise. No explanation is given for this radical change in attitude concerning parochial schools other than, perhaps, extreme pleasure in the results of the brothers' and sisters' teaching methods under the guidance of Brother Lucian and Mother Mary Ligouri. All looked well for the schools, but in the same month as the editorial's publication, the country erupted into the Civil War.

The intensity of tensions between the North and South had been building steadily since the Compromise of 1850. Because of the strong anti-Catholicism that was prevalent across the country at mid-century, most Catholic leaders had refrained from political discussions that did not have a direct bearing on the Catholic Church. On January 4, 1861, however, Bishop Verot delivered a sermon at the church in St. Augustine that launched him into the political arena. The occasion was the Day of Public Humiliation, Fasting, and Prayer proclaimed by President Buchanan in a spiritual effort to avert the disintegration of the Union. Verot's message, "Slavery and Abolitionism," strongly condemned the North for the widespread practice of refusing to assist in the capture and return of runaway slaves, a rebelliousness that flagrantly violated the Fugitive Slave Act of 1850 and justified the South's consideration of secession. The sermon also denounced abolitionists for blasphemously trying to use the Bible to condemn slavery as a "moral evil, and a crime against God, religion, humanity, and society." Verot countered that slavery had "received the sanction of God, of the Church, and of Society at all times, and in all governments,"[28] and cited biblical and historical examples to support his argument. Verot's

28. The Right Rev. A. Verot, *A Tract for the Times: Slavery and Abolitionism Being the Substance of a Sermon, Preached in the Church of St. Augustine, Florida, on the 4th Day of January 1861, Day of Public Humiliation, Fasting and Prayer*, new ed. (New Orleans: Printed at the "Catholic Propagator" Office, 1861), 5.

defense of slavery and states' rights was published and widely quoted throughout the South and gained him the reputation of being a "rebel bishop."[29]

Verot defined slavery as a "state of dependency of one man upon another 'so as to be obliged to work all his life for that master with the privilege in the latter, to transfer that right to another person by sale.'" The master, however, did not own the slave, but only had a right to the slave's labor and that of the slave's children.[30] According to Verot, masters also had responsibilities toward their slaves. Some treated their slaves like animals, but the bishop said,

A man, by being a slave, does not cease to be a man, retaining all the properties, qualities, attributes, duties, rights and responsibilities attached to human nature, or to a being endowed with reason and understanding, and made to the image and likeness of God. A master has not over a slave the same rights which he has over an animal, and whoever would view his slaves merely as beasts, would have virtually abjured human nature, and would deserve to be expelled from human society.[31]

Verot's sermon also delineated six conditions under which slavery could be considered "legitimate, lawful, approved by all laws, and consistent with practical religion and true holiness of life in masters who fulfil those conditions:"[32] (1) repudiate the slave trade, for slaves brought into the country from Africa had not really been captured in war, but were caught and sold as trade items; (2) respect the rights of free colored persons; slavery was not based on color, but on property rights, and it was unjust to re-enslave a free person; (3) do not take advantage of colored females, who were frequently subjected to immorality; (4) honor, respect, and encourage slave marriage and keep families

29. Gannon, *Rebel Bishop*, 31.
30. Gannon, *Rebel Bishop*, 40.
31. Verot, *A Tract*, 15.
32. Verot, *A Tract*, 5.

together; (5) provide adequate food, clothing, and shelter; and (6) provide a means for slaves to know and practice religion. To seal these reforms, Verot proposed that the Confederacy adopt a servile code to outline the rights and duties of slaves.[33]

Verot frankly addressed the immorality some masters forced upon their female slaves:

It is but right that means should be taken to check libertinism and licentiousness, and that the female slave be surrounded with sufficient protection to save her from dishonor and crime. The Southern Confederacy, if it should exist, must rely on morality and justice, and it could never be entitled to a special protection from above unless it professes to surround Slavery with the guarantees that will secure its morality and virtue.

Such concern for female slaves and the open admission that the sexual abuse they often suffered was criminal was startling, especially coming from a Southern bishop. Verot, however, also held racist ideas. His emphasis on the need to keep slave families together to avoid sexual immorality was based on the belief that "the strength and violence of animal propensities is in the inverse ratio of intellectual and moral faculties, which are decidedly weaker in the African race, as all persons of experience will testify."[34]

On January 10, 1861, six days after Verot delivered his sermon, Florida seceded from the Union; little more than three months later, the Civil War began with the Confederacy's firing on Fort Sumter. Union troops took possession of St. Augustine on March 10, 1862. So many people fled the city that the Sisters of Mercy closed St. Mary's Academy in May, though "the [local] children continued to come on Sundays for instruction, and the blacks were cared for as usual." Great uncertainty gripped St. Augustine. There were rumors the city was to be shelled and the convent destroyed. Convinced that the sisters were in

33. Gannon, *Rebel Bishop*, 45–48, 52.
34. Verot, *A Tract*, 18–19.

great danger, despite their desire to remain in the Ancient City, Bishop Verot determined to remove them to a safer place. On August 17, 1862, Verot personally conducted seven of the eleven Sisters of Mercy, including Mother Liguori and Mother Agnes, to Columbus, Georgia, at the western edge of his diocese for the duration of the conflict.[35] The four who remained in St. Augustine lived in great poverty, and the work that had been going very well before the war suffered a major setback.[36] During the Civil War, Sister Mary Ann, one of the St. Augustine Sisters of Mercy, provided nursing care at the Savannah Hospital and at the prison camp at Andersonville after the Battle of Olustee. The battle, the largest confrontation in Florida during the war, took place near Lake City, a community west of Jacksonville, in February 1864.[37]

The bishop and sisters arrived in Columbus on September 4, 1862. In spite of Verot's best intentions, Columbus failed to provide the safe haven he had anticipated. The winters were much colder than they had been in St. Augustine, and the sisters suffered from a lack of fuel and food. Breakfasts consisted of one slice of cornbread for each one, two spoonfuls of hominy, and tea made from blackberry leaves or coffee made from parched corn without milk or sugar. The midday meal often included beef with a little rice or a few sweet potatoes, and suppers were cornmeal gruel or buttermilk, or sometimes nothing. Sleeping accommodations were nearly nonexistent; two sisters shared a quilt, and others slept on the floor until a friend gave them some

35. An account of the trip to Columbus, which is described by Michael Gannon as "a pure classic for error and misadventure" (Gannon, *Rebel Bishop*, 66), is masterfully told by Sister Austin Carroll in *Leaves*, 4:335–44. The Christian Brothers sent their boarders home. With their major source of income gone, they could no longer sustain themselves. On May 1, 1863, they abandoned their house, furnishings and all, never to return; Justin Lucian, *Brothers of the Christian Schools* [7, 35, 37–38].

36. Jane Quinn, *The Story of a Nun: Jeanie Gordon Brown* (St. Augustine: Villa Flora, Sisters of St. Joseph, 1978), 73.

37. Edward F. Keuchel, "Sister Mary Ann: 'Jacksonville's Angel of Mercy,'" in *Florida's Heritage of Diversity: Essays in Honor of Samuel Proctor*, ed. Mark I. Greenberg, William Warren Rogers, and Canter Brown Jr. (Tallahassee: Sentry, 1997), 100.

dry goods boxes to use as beds. For shoes, the sisters saved one special pair each to wear to Mass; otherwise, they "made slippers of any stuff they could get, with thick paper soles." One day they were given a box of shoes that were made by slaves. "They took any sizes they could get; as none fitted there was little choice; one sister who wore twos was glad to get into sevens, but the noise she made walking, flip-flap, was intolerable." Somehow, they managed to piece together their habits, which were falling apart, or replaced them with cotton habits dyed black, as no serge was available.[38]

As if such conditions were not bad enough, federal troops descended upon Columbus on April 16, 1865, Easter Day, intent on taking the Confederate-held bridge that crossed the Chatta-hoochee River. Some women and children sought refuge at the convent. "All night long the Sisters remained in prayer before the Blessed Sacrament, disturbed by the yells and shouts of the victors, and the groans and cries of the vanquished." Unaware that the Confederacy had surrendered on April 9, the Union soldiers were given permission to rampage through the little city for the next three days, pillaging and destroying it, leaving nothing for its inhabitants. In the aftermath, bartering was the only means of exchange until the winter. The sisters reopened their schools, but soon closed them, as they needed to tend to other needs in the miserable community where "every one was in trouble; poverty, suffering, bereavement were everywhere."[39]

With war's end in 1865, some of the Sisters of Mercy remained at the Columbus house established in 1862, while others returned to St. Augustine, where St. Mary's Academy resumed its place as the favored institution dedicated to the education of the Ancient City's white girls to make them refined young women. According to their advertisements in the *Examiner* in

38. Austin Carroll, *Leaves*, 4:344–45.
39. Austin Carroll, *Leaves*, 4:347–51.

1866, the Sisters of Mercy offered a full course of instruction for young ladies that would meet these expectations. They taught reading, writing, grammar, orthography (spelling), arithmetic, geography, history, rhetoric, natural philosophy, algebra, geometry, chemistry, astronomy, French, German, and Spanish languages, music, vocal and instrumental, drawing, and plain or ornamental needlework. Tuition for boarders was four hundred dollars a year, with extra charges for instruction in the foreign languages, art, and music. Needlework was offered free of charge to the boarders.[40]

Because the school was a parochial school, its curriculum was steeped in strong Catholic teaching. The basic goal of Catholic schools was to "fortify the soul with Christian education" by "training the intellect and memory in truth, teaching the heart and will—which are the springs of moral action—to obey the dictates of conscience and thus acquire virtue, and enlightening and controlling the conscience by the sanction of religion, so as to make it an effective guide to conduct." In addition to academic training, therefore, there would have been daily prayers and religious instruction.[41]

The excellent reputation of the academy was reflected in a report that appeared in the *Examiner* in the fall of 1868. Bishop Verot had gone to the North and returned with three new Sisters of Mercy to join the faculty at St. Mary's. According to the paper, the sisters, "yielding to motives of zeal and feeling the impulse of the missionary spirit,... cheerfully renounced the comforts, blandishments and advantages of home and changed them with the sacrifice, privations and comparative poverty of a country lately desolated by evil disaster and war." Speaking of their work at the academy, the paper continued,

40. *Examiner*, November 10, 1866.
41. Sister Mary Alberta, SSJ, "A Study of the Schools Conducted by the Sisters of St. Joseph of the Diocese of St. Augustine, Florida, 1866–1940" (Master's thesis, University of Florida, 1940), 49.

They have already commenced to teach the young daughters of the "Ancient City" in St. Mary's Academy, which has now been in existence for ten years and earned a just reputation throughout Florida for the solid and accomplished education which it gives to young ladies. With the addition of these three new members, the school cannot fail to become more prosperous; doubtless it will sustain its reputation of a first class school for young ladies, and we hope it will draw large numbers of young ladies from the county and neighboring cities.

The editors strongly encouraged parents to send their daughters as boarding students, claiming that they would "receive more fully all the benefits of the Institution," and pointing out what a bargain it was at only two hundred dollars a year, half of the pre-war rates.[42]

The academy did have to compete with other schools that advertised in the *Examiner*: Mrs. M. M. Reid's Boarding and Day School for Young Ladies in Palatka, Florida, and the Bay Side Seminary, A Home School for Young Ladies, in Oyster Bay, Long Island, New York. A citizen identified only as Observer wrote the editor of the *Examiner* in 1867, extolling the work of the Sisters of Mercy: "We willingly take this opportunity of congratulating with our fellow citizens of St. Augustine and the country around for the good opportunity they enjoy of giving a thorough, classical scientific and above all genteel and moral education to their daughters." The Observer thought "it was a very superfluous and rather dangerous experiment to send those young plants of the South to Northern latitudes in the hostile soil, with so good and substantial opportunities of a good education at home."[43] Such accolades regarding St. Mary's Academy were common in the *Examiner*.

Another laudatory remark regarding St. Mary's Academy commented that the sisters had succeeded in making the girls not

42. *Examiner*, October 17, 1868. St. Mary's Academy was established in 1859, nine years before.
43. *Examiner*, August 17, 1867.

only graceful but also intellectual.[44] A review of other comments about the academy, however, demonstrates that special appreciation was accorded the training the girls received in the finer arts and skills, such as needlework and other handiwork. The prevailing attitudes toward what were suitable activities for young ladies were represented in the *Examiner* in an article entitled, "Woman's Scepter, the Needle," in which the writer asserted,

There is something extremely pleasant; and even touching ... if very sweet, soft and winning effect—in this peculiarity of needle work, distinguishing woman form [*sic*] man. Our own sex is incapable of any such by play, aside from the business of life; but women ... have always some handiwork ready to fill the tiny gap of every vacant moment.... A needle is familiar to the finger of them all ... and they have greatly the advantage of us in this respect. The slender thread of silk or cotton keeps them united with the small, familiar, gentle interests of life.... Women of high thought and accomplishments love to sew.[45]

With the education of the white Catholic girls so well in hand, Bishop Verot turned his attentions toward educating the newly freed slaves. The addition of this new field of labor, however, was too much to ask of the Sisters of Mercy. It was difficult to recruit new Mercy Sisters, for St. Augustine, though not destroyed by the war, was impoverished; and the Sisters of Mercy were now divided between St. Augustine and Columbus, separated by hundreds of nearly impassible miles. Under such straitened circumstances, it was impossible for the Sisters of Mercy to continue with their teaching and catechizing and to assume the added burden of establishing schools for the freedmen.[46] Verot, therefore, looked for others to take on the task, and in June 1865 he turned to his mother country, France, to find new laborers to work among the blacks.

44. *Examiner*, July 6, 1867.
45. *Examiner*, November 3, 1866.
46. Sister M. Aquin McEervey, "History of the 'Macon' Novitiate, Mount De Sales Academy," copy in SSJ Archives, 301.2, pasted in back of Record Book; on file at the Archives of the Sisters of St. Joseph of St. Augustine, St. Augustine, Fla. Hereafter cited as ASSJSA.

Chapter 2

"Notre Chère Mission d'Amérique"

The French Sisters
of St. Joseph's Mission
in Florida

⌐

In 1865, Verot went to Le Puy, France, to recruit additional sisters to teach the freedmen and to instill in them a strong Catholic faith in St. Augustine. Le Puy, itself an ancient city, dates from at least 420 A.D., when a church was built there. Le Puy's great Notre Dame Cathedral dates from the tenth century, and the present city was built around it.[1] The city is located in the heart of the Massif Central, a remote, huge plateau, filled with isolated valleys in the center of southern France. Its altitude is about 2,000 feet above sea level.

Le Puy is the seat of government for Haute-Loire, one of the departments created by the National Assembly in 1790. Its winters are harsh and its terrain rugged. Its isolated people were slow to take up modern ways. The region, and Le Puy in particular, was known for its strong religious life, with many inhabitants entering the religious life or participating in pious

1. Noel Graveline, *Le Puy-en-Velay: Excitement, Colours and Fun* (Beaumont, France: Editions Debaisieux, 2003), 13, http://www.meteo.fr/meteonet/meteo/pcv/cdm/dept43/images/zcdm24.gif.

associations. Many of those religious groups, persecuted during the French Revolution, were reconstituted soon after the Revolution ended.[2]

Among the many women's religious orders in Le Puy was the Sisters of St. Joseph, founded there in 1650 and refounded all over France in 1807. One of the order's primary ministries was to teach in the public schools. It was to these Sisters of St. Joseph that Bishop Verot went in mid-July 1865, seeking teachers. He made it clear that they were to instruct newly liberated slaves in Florida and Georgia, saying, "I have five or six hundred thousand [sic] Negroes without any education or religion ... for whom I wish to do something."[3] He was compelled not only by genuine concern for the "Negroes," but also by the Florida legislature's recent action to provide schools for blacks and by the efforts already in place by Protestant teachers from the North. In explaining the urgent need for teachers, he told his French audience, "We must make a beginning by establishing schools—a necessity. The Protestants have anticipated us here: they have opened free schools which the Negroes attend in great numbers.... We must, therefore, prepare for the contest ... in procuring religious instruction for this simple and docile race."[4] The work of the Protestant missionaries in competition with the Catholic efforts in St. Augustine is the subject of chapter 3.

Of the sixty Sisters of St. Joseph from Haute-Loire who volunteered, eight were chosen from throughout the department. The oldest and the one appointed to be the mother superior for the colony in Florida was Sister Marie Sidonie Rascle, age forty. She had taught in Le Puy's convent school for twenty years, was especially gifted in working with younger students, and was well liked by both her charges and their parents.[5]

2. Pierre-François Aleil et al., *Haute-Loire* (Paris: Christine Bonneton, 2001), 53–60.
3. Gannon, *The Cross in the Sand*, 183–84.
4. Gannon, *Rebel Bishop*, 117.
5. Congrégation de Saint-Joseph du Puy, *Religieuses Décédées, Depuis le mois de*

Mother Sidonie was accompanied by two other seasoned sisters, Julie Roussel (Roussell), age forty-one, and Joséphine Deleage, age thirty-six. The remaining five members of the chosen eight were all second-year novices who had made their first vows on July 19, 1866, about two weeks before they set out for Florida. While the three older sisters provided steady guidance, the newly minted sisters were sought for their enthusiastic and adventuresome spirits. Sister St. Pierre Borie, age twenty-eight, was one of the first to volunteer for the Florida missions. The others were: Sister Clémence Freycenon, age twenty-six; Sister Julie Clotilde Arsac, age twenty-four; Sister Célenie Joubert, age twenty-two; and Sister Marie Joseph Cortial, age twenty-one.[6]

On the day the sisters were to depart for America, the little company was blessed and exhorted by the bishop of Le Puy and, after a last Eucharist in the convent chapel, departed for their mission in "La Floride." These missionaries were the first ever sent out from the Le Puy community of the Sisters of St. Joseph and the only Catholic religious ever specifically charged to minister to the former slaves in America. They were accompanied partway by Mother General Léocadie Broc and Mother Agathe, the mistress of novices, to Paris and then on to Le Havre,[7] where the sisters boarded a steamer bound for New York City on August 2.[8] Sister Julie Roussel wrote the Le Puy community the next day, describing the parting:

After we had given them our last farewells, through a few signals which we were interrupting in order to wipe our tears, we soon took courage; gaity showed on all the faces again, and it no longer disappeared, . . .

Janvier jusqu'au mois de Juillet 1889. On file at the Archives of the Sisters of St. Joseph, Le Puy, France. Hereafter cited as ASSJLP.

6. Table created by Sr. Louis Marie Briat, Archivist, Sisters of St. Joseph in Le Puy.

7. Letter no. 10, Mtr. Sidonie Rascle to Rev. Mtr. Léocadie Broc, September 14, 1866, ASSJSA.

8. Letter no. 1, Mtr. Sidonie Rascle to Rev. Mtr. Léocadie Broc, August 2–3, 1866, ASSJSA. Coincidentally, the steamer was the "Lafayette," named for the French hero of the American Revolution, who was born near Le Puy.

our hearts are not indifferent on seeing the ship carry us so far from those whom we cherish; however, we are pleased to have made the first step, and if it were still to be done, we would not hesitate a moment.[9]

The voyage lasted nearly three weeks. Although most of the sisters suffered from seasickness, the trip gave them an opportunity to adjust to aspects of the new culture they were about to enter. During that time, they were "agreeably surprised to find waiters and other help were negroes, as they had come to teach them, but having never seen them before they were pleased to have the opportunity of observing the negroes unnoticed." They particularly liked the blacks' soft voices and polite manners.[10] They also were exposed to Americans, most of whom were Protestants, for the first time. Sister Julie Roussel's description of the Americans onboard reveals not only her impressions of them, but also gives a taste of her dry sense of humor: "Each time we went to table we could hardly wait to leave the dining room so we could laugh freely. The Americans in their turn must laugh at us if, however, they are capable of unbending a bit. What a serious race! They would make good religious, at least silence would cost them very little."[11] Aware of the anti-Catholicism of many Americans, the sisters had debated whether to wear their habits on the trip. The decision to don them proved a good one, for because of them they were met with curiosity rather than hostility and were treated with great respect rather than derision.[12]

In New York, the sisters were met by three Florida priests who then traveled with them to Savannah. While there, the sisters stayed with the Sisters of Charity of Our Lady of Mercy.[13]

9. Letter no. 2, Sr. Julie Roussel to Le Puy Community, August 4, 1866, ASSJSA.
10. [Sister Julia Mickler, SSJ], *Sheaves Gathered from the Missionary Fields of the Sisters of St. Joseph in Florida, 1866–1936* (St. Augustine: Diocese of St. Augustine, 1936), 9.
11. Letter no. 7, Sr. Julie Roussel, Savannah to her family, August 31, 1866, ASSJSA.
12. Letter no. 6, Sr. Julie Roussel to Rev. Mtr., August 23, 1866, ASSJSA.
13. Mother Sidonie explained to Mother Agathe in Le Puy that the Sisters in Savannah were not from the same order as the Sisters of Mercy in St. Augustine, whose founder was Catherine McAuley; Mtr. Sidonie, St. Augustine, to Mtr Agathe, Le Puy, November 27,

Bishop Verot, from his house in Savannah, wrote to the bishop of Le Puy:

It is an indescribable pleasure for me to report that the good daughters, or rather the glorious heroines of your diocese, arrived in Savannah, after many days, all in good health, and with an admirable enthusiasm to consecrate themselves to the service of the poor black people, of whom they have already seen a large number.... I hope the good God will give them His blessing, and that the Blacks will run to them in crowds to be instructed. It will be necessary to open an orphanage for the young black boys and girls [in Savannah]; that will be the means of doing much good. Unfortunately, the black people are poor, and that enterprise will entail much expense; but Providence never is lacking toward its children, and I foresee that already in a short time I will have to request from Your Excellency another colony of Missionaries *in veils*.[14]

Just over a month later, Bishop Verot attended the Second Plenary Council of Catholic Bishops in Baltimore, from October 7 to October 21, 1866. The pastoral letter issued by the bishops after the council strongly addressed the church's responsibility to provide ministries to the newly freed slaves: "We must all feel, ... that in some manner a new and more extensive field of charity and devotedness has been open to us by the emancipation of the immense slave population of the South.... We urge upon the clergy and people of our charge the most generous co-operation

1866, ASSJSA. The Sisters in Savannah were an order created in Charleston by Bishop England in 1829 "'to educate females of the middling class of society; also to have a school for free colored girls and to give religious instruction to female slaves' and to care for the sick"; Mary Jane BeVard, ed., *One Faith, One Family: The Diocese of Savannah, 1850–2000* (Syracuse, N.Y.: Signature, 2000), 27. They are not to be confused with the Sisters of Mercy founded by Catherine McAuley in Ireland in 1831. At the suggestion of Rome, the Savannah Sisters of Mercy adopted the Constitution and habit of the McAuley Sisters of Mercy in 1892; "The Mother McAuley Sisters of Mercy," page 4; typescript on file in the Sisters of Mercy Archives, Macon, Georgia.

14. Letter no. 8, Bishop Verot, Savannah, to Bishop Le Breton, bishop of Le Puy, September 3, 1866, ASSJSA. Mother Sidonie Rascle wrote Mother Léocadie on September 14, 1866, that the plans to leave four Sisters of St. Joseph in Savannah to open the orphanage for small colored girls had to be postponed because the sisters did not yet speak English well enough.

... to extend to them that Christian education and moral restraint which they so much stand in need of." Shortly thereafter the newly founded Fathers of the Society of St. Joseph [Josephites] were designated to serve blacks in the United States.[15] Thus, the Sisters of St. Joseph's mission was in keeping with the goals of the Roman Catholic Church in America.

On September 2, 1866, the eight French Sisters of St. Joseph arrived in St. Augustine, a tiny town compared to Le Puy, located on the east coast of Florida, barely five feet above sea level. Aside from its European flavor, it was a place vastly different from Le Puy. At first, they stayed with the Sisters of Mercy, who warmly welcomed them.

The mother superior for the Mercy sisters was then Sister Aloysius, Mother Liguori having transferred elsewhere after the Civil War. Bishop Verot's diary records the personnel changes:

Feb 1866.... During my visitation of the convents of Columbus and St. Augustine, I perceived it was necessary to change the superioress, and having asked from Mother Bernard of Hartford, Ct., I obtained Sister Bonaventura, whom I appointed Mother and who went to Columbus to govern the community. The former superioress, Mother Liguori, left St. Augustine with Mother Agnes and Sister Frances. I appointed Sister Aloysius to govern the house of St. Augustine and letters reached me that the houses of Columbus and Augustine have peace and do very well.[16]

A series of articles about the Sisters of Mercy published in 1925 sheds a little more light on what prompted Mother Liguori's departure:

---

15. Miriam T. Murphy, "Catholic Missionary Work among the Colored People of the United States, 1776–1866," *Records of the American Catholic Historical Society* 35, no. 2 (June 1924): 127.

16. *Brief History of the Churches of the Diocese of Saint Augustine, Florida*, part 6, "Record of the Episcopal Acts of Rt. Rev. Augustine Verot, Bishop of Savannah and Administrator Apostolic of Florida" (Saint Leo, Fla.: Abbey Press, 1923), 167.

The Convent in St. Augustine was again opened, but two small convents under one Superior and so far distant from each other could not function satisfactorily. The exigencies of the times, the paralysis of all industries caused by the war, and the restrictions placed on the South by the Federal Government made life from day to day one long anxiety. In 1866, Mother Liguori returned North with her Sister Mother Agnes, whose health had become greatly impaired.[17]

For several months, the Sisters of St. Joseph stayed at the Mercy sisters' old convent located next to the new Mercy convent, the one completed in August 1861. During their first week there, the Sisters of Mercy sent meals over to the Sisters of St. Joseph, and the two communities shared their daily recreational periods in a garden between the two houses.[18] The arrangement worked very well. Mother Sidonie wrote:

The good Sisters of Mercy are perfect to us, and we are anything but perfect; we do not even know how to say "Thank you." Happily for us there is a French aspirant whom Bishop Verot brought from Paris seven years ago; she is 50 years old. She teaches piano and French. Miss Laura de Bertheville is therefore our interpreter; and [when] we cannot understand our excellent and holy little Sister Aloysia, Superior, we go to our "mouth-piece."[19]

The Sisters of St. Joseph hoped to set up their own household, but without the necessary provisions yet in hand, it seemed good to continue with the Sisters of Mercy. They consulted with Father Aubril, the Mercies' chaplain, and decided to stay longer, sharing expenses, including that of hiring a black woman to assist the lay sisters who performed housekeeping chores. Sister

17. Chapter 4, "The Sisters of Mercy of Macon," *The Bulletin of the Catholic Laymen's Association of Georgia*, December 12, 1925, 5, hereafter cited as "Sisters of Mercy of Macon"; according to Sister Aquin McEervey, Mother Agnes had had a nervous breakdown; "History of the 'Macon' Novitiate." Mother Liguori later was sent to establish a Sisters of Mercy community in Lacon, Illinois; "Sisters of Mercy of Macon," October 24, 1925, 6.

18. Letter no. 7, Sr. Julie Roussel, Savannah, to her family in France, August 31, 1866, ASSJSA.

19. Letter no. 10, Mtr. Sidonie Rascle, St. Augustine, to Rev. Mtr. Léocadie Broc, Le Puy, September 14, 1866, ASSJSA.

Mary Ann, a lay Sister of Mercy, did the laundry for both communities.[20] Under the new arrangement, the Sisters of St. Joseph ate with the Mercy sisters. It was customary for religious to listen to readings during meals, rather than conversing. The readings in English that the Sisters of St. Joseph heard and their conversations with the American Sisters of Mercy during the recreational periods greatly facilitated the French sisters' acquisition of English, though that remained a daunting task. Mother Sidonie continued, "We find ourselves perfectly at ease with those good religious. What a wholesome spirit in this country. When we asked to take our meals with the community, we were already sure our suggestion would be accepted. Miss Laura told us that Sister Superior would be happy to make one community with us."[21] Indeed, the two communities worked so well together that Mother Sidonie reported to her superiors in France, "We are almost Sisters of Mercy." Sisters Joséphine and Marie Joseph assisted the Mercy sisters by teaching a class for the novices for three days, while Sister Célenie tended to the sick, Sisters Clemence and Clotilde helped in the kitchen, and Sister St. Pierre swept the chapel and refectory (dining room).[22] Sister Joséphine DeLeage shared the enthusiasm toward the Sisters of Mercy when she wrote Mother Léocadie, "In St. Augustine the [Mercy sisters] are few [there were only four of them] which does not follow for their fervor; the Superior seems an angel in church. How edifying she is to me! How she confounds me! We are sharing in spiritual rapport."[23]

In addition to helping the Sisters of St. Joseph with their

20. Letter no. 16, Mtr. Sidonie Rascle, St. Augustine, to Rev. Mtr. Léocadie Broc, Le Puy, November 5, 1866, ASSJSA.

21. Letter no. 10, Mtr. Sidonie Rascle, St. Augustine, to Rev. Mtr. Léocadie Broc, Le Puy, September 14, 1866, ASSJSA.

22. Letter no. 15, Mtr. Sidonie Rascle, St. Augustine to Rev. Mtr. Léocadie Broc, Le Puy, October 12, 1866, ASSJSA.

23. Letter no. 12, Sr. Joséphine DeLeage, St. Augustine, to Mtr. Léocadie Broc, Le Puy, September 15, 1866, ASSJSA.

English, the Sisters of Mercy introduced them to the blacks of St. Augustine, the object of their mission. The Sisters of Mercy, in addition to running the schools for whites, had also been instructing blacks in the Catholic faith. Every Thursday night, black women in the Society of Monica, a sodality, met at the convent, where Sister Aloysia taught them the catechism. On Friday nights, girls in the Society of Holy Angels met there. The best students were awarded with a large white ribbon, worn like a scarf, with a medal at the shoulder.[24]

As the cooler months approached, Mother Aloysius took Mother Sidonie with her to visit a black man who was sick with swollen feet and was so impoverished that he had no fire to ward off the cold. Mother Sidonie wrote of the visit as her "apprenticeship," saying, "I wish, my dear Sisters, you could have seen the emaciation of the hands and face of that man; what an effect it made with that black skin! And yet, under that sad exterior what a beautiful soul! What resignation in his poverty, in the length of his sufferings."[25] After Mother Aloysius encouraged him and prayed for him, he addressed Mother Sidonie, saying, "French Sister, thank you for your visit, pray for me." Mother Sidonie was greatly touched and declared in her letter, "Oh, how happy I will be when I am able to speak comfortably in English, and to go to my good black people, to tell them about how great is the goodness of God toward His children!!" Her reference to the black man's soul is significant. One of Bishop Verot's convictions in caring for the blacks under his charge was that "negroes" did, indeed, have souls. He made his most public argument in support of the former slaves' full humanity and possession of souls when he addressed the Vatican Council that began December 8, 1869, and continued until July 1870, when it was

24. Letter no. 14, Mtr. Sidonie Rascle, St. Augustine, to Mr. Bonhomme, Le Puy, September 21, 1866, ASSJSA.
25. Letter no. 23, Mtr. Sidonie Rascle, St. Augustine, to the Sisters of St. Joseph in France, December 1, 1866, ASSJSA.

interrupted by the Franco-Prussian War. His long argument before the assembly can be summarized by his statement, "'But especially do we condemn the inept error of those who dare to assert that Negroes do not belong to the human family, or that they are not endowed with spiritual and immortal souls.'"[26] Mother Sidonie's exclamation, so similar to expressions used by the other sisters in describing their work with the blacks, shows how Verot had imbued them with a love for the former slaves and how ready they were to embrace the poor freedmen they had come to serve.

Although the Sisters of St. Joseph desired to move on into their own ministries to the freedmen, there was great contentment in working with the Sisters of Mercy. Apparently, Father Aubril, the Mercy sisters' chaplain, had even devised plans for joining the two communities,[27] but it was not to be. A month later, the Sisters of St. Joseph left to be on their own. The Sisters of Mercy were in tears. Mother Sidonie wrote, "We had a visit today from the Sisters of Mercy; they cried, poor Sisters; I pity them! They are not numerous enough.... How troubled I was those days to have nothing to give those good religious and to those [Sisters of Mercy] who did so much for us."[28] Even though they had separated, the Sisters of St. Joseph continued to help the Sisters of Mercy by teaching their students French.

The Sisters of St. Joseph progressed in their work but were still greatly hampered by their inability to speak English well, a handicap that would be vexing to all of them and to Bishop Verot in their first year. In November, however, six new postulants from Savannah, some of whom were Americans, helped them overcome the language barrier, and the sisters opened a

26. Gannon, *Rebel Bishop*, 206.

27. Letter no. 24, Sr. Joséphine Deleage, St. Augustine, to Mtr. Léocadie Broc, December 1, 1866, ASSJSA.

28. Letter no. 35, Mtr. Sidonie Rascle, St. Augustine, to Mtr. Léocadie Broc, Le Puy, January 1, 1867, ASSJSA.

school for black children in St. Augustine.[29] Mother Sidonie said that the black children were "proud of being taught by French Sisters, whom the people [of St. Augustine] despised on that account." In February 1867, Mother Sidonie was able to send five sisters to establish a similar school in Savannah. Sister Julie Roussel was the superior, and the teachers were Sisters Josephine and Marie Joseph; Sisters St. John and St. Paul, both new novices, were also part of the faculty. They taught out of a "rickety frame building on the grounds of St. John's Cathedral."[30]

As in St. Augustine, most of the white citizens of Savannah were unhappy at having a school for blacks and did not welcome the sisters, some referring to them as "nigger Sisters." Bishop Verot's announcement of the school's opening was met with "whispering of disapproval" throughout the congregation.[31] Even so, the school opened with fifty students and went on to provide night classes for adults. In October, four more sisters arrived, and Mother Julie returned to St. Augustine with three new sisters. Back in the Ancient City, they established a school for white boys.

If the whites of St. Augustine at first looked askance at the sisters, Mother Sidonie was not very well impressed with the Americans, either. She wrote:

St. Augustine is an extremely poor country; they are very lazy here; there is no commerce, no industry. Culture is entirely neglected. They bring in grain from Savannah or New York ... also everything is for a crazy price.... The people of St. Augustine live almost like patriarchs of old. Each one bakes bread; each one does care for his house, each cultivates his garden, then strolls along the riverside. The poor go fishing every day to seek their nourishment for the next day. If fishing is

29. Sister Thomas Joseph McGoldrick, "A Study of the Contributions of the Sisters of St. Joseph of St. Augustine to Education, 1866–1960" (unpublished Master's thesis, University of Florida, 1961), 24.
30. Sister Mary Alberta, "Study of the Schools," 3.
31. Sister Mary Alberta, "Study of the Schools," 3.

Bishop Augustin Verot.
Courtesy of the Archives of the Sisters of St. Joseph of
St. Augustine, St. Augustine, Florida.

good, they eat; if they are not successful, they patiently wait for the following day; they never have provisions on hand. One lives from day to day; they are perfectly detached from life; they die; very well!!!![32]

Of the blacks, however, she wrote:

Except for a few families, the negroes are almost as well off as the white people; the latter were accustomed to being served before the abolition of slavery and they cannot be reconciled to work; the black people were their bread winners, while these freed men now work for themselves zealously. With them they have everything to gain; … These poor people are despised; they are allowed to have nothing to do with white people except to serve them.[33]

32. Letter no. 26, Mtr. Sidonie Rascle, St. Augustine, to Sr. Louis Gonzaga Bache, Assistant, n.p., December 3, 1866, ASSJSA.
33. Letter no. 15, Mtr. Sidonie Rascle, St. Augustine, to Rev. Mtr. Léocadie Broc, Le Puy, October 12, 1866, ASSJSA.

Within a year, the Sisters of St. Joseph were well established in their St. Augustine schools. Although there was some initial opposition to their work with the African Americans, St. Augustine soon embraced the French nuns. In August of 1867, a citizen commented on their work among the freedmen: "We hear ... that the Sisters of St. Joseph have met with success in training the coloured children of St. Augustine.... [We] cannot give too much praise to these devoted Sisters of St. Joseph, for having left their happy country and all the comforts of 'la Belle France' to assist in the great work of the moral regeneration of the African race."[34] Coming from France placed the sisters at a great advantage in the larger, more prosperous city of Savannah also. Sister Julie Roussel wrote:

You would not believe the honor which Americans extend to our beautiful France. I think they look on her as queen of all the countries in the universe. Everything that is perfect in goodness, beauty, stability, and even holiness comes from France. A family which is sufficiently comfortable to have a regular servant would not want to admit the servant was not French; a ball gown that does not come from Paris is nothing; the sardines of which they are so fond here, are not good if one does not read on the little tin box the name of our French towns, of Lorient above all.[35]

The sisters in general expressed great satisfaction with their work. They were appalled at the African Americans' need for good Catholic instruction. Mother Sidonie wrote to the bishop in Le Puy that the black children who they taught were "among the most profoundly ignorant," especially concerning religion, not even knowing how to make the sign of the cross. The "negroes" had great desire to learn and were particularly attracted to singing and "learn[ed] airs with amazing ease." The sisters

34. *Examiner*, August 17, 1867.
35. Letter no. 51, Sr. Marie Julie Roussel, Savannah, to Sisters in Le Puy, July 5, 1867, ASSJSA.

seemed to concentrate on religious instruction, but also taught them the basic ABCs and arithmetic.[36]

Most of the sisters expressed great warmth and love for their new black charges. Sr. St. Pierre, for example, wrote she had "no regrets from leaving our dear France" and that she was "happy to have been chosen for such beautiful work." She looked forward to teaching the black children, and later was assigned to teach girls.[37] Sr. Célenie, who taught small children with Mother Sidonie, wrote, "I have one desire only, that is to become useful and to procure the glory of the good God by teaching His poor little blacks whom I already love and am attracted to although they may be very unhandsome; but they have a soul created in the image of God!!"[38] Such expressions were typical of most of the sisters. Some, however, had to overcome negative feelings. For example, Sister Lazarus L'hostal, who had just arrived from Le Puy in December 1867, wrote about her first impressions:

I must tell you, good Mother, the pain I felt seeing the black people. The day after our arrival in Savannah, we went into the classes; when I saw all those black faces, where only eyes and teeth show white, I couldn't look at them; I didn't go near them; I was afraid of them; we stayed there almost a half quarter hour [?] and I was anxious to leave those classes; and I asked myself how would I ever teach class; I felt such repugnance it seemed that would be what I would have the most trouble about, then I consoled myself thinking that as yet I didn't have to begin, and I would have the time to get used to them; and already I fear them less."[39]

36. Letter no. 88, Mtr. Sidonie Rascle, St. Augustine, to the bishop [of Le Puy], December 10, 1867, ASSJSA.

37. Letter no. 18, Sr. St. Pierre Borie, St. Augustine, to Rev. Mtr. Léocadie Broc, November 25, 1866, ASSJSA.

38. Letter no. 28, Sr. Célenie Joubert, St. Augustine, to Rev. Mtr. Léocadie Broc, Le Puy, December 3, 1866, ASSJSA.

39. Letter no. 84, Sr. Lazarre Lostal [sic], St. Augustine, to Sr. Marie de Sales, Le Puy, June 18, 1870, ASSJSA; "Soeur Lazare," *Notices Nécrologiques des Soeurs de St. Joseph de 1912 á 1942*, p. 6; original at ASSJLP.

Sister Lazarus did, indeed, overcome her aversions, and loved the forty-five black girls she later taught. She eventually became the local superior and provincial superior in St. Augustine.

Suffering was considered part of the missionary experience. Sister Julie Clotilde, however, wrote in November 1866, "Suffering seen from a distance [has] much attraction, but near at hand it is not so easy, but this still does not give a moment of regret; I have not come to have what I would like thus I am not disturbed to have to suffer."[40] Indeed, suffering was expected, perhaps even anticipated, for as Mother Sidonie wrote, "If we had nothing to suffer, we would not be true missionaries"[41] They were not disappointed. Physically, they endured poor food, long hours, heat and humidity, and attacks from mosquitoes. Emotionally, they suffered from the strain of teaching students who were despised by the general population; their initial difficulties in speaking English, that "villainous language";[42] and the strain of being so far from all that was comfortable, familiar, and secure. Teaching, itself, could also be quite trying. Sister Julie Clotilde confessed in a letter to Mother Agathe, "I often think of what you said, that the mistake of young teachers is to scold too much; however, I am driven to that sad necessity. I am almost always with students; in the day with 'the girls,' the evenings with 'the Women'; just the same I am content in spite of my little troubles; but I need patience."[43] Her sufferings culminated in July of the next year, when she died of typhoid.

The first death in the little community, however, was the death of their youngest member, Sister Marie Joseph Cortial,

40. Letter no. 16, Sr. Julie Clotilde, St. Augustine, to Mtr. Léocadie Broc, Le Puy, November 18, 1866, ASSJSA.
41. Letter no, 15, Mtr. Sidonie Rascle, St. Augustine, to Rev. Mtr. Léocadie Broc, Le Puy, October 12, 1866, ASSJSA.
42. Letter no. 7, Sr. Julie Roussel, St. Augustine, to her family in France, August 31, 1866, ASSJSA.
43. Letter no. 47, Sr. Marie Clotilde Arsac, St. Augustine, to Mtr. Agatha Deschayeux, Le Puy, May 11, 1867, ASSJSA.

who died from tuberculosis in March 1868. Marie Joseph had been assigned to Savannah, but had returned to St. Augustine, where she died. Mother Sidonie's account of her death shows the devotion felt by her black neighbors:

There was a dispute at the parish Church about the question of decorating the catafalque of our poor Sister! The ladies of the City, who are in charge of decorating the church were preparing to do it in their best manner; but Marie Pappet, the head of the black women, opposed them about it; she said to those ladies: "Sister Marie Joseph came for us and not for you, ladies, so it is right for us to take charge of her funeral, and we are the ones who will walk first in the procession."

Marie Pappet prevailed, and the blacks led the impressive procession. Sister Bertrand continued:

That dear Marie did very well; she put out all the lights and candles she could find in the church and at the Mercy Convent (that woman has "white feet" although her skin is black). When I wanted to know how much I owed her for the candles she answered: "There is no question of that! The preacher said it well; you have made enough sacrifices for us; the church can very well furnish the lights in this circumstance," and she wiped her eyes with her shawl; then she added: "The whites were upset because we were first in the procession; but it was only just. Sister Marie Joseph was first a teacher of the black children." That word "first" flatters them. They believe they were honored in the procession; since that day they feel ennobled.[44]

With such a strong relationship established with the black community, the sisters were able to work effectively in St. Augustine.

In addition to teaching the black children, the sisters also taught classes for adults in the evenings. The women met on Mondays, Tuesdays, and Fridays; the men met on Thursdays, Saturdays, and Sundays; and everyone met together on Wednesdays. Mother Sidonie described the mid-week session:

44. Letter no. 8, Tome II, Mtr. Sidonie Rascle, St. Augustine, to Rev. Mother, Le Puy, March 24, 1868, ASSJSA.

After Wednesday session we have Benediction of the Blessed Sacrament in the chapel; all sing—men, women, postulants, and Sisters.... Black people learn the melodies easily and sing well. How I love to hear God's praises sung by all these poor people. Young and old shout, sing with all their heart and soul. How much good we could do among these poor people if we knew how to speak [English] and above all if we were true apostles.[45]

In their letters, the sisters often commented on the blacks' love of singing, and how useful it was in teaching them. Another useful tool was the establishment of sodalities for the children as well as adults. The Sisters of St. Joseph continued the sodalities established by the Sisters of Mercy, the societies of St. Monica for black women, Holy Angels for black girls, and St. Joseph for young black boys. They also established some new ones: St. Frances of Rome and the Ladies of the Sacred Heart in St. Augustine. The latter was composed of the mothers of the black families. The group had about forty-eight members who met monthly at the convent and discussed ways to assist the poor and sick. They took up small collections for the needy, and members would sit up with the sick through the night as needed.[46] Other sodalities met monthly or weekly and took part in services on feast days and in special ceremonies with much pageantry enlivened with official badges and colorful banners and sashes distinctive to each society.[47]

The loving partnership between the Sisters of Mercy and Sisters of St. Joseph continued for two years. By August 1869, however, it had become clear that the Sisters of Mercy were too small in number to sustain their ministries in St. Augustine.

45. Letter no. 38, Mtr. Sidonie Rascle, St. Augustine, to Rev. Mtr. Léocadie Broc, Le Puy, February 17, 1867, ASSJSA.

46. Letter no. 41, Tome II, Mtr. Stanislas, St. Augustine, to Mtr. Léocadie Broc, Le Puy, August 5, 1873, ASSJSA.

47. Letter no. 39, Sr. Marie Julie Roussel, St. Augustine, to Community in Le Puy, January 6, 1873, and Letter no. 14, Mtr. Sidonie Rascle, St. Augustine, to the Community in Le Puy, September 20, 1866, ASSJSA.

After much discussion and fervent prayer, the Sisters of Mercy regretfully decided they would have to give up their work in the Ancient City. St. Augustine's Sisters of Mercy left to join their fellow sisters in Columbus. They gave St. Mary's Academy over to the Sisters of St. Joseph, who renamed the school St. Joseph's Academy. At the request of Bishop Verot, the two lay Sisters of Mercy, Sisters Monica and Mary Ann, remained in St. Augustine and became Sisters of St. Joseph. The Sisters of Mercy remained in Columbus until that entire religious community relocated to Macon, Georgia, in 1876.[48]

The decision for the Sisters of Mercy to leave was final after the vicariate apostolic of Florida, attached to the Diocese of Savannah, was erected as a separate Diocese of St. Augustine on March 11, 1870. Bishop Verot, who had been the bishop of Savannah since July 14, 1861, was given the choice of maintaining his bishopric in Savannah or leading the new Florida diocese. He chose to stay in St. Augustine, and the Right Reverend Ignatius Persico, D.D., became the new bishop of Savannah in 1871.[49]

Over the next several years, the French Sisters of St. Joseph established other schools for freedmen in St. Augustine and nearby communities. The second foundation, after St. Augustine, was in Savannah, Georgia. In 1867, Mother Sidonie sent Sister Joséphine, one of the original Sisters of St. Joseph in St. Augustine, along with several other sisters to establish a colony there. Sister Joséphine became the third mother superior of the community in 1870. The next year, 1871, Bishop Persico broke the sisters' tie to the motherhouse in St. Augustine and changed their name to the Sisters of St. Joseph of Georgia. The sisters maintained loving relations with the Sisters of St. Joseph in St. Augustine, even though their administrative ties had been

48. McEervey, "History of the 'Macon,'" 1.
49. "Sisters of Mercy in Macon," 5.

cut. Their story at this point diverges from that of the Sisters of St. Joseph of St. Augustine and is, therefore, addressed separately in chapter 8.

Meanwhile, back in Florida in 1867, Verot and the sisters in St. Augustine had considered establishing a new foundation in Jacksonville, a place where there was little Catholic presence. Mother Sidonie looked forward to the new colony, for she felt it would be a base of operations for the sisters in Savannah and St. Augustine. As a small but growing commercial town, there would be more opportunities for the sisters to support themselves as they taught free classes for the blacks. Writing to Reverend Mother Léocadie in Le Puy on September 1, 1867, she told how she persuaded Verot that it would be important for them also to teach whites, saying that they would be "little esteemed [in Jacksonville] if we had no white classes."

Before the Jacksonville foundation was established, however, Bishop Verot desired the sisters' work to begin in Mandarin, a small community of the east side of the St. Johns River, southeast of Jacksonville (now a part of Jacksonville). On February 3, 1868, Sister Julie Roussel and Sister Mary Bernard, who was still a novice, went to Mandarin to open schools for white and black children. On February 10, classes began; forty white students were taught in the main part of the church and twenty-seven black children were taught in the sacristy, a 12 x 16-foot room with one window. The sisters stayed at the home of a Mrs. Hartley nearly a mile away and walked this distance four times a day. This exertion, coupled with a poor diet of hominy, sweet potatoes, molasses, cabbage, and occasional salt pork, soon left Sister Julie in extremely poor health. The mission in Mandarin was, therefore, abandoned until 1873. Sister Julie Roussel, along with another sister and a lay teacher, returned at that time and lived in their own house, greatly assisted by Father Langlade, who provided priestly services and remodeled the house for them to be able to accommodate boarders. Sister Julie reported that there were then four public schools, two for whites and two for blacks. The sisters had twenty-one students who met from 9:00 a.m. until 4:00 p.m.[50] At first, the sisters had girl boarders, but beginning in 1881, only boys were taken as boarders, while the girls continued as day students. A new convent was constructed in 1884.[51] Sister Julie died in Mandarin on December 10, 1886.

Shortly after the first mission to Mandarin was initiated, Mother Sidonie's desire to establish the foundation in Jacksonville was achieved. She had drawn up plans for a convent and school, and work on their construction began in 1868. They were completed in time for Mother Sidonie's November 15, 1869, arrival to be the superior in Jacksonville. She was accompanied by Sister Célenie Joubert, who had come with her from France in 1866; Sister Mary Ann Hoare, the lay Sister of Mercy who at Bishop Verot's request had joined the Sisters of St. Joseph when the other Sisters of Mercy left St. Augustine; Sister Clavéry Chambouvet; and a novice. The five sisters who made up the community were very pleased with the new convent Mother Sidonie had designed and soon began teaching. Sister Clavéry reported that a number of their students were Protestants who had "a thousand questions about our religion."[52]

The work in Jacksonville was quite difficult. Mother Sidonie reported:

We can do nothing with the blacks; all belong to different religions. The population of negroes is composed of 5,000 souls, of which only 30 are Catholic.... They have eight different churches of their own. Their ministers preach constantly. They have their Bishops also. From time to time there are missions, *of their fashion,* ... they have extraordinary times of prayer. Thus they pass almost the entire Sunday at

50. Letter no. 39, Sister Marie Julie, Mandarin, to Le Puy, March 12, 1873, ASSJSA.
51. Mickler, *Sheaves,* 42–45.
52. Mickler, *Sheaves,* 33; Letter no. 31, Sr. Clavéry Chambouvet, Jacksonville, to Mother Agathe Deshayeux, Le Puy, December 23, 1869, ASSJSA.

First Sisters of St. Joseph of St. Augustine from Le Puy, France.
Courtesy of the Archives of the Sisters of St. Joseph of St. Augustine,
St. Augustine, Florida.

church; they sing there; one preaches; this lasts until midnight. The devil does his work well there! Truly, without the aid of satan the poor people would not be able to resist fatigue; on certain occasions they resemble fanatics; they make a hellish noise. We have no hope.

With such despair of ever reaching the African Americans in any great numbers, the sisters turned toward the whites. Jacksonville had a population of about five or six thousand, five hundred of whom were counted as Catholics. Of those, only thirty regularly attended church. Mother Sidonie reported, "The best don't have religious instruction; they have false principles, little faith; the love of pleasure and money dominates." Their strongest hopes lay in reaching the young people.[53] By 1874, the sisters had made some progress; the city then hosted twelve Protestant churches and two Catholic churches. The many schools already existing in Jacksonville, however, hampered their educational work there.[54]

In 1871, the sisters in Jacksonville fulfilled the wish of the pastor of the Catholic church in Fernandina to have two sisters assist in preparing children for their First Communion. Sister Célenie and a Sister Hélène left for Fernandina on May 12. There, they lived in the church and taught the children. The children's parents took turns providing meals for the sisters. Mother Sidonie expressed her excitement about the new foundation and described the mission for the sisters in France:

I am happy to have … some good news to tell you. It is about a fifth foundation, a new field where your daughters will be able to work in the vineyard of the Lord. On the 12th of this month, May, my very good and dear Sister Célenie and Sister Hélène, novice, left for their mission, Fernandina.

Fernandina is a pretty little town between Savannah and Jacksonville. It has a port on the Atlantic; the largest ships may land there. The place is charming; it has always smiled at me. Surrounded like Jacksonville with great evergreen trees, it has a delightful aspect.

For the moment, our Sisters have only a single room for the two of them and two others for their classes; that is all they possess. In order to attract children, the classes will be free until the opening of school in September. Seven families have undertaken to provide for the needs of the Sisters; each family has a day assigned for sending the Sisters their three meals, which they take in their little bedchamber.

53. Letter no. 31, Mtr. Sidonie, Jacksonville, to Msgr. Le Superieur, Le Puy, December 18, 1872, ASSJSA.

54. Letter no. 5, Mtr. Marie Sidonie, Jacksonville, to Our Rev. Mother, [Le Puy], May 17, 1871, ASSJSA.

She also noted the competition they would have with the Episcopalians:

Fernandina is the Episcopal city of the bishop of the Episcopalians; he has a pretty temple [church] and a magnificent home, but what is most distressing is that he has a boarding school or seminary for young girls; he has distinguished teachers, English and French, and excellent musicians. It will be necessary for our poor Sisters to compete with Bishop Young.[55]

Mother Sidonie was referring to St. Mary's Priory, a boarding school for white young ladies established by Bishop John Freeman Young. It was started with a personal loan from the bishop himself and received support from other parishes in the Episcopal Diocese of Florida. It was the Episcopal Church's first such school in Florida. As revealed by the September 15, 1866, *St. Augustine Examiner*, St. Mary's Priory was established explicitly as a countermeasure to the Sisters of Mercy's successful St. Mary's Academy in St. Augustine: "One of the aims of the new priory at Fernandina was to draw the Protestant students in St. Augustine to it and to the Episcopal Church." Their rivalry lasted throughout most of the Reconstruction period, though St. Mary's Priory was at a disadvantage because its teachers were not teaching sisters, resulting in much higher tuition fees. Many of the Episcopalians in St. Augustine, therefore, continued to send their children to St. Mary's Academy.[56] Bishop Young's dream of staffing the priory with an Episcopal teaching order was never realized.

In 1870, through generous donations, St. Mary's Priory was able to purchase ten acres for an improved facility; it began to increase in stature and enrollment. By 1873, the priory had sixty

55. Letter no. 5, Tome II, Mtr. Marie Sidonie, Jacksonville, to Our Rev. Mother, [Le Puy], May 17, 1871, ASSJSA.

56. Joseph D. Cushman Jr., *A Goodly Heritage: The Episcopal Church in Florida, 1821–1892* (Gainesville: University Press of Florida, 1965), 87–89.

girls enrolled and a staff of six. It was during this time of the school's prosperity that Mother Sidonie bemoaned the competition the sisters faced from the Episcopalians. In reality, they had nothing to fear. Although the Episcopal Church supported several schools, the nationwide financial panic in 1873 and mismanagement kept the schools quite small. The Episcopal Church in Florida was never able to successfully compete with the combined forces of the Roman Catholic academies and the schools of the emerging public-school system.[57]

By May of 1871, Sister Célenie's health was so impaired from a lack of proper diet that the sisters temporarily left Fernandina. Célenie returned with additional sisters in October, however, with the intent to remain permanently, and they settled into a rented cottage. Among the newcomers under Mother Célenie were Sisters Marie de Sales, Marie Louise, and Xavier.[58] By the end of the decade, the sisters had established two free schools for blacks and whites in 1872: St. Peter Claver School for blacks in 1874 and a St. Joseph's Academy for whites in 1879.[59]

In 1873, Bishop William Gross succeeded Persico as the bishop of Savannah, and in May 1874, Gross severed the sisters' ties with the motherhouse in Le Puy. This pronouncement took the sisters in Le Puy by surprise and rocked the order. He gave the Sisters of St. Joseph in Georgia twenty-four hours to accept the new diocesan status under him or to leave the diocese. Mother Joséphine chose to leave. She resigned from her position and returned to St. Augustine briefly before returning to Le Puy, France. In October 1875, she returned to St. Augustine in the company of Mother Léocadie Broc, then assistant general from the motherhouse in Le Puy. Mother Léocadie came for a

57. Cushman, *A Goodly Heritage*, 90–93.

58. Mickler, *Sheaves*, 50.

59. *The Sisters of Saint Joseph of Saint Augustine, Florida: Our First One Hundred Years, 1866–1966, 2000* (St. Augustine: Sisters of St. Joseph, 2000), unpaged. Hereafter cited as *Our First One Hundred Years*.

lengthy visitation to the sisters in Florida. In January, she, accompanied by Mothers Lazarus L'hostal and Stanislas Bertrand, went to investigate the possibilities of establishing a house in Palatka, Florida. The order bought land at the corner of Lemon and Fourth streets to establish a convent; it was built by the end of the year. The colony was founded in 1876 by Sisters Joséphine, Mary Regis Defour, and Mary Joseph Canova, Sister Joséphine serving as the superior for nearly two years. During that time, they established a girls' academy. Mother Joséphine returned to the motherhouse in St. Augustine in November 1877 and served as the procurator (financial administrator).

The Sisters of St. Joseph continued to establish new foundations for the next several decades, expanding their number to ten by the first decade of the twentieth century: first, St. Augustine in 1866; second, Savannah, Georgia, in 1867; third, Mandarin in 1874; fourth, Jacksonville in 1869; fifth, Fernandina in 1872; sixth, Palatka in 1876; seventh, Elkton in 1882; eighth, Orlando in 1889; ninth, Ybor City in 1891; and tenth, Miami in 1905.

By 1920, the Sisters of St. Joseph had opened day schools in Palatka (1876); St. Ambrose School in Elkton, southwest of St. Augustine (1882); St. Agnes School, North City, a suburb of St. Augustine (1889); St. Joseph Academies in Orlando (1891) and in Ybor City (now part of Tampa) (1892); and St. Cecelia's School, a school for black students, in St. Augustine (1898).

The Ybor City foundation was on the west coast of Florida, over two hundred miles away from St. Augustine, but its difference from the other missions went beyond geography, and a fuller discussion of the sisters' work there is warranted. Unlike the earlier missions, which established schools for whites and blacks, the work in Ybor City focused on the community's large number of cigar factory workers, most of whom were Spanish, Cuban, Sicilian, or Italian and had been brought up in the Catholic Church. The large influx of these ethnic groups came to the

Tampa area in 1885, when Vicente Martinez Ybor, a Spaniard by birth, moved his cigarmaking enterprises from Key West to establish factories and a company town two miles northeast of downtown Tampa. Other cigar manufacturers also relocated to Tampa after two major fires in Key West. By 1900, the number of factories and workers surpassed the numbers in Key West. Of the immigrants, Cubans made up the largest group.[60]

A concerted Catholic effort to work with the people of Tampa began as result of yellow fever epidemics in 1887 and 1888. Jesuit priests were sent to Tampa and were so successful that Bishop John Moore, the second bishop of the Diocese of St. Augustine, asked them to stay. The first Catholic church in Ybor City was Our Lady of Mercy, built in 1890, five years after the founding of Ybor's company town, with the expectation of meeting the spiritual needs of the 2,500 Cubans, plus the Italian and Spanish Catholics.[61]

In response to a request from the Jesuit priests, Bishop Moore asked that some Sisters of St. Joseph be sent to minister to the Cubans in Ybor City. In September 1891, Mother Lazarus L'hostal, the provincial superior of the Sisters of St. Joseph in Florida, accompanied three sisters to open a house there. They were: French Sister Onésime Vedrine, age thirty-seven, who came from the academy in Jacksonville, as the superior; Mary Catherine Byrne, age thirty-two, from the Orlando house, where she had been the superior; and Theophelia Sullivan, a novice in her twenties, from Massachusetts.

A different group of Catholic sisters, Sisters of the Holy Names of Jesus and Mary, had established an Academy of the Holy Names in Tampa in 1881 and were quite successful with their white, English-speaking students. Those sisters also ran a

60. Gary Mormino and George Pozzetta, *The Immigrant World of Ybor City: Italians and Their Latin Neighbors in Tampa, 1885–1985* (Urbana and Chicago: University of Illinois Press, 1987), 63–67, 76.

61. Mormino and Pozzetta, *Immigrant World of Ybor City*, 210.

school for black children: St. Peter Claver Catholic School.[62] The Sisters of St. Joseph's mission to the immigrants of Ybor City was quite different from the one in Tampa. Living in a tiny three-room cottage next to the church, they managed to begin classes a week after their arrival, using various areas in the church building as their classrooms, where they taught the usual curriculum of academic and religious subjects. As with the first sisters who came to Florida in 1866, language was a barrier; none of the sisters spoke Spanish or Italian. Even so, Vicente Ybor, the great cigar manufacturer, and many factory employees sent their children to the sisters' school.

The sisters found the children to be "intelligent but utterly ignorant of their religious duties," practicing various forms of popular religious piety, but with little understanding of standard, church-sanctioned religious practices. Few ever attended Mass, and those who did were usually women and children. Concerning masculine participation, the sisters observed, "The men, with very few exceptions, have no faith." Discipline was also a problem: "Teaching ... was difficult. The children were bright but not accustomed to restraint. They would speak aloud in school, leave their places without permission and, as it was necessary to have someone interpret all that was said by teachers or pupils, there was unending confusion." The teaching environment was so difficult that two novices quit, abandoning their aspirations to become sisters.[63]

In 1892, with money borrowed or raised through fairs, the sisters built a small frame building to serve as St. Joseph's Academy. It was completed in October, and the following spring there were 176 students. The academy offered the same classes as were provided in the initial classes, but now the sisters also offered

62. Jane Quinn, "Nuns in Ybor City: The Sisters of St. Joseph and the Immigrant Community," *Tampa Bay History* 5, no. 1 (Spring/Summer 1983): 26.

63. Annals of the Sisters of St. Joseph in Ybor City on file at ASSJSA; quoted in Quinn, "Nuns in Ybor City," 28.

instruction in music, drawing, calligraphy, phonography (a phonetic writing system), typewriting, sewing, and embroidery. The lack of money, however, was always a problem, and it was not until 1895 that a real convent was built for the sisters.[64]

By 1895–96, the sisters began teaching English to Italian immigrants, but at the same time, the war between Spain and its Cuban colony impacted the sisters' work. Many of their Cuban students stopped paying their tuition or stopped attending altogether because their families were sending funds to support the Cuban revolution. When the United States entered the conflict in 1898, many American troops were stationed in Tampa and Fernandina. The Sisters of St. Joseph were among those who helped to tend to the soldiers' medical needs. At the convent, Mother Onésime left to become the superior at the Orlando house; she was replaced by Mother Marie Louise Hughes.[65]

The chronicles recorded by the sisters in Ybor City mention the difficulties they encountered but give no hint of the deep-seated hatred with which they were viewed by the radicals in the community. In their book *The Immigrant World of Ybor City: Italians and Their Latin Neighbors in Tampa, 1885–1985*, Gary Mormino and George Pozzetta provide a grimmer description of the sisters' experiences in Ybor City. The difficulties extended beyond the challenge of teaching unruly children who did not speak the sisters' language.

The late nineteenth and early twentieth centuries were a time of challenges to the old order by radical ideas such as anarchism, socialism, and communism coming out of Southern Europe. A part of the old order that was rejected was formal religion, especially that espoused by the Roman Catholic Church. This antipathy grew out of many immigrants' experiences with a

64. Quinn, "Nuns in Ybor City," 29–30.
65. Sister Thomas Joseph, McGoldrick, SSJ, *Beyond the Call: The Legacy of the Sisters of St. Joseph of St. Augustine, Florida* (n.p.: Xlibris, copyright held by the author, 2008), 301; Quinn, "Nuns in Ybor City," 32; Mickler, *Sheaves*, 66–69.

corrupt church in Europe, whose priests and bishops, they said, had built temporal empires at the expense of the poor.[66]

The Cuban, Sicilian, and Italian workers in Ybor City were particularly hostile toward the local Roman Catholic priests because they had accepted donations from the Spanish factory owners who dominated the church. Their privileged place of power was particularly odious to the Cubans who supported the Cuban rebellion against Spain. They considered the Catholic Church and the colonial Spanish government both to be oppressors of Cuba. In addition to the class struggles, adherents of the prevailing radical ideologies fomented hatred of the Catholic Church, seeing it as "an even greater foe than capitalism." According to Mormino and Pozzetta, "Parish priests, missionaries and the Sisters of St. Joseph ... battled a stream of anticlerical invective which filled the pages of leftist newspapers and frequently spilled over into street-corner rhetoric."[67] The authors assert that although churches and schools were built, the Catholics actually realized little success in their efforts to overcome apathy or outright hostility until later in the twentieth century. This evaluation seems to be supported by Bishop Patrick Barry, the prelate over the Diocese of St. Augustine, who wrote in 1935, "For fifty years and more, zealous, unselfish priests and Sisters here exhausted themselves in trying to save these people [of Ybor City], and their reward must be sought in heaven for they receive no earthly one."[68]

Protestant missionaries also sought to reach the souls of the Ybor City immigrants. Seeing the difficulties encountered by the Catholic Church, various Protestant denominations tried to break through the antagonism toward organized religion: Congregationalists from 1893 to 1904, Episcopalians from

---

66. Mormino and Pozzetta, *Immigrant World of Ybor City*, 23.
67. Mormino and Pozzetta, *Immigrant World of Ybor City*, 212.
68. Bishop Patrick J. Barry to Amleto Giovanni Gicognani, August 25, 1935, ASSJSA; quoted in Mormino and Pozzetta, *Immigrant World of Ybor City*, 221.

1894 to ca. 1897, Baptists from 1902 to the 1930s, Presbyterians from 1908 to ca. 1910, and Methodists (the Methodist Episcopal Church, South) from 1886 to 1939. They tried to minister to the Cubans, Sicilians, and Italians with varying degrees of success until about 1940. With such hostility toward formal religion getting in the way of many of their efforts, the successes they achieved came through the schools, including nursery schools and kindergartens that assisted the working mothers, rather than through the churches.[69]

In many respects, the missionary efforts in Ybor City repeated the experiences of the Sisters of St. Joseph and the missionaries of the American Missionary Association who competed with each other to reach the freedmen after the Civil War. In Ybor City, however, the cultural differences exceeded the language barriers for the sisters. Both the sisters and their rivals, the Protestant missionaries, faced adherents of radical ideologies that included a virulent anticlericalism based on Old World experiences with the Catholic Church. The ideologies created a hatred for formal religion that the even the sisters' rivals could not overcome, as evidenced by their relatively short-lived efforts. The Catholic Church, however, persevered. The Sisters of St. Joseph left Ybor City in 1944 and turned their work at St. Joseph's Academy over to the Sisters of Notre Dame; their work at St. Benedict the Moor School, a school for African Americans they had opened in February 1903, was turned over to the Sisters of St. Francis.[70]

Because of the tensions associated with the cultural and political climate of Tampa, the school in Tampa presented the Sisters of St. Joseph with challenges unlike those experienced at the other schools they had established in Florida. Despite those challenges, however, the establishment of St. Cecilia's School for

69. Mormino and Pozzetta, *Immigrant World of Ybor City*, 225–27.
70. McGoldrick, *Beyond the Call*, 301.

The Sisters of St. Joseph's First Class in St. Augustine, 1867.
Courtesy of the Archives of the Sisters of St. Joseph of St. Augustine,
St. Augustine, Florida.

the black children in St. Augustine was the crowning achievement of the sisters' work to educate African American children in Florida.

From the very beginning of the Sisters of St. Joseph's ministry to the people of St. Augustine, the spiritual and secular education of the newly freed slaves was their primary objective. Over the years until 1898, the sisters taught in a variety of locations. Their first school, one for black boys, opened in November 1866 in a small coquina and tabby building located just south of the southeast corner of Cadiz (formerly known as Green) Street and St. George Street. The sisters began with twenty students, but by February 1867, there were sixty boys enrolled. They also taught girls in a separate class. The black adults met for class at night on the first floor of the convent, the O'Reilly House.[71] In 1869, after the Sisters of Mercy left, the Sisters of St. Joseph purchased the convent and its furnishings and opened a free school for white girls there.[72] In September 1883, the sisters opened a school for the black children on the third floor of the old convent that had been used by the Sisters of Mercy. This school was the best facility the sisters had ever had for their black students, and for the first time one that was worthy of a name, St. Cecilia's School. In 1895, the old St. Mary's Convent became a cigar factory, and St. Cecilia's moved into the former public school for blacks.[73]

Although the sisters at first were greatly hampered by their inability to speak English, within a year or so, they had gained enough proficiency to provide a basic secular curriculum in addition to religious instruction. Black students received the same instruction as the students in the sisters' free white schools: reading, writing, arithmetic, social studies, and catechism.[74]

In 1890, a Mlle. Dumas deeded the "Dumas Block" to the Diocese of St. Augustine. It was bounded by Central Avenue on the east, Sanford Street on the west, St. Francis Street on the north, and De Haven Street on the south, in the middle of Lincolnville, the historic black section of St. Augustine. Bishop John Moore saw this donation as an opportunity to build a school and eventually a church there, as well as houses that could provide rental income to pay a resident priest.[75] Mlle. Dumas died in 1896.

71. McGoldrick, *Beyond the Call*, 130–31. The little house where the boys were taught was torn down in 1908.

72. McGoldrick, *Beyond the Call*, 272.

73. McGoldrick, *Beyond the Call*, 305.

74. Personal communication, Sister Thomas Joseph McGoldrick, St. Augustine, to Barbara Mattick, September 26, 2007.

75. "St. Benedict the Moor," in *Brief History of the Churches of the Diocese of St. Augustine, Florida*, part 2 (St. Leo, Florida: Abby Press, 1923), 26, hereafter cited as "St. Benedict the Moor," *Brief History*; *1911–1936 Silver Jubilee of the Church of St. Benedict the Moor, February 2nd, 1936* (St. Augustine: 1936), unpaged; hereafter cited as *Jubilee*.

In 1898, the bishop took steps to provide a better facility for the sisters' African American students and proposed the construction of a new school in an unidentified report:

There is the greatest need of a school in St. Augustine, as the present one is an old building loaned to us by Mr. H. M. Flagler. We own a whole block in a part of the city called Lincolnville, which is the center of the colored population. The property measures 310 x 253 and I could erect on it at a cost of about $8,000 a two story building, with classrooms on the first floor, and a hall on the second floor, which would be used for meetings.[76]

In 1895, Bishop Moore had successfully appealed to Sister Katharine Drexel for funds to complete a school for African Americans in Tampa.[77] Katharine Drexel was the founder of the Sisters of the Blessed Sacrament, a Catholic order whose specific mission was to serve Native Americans and African Americans. Such efforts were funded by the huge inheritance she received after the death of her father, Philadelphia banker Francis Drexel, who died in 1885.[78]

Bishop Moore returned to the Sisters of the Blessed Sacrament well in 1898, this time on behalf of St. Cecilia's School in St. Augustine, and was again successful. Writing to Mother Katharine on March 9, 1898, to thank her for the five-thousand-dollar check he had just received from her, he reported on the status of the project: "Within two weeks it will be completed, and dry enough to transfer the children to it. As soon as the work is finished the St. Cecilia Society composed of young colored girls, proposes to give a few entertainments in it. We will then have an

76. McGoldrick, *Beyond the Call*, 309.
77. John Moore, D.D., bishop of the Diocese of St. Augustine, St. Augustine, to Mother Katharine Drexel, January 6, 1894; March 13, 1894; April 19, 1894; May 14, 1895; and Bishop John Moore, D.D., to Mother M. Magdalen, June 9, 1895; photocopies provided by Archives of the Sisters of the Blessed Sacrament, Bensalem, Pennsylvania.
78. Mary van Balen Holt, *Meet Katharine Drexel: Heiress and God's Servant of the Oppressed* (Ann Arbor, Mich.: Charis, Servant Publications, 2002), 44–46.

opportunity to see how proud our Colored Catholics are of their 'House of Refuge.'"[79]

The Sisters of St. Joseph considered St. Cecilia's School a great triumph. The school's records show that, from 1895 to 1899, 117 students, representing sixty families, were enrolled.[80] The Diocese of St. Augustine continued in Sister Katharine Drexel's good graces for years. In 1903, Bishop Kenny successfully appealed for funds for a black school in Jacksonville and received twelve hundred dollars from the benefactress.[81] Katharine Drexel's passion for the Catholic evangelization of African Americans was well represented in the Diocese of St. Augustine and provided excellent facilities for the work of the Sisters of St. Joseph.

St. Cecilia's was fully completed in April 1898, and the closing exercises were held in the hall on the second floor. If a program from the closing exercises held in 1910 is any indication, the 1898 festivities were similar to those held for all of the sisters' schools, with students' singing, recitations, and piano solos.[82] The Sisters of St. Joseph taught many generations of St. Augustine's blacks, many of whom were not Catholic, in this building until 1964. That year, the institution for students in kindergarten through the eighth grade, then known as St. Benedict the Moor School, was closed after the advent of integration during the Civil Rights era.[83]

79. John Moore, D.D., bishop of the Diocese of St. Augustine, St. Augustine, to Sister Katharine, March 9, 1898. In the same letter, Moore told her how pleased blacks in Mandarin were with a new schoolhouse, apparently not funded by Mother Katharine. Moore said the white children at the local public school were jealous that the "colored children's" schoolhouse was better than theirs, and added, "The colored people are flattered and encouraged when they see such attention paid to their wants"; photocopy provided by Archives of the Sisters of the Blessed Sacrament, Bensalem, Pennsylvania.

80. McGoldrick, *Beyond the Call*, 306.

81. M. M. Katharine Drexel, Convent of the Blessed Sacrament, St. Elizabeth's, Mand, P.O. Pennsylvania, to Bishop Wm. J. Kenny, St. Augustine, 1903; Records of the Diocese of St. Augustine, Microfilm, Reel 3 (2Ci), P. K. Yonge Library, Gainesville: University of Florida.

82. Program from Closing Exercises, St. Cecilia's School, St. Augustine, Fla., Monday, May 23, 1910; in McGoldrick, *Beyond the Call*, 307.

83. McGoldrick, *Beyond the Call*, 307.

In the mid-nineteenth century, the focus of the Sisters of St. Joseph was freed black people and whites. By 1872, it was clear that the Sisters of St. Joseph's greatest victories with the freedmen would be in St. Augustine, where many of the black people were already Catholic. In Jacksonville, of the 5,000 black residents, only thirty were Catholic, and there was little hope that the other blacks could be dissuaded from attending their own African American churches. The Jacksonville mission, therefore, was primarily to the white population, and that, too, was a challenge.[84] Their successes throughout the state were many and varied but lay primarily in the establishment of schools that became the seeds of a statewide parochial school system.

84. Letter no. 31, Tome II, Sr. Sidonie Rascle, Jacksonville, to Msgr. Le Superieur, Le Puy, December 18, 1872, ASSJSA.

Chapter 3

The Competition for Black
Souls and Minds

The Sisters of St. Joseph vs.
the American Missionary Association
and Other Protestants

⟜

Many of the freed slaves in St. Augustine were practicing Catholics, having followed the religion of their former owners. Some were descendants of runaway slaves who had found refuge among the Spanish at Fort Mose during the seventeenth and eighteenth centuries.[1] When Bishop Verot went to France to recruit Roman Catholic sisters to work among the freedmen in Florida and Georgia, he was ready to pitch battle with the Northern Protestant missionaries who had already established a strong foothold among the freedmen in Florida. He was confident that Catholic blacks would remain faithful to the church

1. The Spanish had promised freedom to fugitive slaves in Florida if they converted to Catholicism. Between 1687 and 1738, about one hundred slaves from South Carolina fled to the Spanish colony. The government established a fort and town, Gracia Real de Santa Teresa de Mose (Fort Mose). Black militiamen manned the fort, providing the first line of defense for St. Augustine. Fort Mose was the "first legally sanctioned free black town in what is now the United States." Fort Mose was abandoned when the British took control of Florida in 1763; Kathleen Deagan and Darcie MacMahon, *Fort Mose: Colonial America's Black Fortress of Freedom* (Gainesville: University Press of Florida, 1995), vii, 19, 37.

and that the others would be drawn to the Catholic Church's liturgy and pomp. Protestants also recognized the potential power of the elaborate Catholic liturgy. What neither Verot nor his Protestant competitors anticipated was the overwhelming victory new African American denominations would achieve over both groups in the quest for black souls.

Bishop Verot wrote to fellow bishop Patrick Lynch in 1865, "The Catholic religion is eminently favorable for attracting and winning the admiration of the Negroes because of the pomp, variety, and symbolism of its ceremonial ritual." Lynch agreed, as did most Southern bishops concerning the freedmen, saying, "The ceremonies of the Church, the Processions, Novenas, etc. would satisfy the cravings of their still tropical nature for pomp and ceremony in a way that would draw many of them from the cold services of Protestant worship." The strongly evangelical American Missionary Association also recognized the potential power of the Catholic liturgy and "expressed the fear that the 'splendors' of the Catholic Church would appeal to the Negro's 'love of display.'"[2] Their assertions were true for at least one young black woman. The Sisters of St. Joseph wrote of a fifteen-year-old girl in Savannah who faithfully came to the convent each morning and evening. They diligently worked with her as she struggled to learn prayers such as the Lord's Prayer and Hail Mary. Sister Julie Roussel wrote:

To encourage her we praised her a little, and . . . , as I told her she would soon know the *Credo* and *Confiteor*, she made an exclamation of joy and said: "Oh Sister, if I knew all my prayers tomorrow I would be baptized! . . . I long . . . to be a Catholic! How 'proud' I will be when I am one. I love to go into your church and see your little children dressed in white who go and return, and you before the priest, greeting him . . . and also the

2. Patrick N. Lynch to the president and members of the Central Council of the Association of the Propagation of the Faith, Lyons, September 7, 1865, Archives of the Diocese of Charleston, box 1865, quoted in Gannon, *Rebel Bishop*, 117fn5; John T. Gillard, SSJ, *The Catholic Church and the American Negro* (Baltimore: St. Joseph's Society Press, 1929), 35.

priest with his beautiful vestments, gesturing and genuflecting; then he turns and prays, "Oh, my Jesus! ..." That poor woman in pronouncing these last words let fall big tears and taking her apron off to wipe them, she added: "Sister, by only thinking of it I feel in my heart something I cannot explain ... we do not feel that in the Protestant churches."[3]

One of Verot's most compelling reasons given in his appeals for support from Roman Catholic sisters, however, was the need to counter the inroads already made among the blacks by Protestants, despite their "cold services." Verot proclaimed, "We must make a beginning by establishing schools—a necessity. The [Northern] Protestants have anticipated us here: they have opened free schools which the Negroes attend in great numbers.... We must, therefore, prepare for the contest ... in procuring religious instruction for this simple and docile race."[4] He was correct in his assessment of the situation. There were, indeed, numerous groups of Protestants at work among the freedmen in Florida. The American Missionary Association was probably the most important of them.

Teachers and ministers from the American Missionary Association (AMA), headquartered in New York City, had begun their work in Florida and Georgia even as the Civil War was still raging.[5] The AMA was created in 1846 by the merging of the Union Missionary Society, the Committee for West Indian Missions, and the Western Evangelical Missionary Society. Its founders were evangelical abolitionists and included George Whipple and Simeon S. Jocelyn. At first the AMA was an interdenominational organization, but after 1865 it became closely tied to the Congregational Church.

3. Letter no. 3, Sister M. Julie Roussel, St. Augustine, to Mother Agatha, Le Puy, after Sr. Julie's return from Savannah to St. Augustine, St. Augustine; the letter commenced on December 29, 1867, and was completed on January 14, 1868; ASSJSA.

4. Gannon, *Rebel Bishop*, 117.

5. Based on the *Freedmen's Journal* at the Boston Public Library, at least seven teachers from other organizations are known to have taught in St. Augustine in 1863; "Letters from St. Augustine," *The Ancient City Genealogist*, St. Augustine Genealogical Society, St. Johns County, Florida, 4, no. 1 (April 1993): 11.

The AMA's work in the South to provide relief and education for slaves began when its agents went to Fortress Monroe, Virginia, in September 1861, five years before the Sisters of St. Joseph arrived in St. Augustine. The numbers of AMA missionaries increased steadily until, by 1868, there were 532 in the South. Their official goal was to enable the blacks to fend for themselves politically and socially and to run their own schools. The AMA's officers also were motivated by religion and patriotism. "Equality before the law was the 'gospel rule,' the AMA concluded, and the country's 'political salvation' depended upon its implementation."[6]

As Bishop Verot had noted in his appeal for French support, the Protestant AMA had sent both men and women to the South to teach the freedmen. Among the first AMA missionaries to work in Florida were Gorham and Harriet Greely, who worked for the AMA in St. Augustine from 1864 to the beginning of 1866. Gorham, born in Maine ca. 1801, was recorded in the 1850 census as a Methodist minister serving in Boston, Massachusetts. Listed with him were his wife Harriet B., age forty-five, and two daughters, Harriet E., age twenty, and Caroline G., age fifteen. The Greelys may have run a boardinghouse, for the household also included nine other adults and one child. Among them were a physician and another Methodist clergyman. The 1859 *New York State Business Directory* listed Gorham A. Greeley as a Methodist Episcopal clergyman in Saratoga Springs, but by the next year, the 1860 census listed his occupation as real estate broker. Apparently, the real estate profession afforded a comfortable living at this time, for he lived only with his wife Harriet and two daughters and employed a live-in servant.[7]

Harriet Greely's letters to George Whipple, the correspond-

6. Joe Richardson, *Christian Reconstruction: The American Missionary Association and Southern Black, 1861–1890* (Athens: University of Georgia Press, 1986), vii–ix.

7. U.S. Census, Population Schedules, 1850 and 1860. Gorham and Harriet's last name appears as Greeley in censuses, but Greely in their letters.

ing secretary of the AMA in New York, provide insight into the interpersonal relationships that existed between the missionaries and their African American students. It was she who taught in the regular school and made home visits, while Gorham took care of official business with the AMA and preached and taught Sabbath School. This was the typical division of labor between men and women missionaries.[8] One letter particularly expresses the nature of their work and Harriet's devotion to her efforts among the freedmen:

It has ... seemed to be my duty to diffuse my [evangelical] influence more generally among the people [only about one-quarter of the Freedman teachers were evangelical] by visiting more among the people from house to house especially the sick, reading the scriptures &c. &c. Still helping forward these elderly persons who have begun to read the scriptures, and looking particularly after the poor—for we have had not a few of the *very poor* ... our house is the resort for help, advice, assistance in their business matters such as making out their bills—contracts, writing letters and *teaching* a few.... I not only feel my heart as much devoted to the cause now as when I first entered into it, but much more so. I better understand the people and their wants, and can better adapt myself to gain their interests and affections.[9]

Occasionally, Harriet made references to the Catholics in St. Augustine. In January 1865, she wrote Brother Whipple, "We have about a dozen Catholics in our school; two of them young men, have lately ventured to our church and Sab[bath] School. There are many Catholics here, some descendants of the Spanish who first settled here, and many curious old relicks of those times."[10] About nine months later, Gorham wrote Whipple,

8. Richardson, *Christian Reconstruction*, 145.

9. H. B. Greely, St. Augustine, to George Whipple, New York, December 9, 1865; photocopy from the American Missionary Association Collection at Fisk University. The originals are now held at the Amistad Research Center (ARC), Tulane University, New Orleans, Louisiana.

10. Harriet B. Greely, St. Augustine, to George Whipple, New York, January 23, 1865, ARC.

"I am informed that the Catholicks are about to open a School for Colored children." Acknowledging the strength of the Catholic influence in the Ancient City, Gorham suggested that rather than struggling against their influences, the AMA would be wiser to focus their efforts on Jacksonville, where the Catholic Church had little presence.[11] This was a full year before the Sisters of St. Joseph arrived in the city.

In early 1866, the Freedman's Bureau bought 8,000 acres on the right bank of the St. Johns River to sell to freedmen at $3.00 an acre. The project developed into the Sammis Plantation Colony, later called the Strawberry Mills Mission. Gorham reported, "About one half of the protestant colored people of this place have engaged lots of land, and are making haste to move.... Probably very few, except the Catholics and the soldiers, will remain [in St. Augustine] by the last of this month."[12] The Greelys left St. Augustine and went to the Sammis Plantation Colony, near Jacksonville. Harriet took over the school there in March. It had been under the care of Carrie E. Jocelyn, daughter of AMA official S. S. Jocelyn, until health concerns caused her to leave.[13] By June 1866, Harriet was teaching at a school in Jacksonville, while Gorham remained at Sammis Plantation. Although many AMA missionaries returned to the North over the hot summers, Gorham wrote in July 1866 that he and Harriet intended to remain through the summer, partly because of cholera outbreaks in the North and partly to ensure that they would not lose any of the religious gains they had made among the freedmen in the previous months.[14] Gorham's next monthly report for July indicated that the name of the colony was changed to

11. G. [Gorham] Greely, St. Augustine, to Whipple, New York, September 10, 1865, ARC.

12. G. Greely, St. Augustine, to Whipple, New York, January 4, 1866, ARC.

13. Mrs. H. B. Greely, Sammis Plantation Colony, near Jacksonville, to Mr. S[amuel]. Hunt, April 1, 1866, ARC.

14. Rev. G. Greely, Sammis Plantation Colony, Jacksonville, to Rev. George Whipple, Cor. Sec. Assn., July 10, 1866, ARC.

Strawberry Mills. Other correspondence indicates he stayed at Strawberry Mills until at least June 1867. The last letter from Gorham, according to the AMA Correspondence Index at the Amistad Research Center, was dated October 1867. The index shows that letters from Harriet continued until December 16, 1867, and came from Belgrade, Maine, indicating they had returned to the state of Gorham's birth. After that, all trace of the Greelys vanishes from the census records and AMA letters.[15]

The husband-and-wife team of Gorham and Harriet Greely was unusual; most of the teachers were single white women in their twenties who were well educated, graduates of normal schools, female academies, or colleges, and hailed from the North.[16] The correspondence of some of the AMA teachers reveals that this description, for the most part, held true in Florida. Besides the Greelys and Carrie Jocelyn, the AMA missionaries who served in Florida in direct competition with the Sisters of St. Joseph were: Miss Lydia P. Auld from East Boston, Massachusetts, who served in St. Augustine from 1868 to 1870; Mrs. Minnie Owen Beale, probably from New York, who taught in the Ancient City from 1872 to 1875; Miss Emma B. Eveleth, possibly from New York, who taught in Jacksonville from 1865 to 1867 and in Gainesville from 1868 to 1873; and Miss Celia E. Williams, from Deerfield, Massachusetts, who served in Jacksonville from 1869 to 1876.[17]

There is little available personal information about most of the AMA missionaries who came to Florida. Celia Williams,

15. G. Greely, Strawberry Mills Mission, Jacksonville, to Rev. Edwd. P. Smith, Genl Field Agent, AMA, June 10, 1867; AMA Correspondence Index, online at http://www.tulane.edu/~amistad/research.htm. The family does not appear in the 1870 census. Gorham, who would have been nearly seventy years old, and Harriet, about sixty-five by that time, may have died. Their daughters may have married and therefore no longer appear in the census under the family name.

16. Richardson, *Christian Reconstruction*, 167; Jacqueline Jones, *Soldiers of Light and Love: Northern Teachers and Georgia Blacks, 1865–1873* (Chapel Hill: University of North Carolina Press, 1980), 30–31.

17. AMA Correspondence Index, online at http://www.tulane.edu/~amistad/research.htm.

whose full name was Lucelia Electa Williams, however, is widely recognized for her work in secondary schools for the freedmen. Born in Deerfield, Massachusetts, in 1824, at the age of forty she began her work among blacks in the South. She taught in South Carolina, Virginia, and Washington, D.C. In 1867, Williams began teaching at the Hampton Normal and Industrial Institute in Virginia, where its founder, Samuel Chapman Armstrong, asked her to organize the Normal School department. She organized it and then went on to develop the physical facilities and curriculum. The Normal School opened in April 1868. In the fall of 1869, the AMA sent her to Jacksonville, Florida, to establish a similar school. The Stanton Normal School opened in November. Its seven teachers and three hundred students comprised the first secondary school for freedmen in Florida. After seven years as principal, Williams retired and returned to Deerfield, where she died in December 1895.[18]

In many respects the AMA missionaries were not very different from the French Sisters of St. Joseph. Both groups were genuinely concerned about the spiritual status of the freedmen, and they shared similar trials and joys in their ministries to them. There were significant differences between them, however, that made the competition between them fierce. Most of the AMA teachers were from New England; few were foreign-born. The most critical difference between them was that most AMA teachers were evangelical Protestants and adamantly anti-Catholic.[19] As an organization, the AMA was driven by a fear that moral society, as defined by members of the main-

18. Ronald E. Butchart, "Williams, Lucelia Electa," in *Encyclopedia of African-American Education*, ed. Faustine C. Jones-Wilson et al. (Westport, Conn.: Greenwood, 1996), 518–19; Obituary, "Miss Lucelia E. Williams," *American Missionary* 50, no. 3 (March 1896): 89. Stanton remains an educational institution and is currently known as the Stanton College Preparatory School, offering the International Baccalaureate Program: http://www.stantoncollegeprep.org/SCPSHistory/StantonHistory.htm.

19. Joe M. Richardson, "'We Are Truly Doing Missionary Work': Letters from American Missionary Association Teachers in Florida, 1864–1874," *Florida Historical Quarterly* 54, no. 2 (October 1975): 184.

stream Northern middle class, was crumbling and identified "Romanism, rum, and ignorance" as major agents of that decline. They considered Roman Catholics to be their chief rivals in seeking the souls of the freedmen.[20] Indeed, Catholicism was a powerful force in St. Augustine, where in 1867, three-fourths of the population was Catholic, including the majority of freedmen.[21]

Catholics tended to be just as strongly anti-Protestant, and the sisters were ready to face the challenge posed by the Northern Protestants described by Bishop Verot. Added to the competition the AMA missionaries faced from Catholicism was the hatred they encountered from Southern whites, not so much because they had come to the South to convert heathen blacks, but because in carrying out their mission work they intended to impart to the blacks their Yankee values. C. B. Wilder, an AMA missionary, described the tense post–Civil War climate in Jacksonville:

The Spirit of Slavery is the "ruling passion" still, among the Southern people, but while fear and poverty holds it in suspense the "set time" is upon us to apply healing remedies & the elevating influences of knowledge & the gospel of the Son of God—Up to within the last six months the old feeling of hatred arrogance and spite was observable often cropping out here and there, sometimes in open insults to northerners, but more generally in suspicions & insinuations, watching for what they had so long asserted, that the Yankees were course [coarse], inbred & revengeful.[22]

Although there had been some initial opposition to the work of the Sisters of St. Joseph with blacks, St. Augustine's Catholic

20. Jones, *Soldiers of Light and Love*, 155. Jones refers to the work of French Catholic sisters in Savannah, mistakenly attributing the efforts there to the Sisters of Mercy rather than the Sisters of St. Joseph.

21. Joe M. Richardson, *The Negro in the Reconstruction of Florida, 1865–1877*, Florida State University Studies 46 (Tallahassee: Florida State University, 1965), 86.

22. C. B. Wilder, Jacksonville, to A. M. Association, New York, January 1, 1868, ARC.

whites soon embraced the nuns. The sisters' acceptance in the Ancient City was made easier because they were everything the AMA missionaries were not: they were Catholic, not Protestant, and were from France, not the North. Furthermore, they were sponsored by the beloved Bishop Verot, who had been such a champion of the Confederacy. Conditions were, however, less favorable for them in other Florida communities such as Jacksonville, where the Sisters of St. Joseph faced strong Protestant opposition.

The Sisters of St. Joseph also had to compete against the work of the Freedmen's Bureau schools that enjoyed the support of the government and private organizations, such as the Peabody Foundation and the AMA. Writing from St. Augustine, Mother Sidonie lamented, "We have mostly to contend with the protestant schools, which are the only recognized by the government, and, by the same, are grandly supported and comfortable, lacking nothing they desire."[23]

Although she had an exaggerated idea of the affluence of the freedmen's schools, she was correct in assessing the recognition and support the AMA missionaries received. The work of the Freedmen's Bureau in St. Johns County was a partnership among the United States government, the local school system, which was supported by county taxes, and several freedmen's aid associations, including the AMA. These organizations maintained primary schools, night schools, Sabbath Schools, industrial training schools, temperance schools, normal schools, and summer schools. Harriet Greely wrote of some of them to

23. Letter from Mtr. Sidonie, St. Augustine, to the Motherhouse in Le Puy, January 29, 1869, published in a report from Maison-Mère de la Congrégation de St-Joseph, Du Puy; on file at Archives, Soeurs de St. Joseph du Puy, France, ASSJLP. From 1868 to 1897, George Peabody, an American philanthropist then living in England, donated $3.5 million to encourage education for all races in the South. Between 1868 and September 1897, Florida received $67,375 from the fund; J. L. M. Curry, *Brief Sketch of George Peabody, and History of The Peabody Education Fund through Thirty Years* (1898) (New York: Negro University Press, 1969), 147.

Secretary Whipple in January of 1865, "The Freedman's Relief Asso[ciation] have four good teachers here and two schools; one primary and one advanced—two teachers at each—all ladies. . . . They are kept in the Meth Col Church, one session each day. They are doing well."[24]

By 1872, the sisters' Protestant competition was even more firmly established. When O. Bronson, St. Johns County's first superintendent of schools, submitted his report to the Florida superintendent of public instruction in Tallahassee, he reported that six schools were in operation in St. Johns County, including a thriving Peabody school. He further reported, "The colored school occupies a commodious building erected by the Freedman's Bureau, and to it is attached a convenient cottage for the teacher's residence, owned by the American Missionary Association, in New York. This school has always maintained a high reputation. It has been a great blessing to those for whom it was established."[25] With so many non-Catholic forces at work, it is no wonder the Sisters of St. Joseph felt greatly disadvantaged and often wrote of their struggle against the ever-zealous Protestants.

Mother Sidonie also lamented that the Protestants apparently paid the parents a dollar a month to send their children to the Protestant schools and that many who went to those schools asserted that in the Catholic schools only the catechism was taught; some wanted to go to the Protestant schools so they would not have to study religion.[26] Because most of the sisters were still struggling to learn English in the early years of their mission to Florida, the charge that they taught only religion

24. Gil Wilson, "Letters from St. Augustine," *Ancient City Genealogist*, St. Augustine Genealogical Society, St. Johns County, 4, no. 1 (April 1993), 11–12; H. B. Greely, St. Augustine, to Whipple, New York, January 23, 1865, ARC.

25. "Dr. Bronson's 1872 Florida School Report, St. Johns County, Florida," online at http://www.drbronsontours.com/bronson1870stateschoolreport.html.

26. Letter no. 88, Mother Sidonie, St. Augustine, to Bishop in Le Puy, December 10, 1867, ASSJSA.

was essentially true. The early letters from the sisters speak of their attempts to teach acts of piety such as how to make the sign of the cross, or how to recite the Lord's Prayer, Hail Mary, or the Creed, rewarding good students with medals or colorful religious cards. They make little mention of academic instruction. The AMA teachers, who had no language barrier, immediately taught reading, writing, arithmetic, and advanced subjects such as geography. In religious instruction they emphasized Bible reading, scripture memorization and recitation, and study at Sabbath Schools.[27] The great desire among many African Americans after the Civil War was to learn to read. Some were eager to acquire the skill to be able to vote, but many were inspired by their longing to be able to read the Bible themselves. Harriet Greely enthusiastically described her class of between forty and sixty-four adult students who were studying reading, spelling, and writing: "With nearly all in my school who can read, the Bible takes the precedence, and with some it is the *only* book."[28] Instead of medals and religious cards, in the AMA schools, New Testaments were a prized reward for many who did well in their studies. AMA missionary Lydia P. Auld noted, however, that the Catholics in her classes rarely owned Bibles.[29]

As dismayed as the Sisters of St. Joseph were by the work of the Protestants, the AMA missionaries, for their part, were equally frustrated by the strong Catholic resistance they experienced in St. Augustine. In 1873, George W. Atwood, the secretary of the Board of Trustees for Public School no. 2, in writing to the AMA to solicit their continued support, said,

I have before informed you that our population is four fifths Roman Catholic and we consequently meet with great opposition, tho'

27. Harriet Greely, Sammis Plantation, Jacksonville, to R. B. Hunt, May 10, 1866, ARC.

28. H. B. Greely, St. Augustine, to Whipple, New York, August 7, 1865, ARC.

29. L. P. Auld, St. Augustine, to Rev. E. P. Smith, December 31, 1868, ARC.

our schools thus far have had a much larger attendance than the RC [Roman Catholic] schools, and our pupils are far ahead of them in their progress of education tho' every effort has been made by the RC to popularize their schools, and the Bishop, Priests and Nuns have threatened all sorts of anathema upon their people who have sent their children to our schools.[30]

A year later he reported, "We continue to have not only vigorous but virulent opposition from our Roman Catholic neighbors, and the Bishop openly proclaims our school a pestilence in this city."[31]

The local newspaper endorsed the sisters' work without any mention of the work of the sisters' Protestant counterparts. Describing a picnic held by the Sisters of St. Joseph for their Catholic Colored School students and the students' parents in May 1874, the paper enthusiastically supported the work of the sisters among blacks. They especially lauded the sisters' success in instilling discipline and order not only in their students, but in the students' parents as well:

The discipline and order, with which the whole affair was conducted, reflected credit upon those who have had the intellectual and moral training of this School.

The parents of the children were in attendance, and deported themselves with such grateful deference, as is in honor due to those who have substantially, and without reward, labored for the enlightenment of the rising generations of this city, "without regard to color or previous condition."

The Colored population of this City are largely Catholic, and ever since the war have had the benefit of liberal educational opportunity which has advanced them in a standard of Citizenship above almost any other city in the South.

---

30. Geo. W. Atwood, St. Augustine, to E. M. Cravath, New York, November 1, 1873, ARC. Statistics for the numbers of students taught by the sisters and the AMA missionaries between 1865 and 1876, gathered from letters and scattered reports, support Atwood's statement that the sisters had fewer students.

31. Geo. W. Atwood, St. Augustine, to E. M. Cravath, New York, October 16, 1874, ARC.

In giving justice where it properly belongs we must say, that the credit for the advancement of this particular class of our community belongs to Catholic influence directed under the auspices of the Right Rev. Bishop Verot.[32]

This evaluation clearly shows the editor's bias toward the work of the Catholic Church and the value he placed on proper deportment among blacks, both young and old.

The men and women who came to Florida from the North as evangelical Protestant missionaries for the AMA and the women who came as Roman Catholic Sisters of St. Joseph, in large measure to counter the AMA efforts, were from extreme ends of the religious spectrum in nineteenth-century America. Even so, their purposes were the same: winning souls for God.

Although their goal was the same, their motives were slightly different. To the Sisters of St. Joseph, salvation was only possible through the Roman Catholic Church; Protestants were heretics. This was consistent with nineteenth-century Catholic doctrine. The Protestant missionaries of the American Missionary Association were dedicated to bringing the former slaves into the Protestant fold, for they, just as adamantly, considered Roman Catholics to be lost souls. Furthermore, as Americans, the AMA missionaries also had a vested interest in teaching African Americans to be good citizens of the United States. To the Sisters of St. Joseph, conversion to Catholicism was a matter of eternal life or death, for blacks as well as whites. Though foreigners, they also had a personal vested interest in their work, for they believed their success or failure in obtaining conversions was a factor in their own salvation and that their efforts as missionaries, including any physical or emotional suffering they endured as a result, gained them great merit with God.

Structurally, the AMA missionary organization and the

32. *Examiner*, May 23, 1874.

Catholic hierarchy over the Sisters of St. Joseph were similar. The AMA missionaries' letters to Secretary Whipple were very much like those the sisters wrote to their superiors in Le Puy. Both passed on their observations and related the trials and triumphs they experienced in the unfamiliar surroundings of the American South in the aftermath of the Civil War. In working with the freedmen, these Protestant and Catholic missionaries also shared a common admiration for the former slaves and disdain for the poor whites of Florida. AMA missionary Emma Eveleth revealed her thoughts in comparing the blacks to the poor whites in Jacksonville. Regarding a white woman who was in dire condition, she wrote:

I could not help think it is *not* the color of skin, that makes anyone degraded, but their *habits*. If people are crushed down all their lives by the heel of oppression can we expect them to rise all of a sudden & be a bright intelligent class of community; without even the dust off their past condition clinging to them? A great many of them *do* shake it off & get up *brighter* than would be expected. The jewels are here, and we have an interesting work to polish them up, for this world & I hope, for the world to come. The poor whites seem to be as much—or *more* degraded and in need than the colored, for the latter are not afraid to work, the others have always thought work degrading; & even now it seems as if they would starve rather than work. There is a hope that when slavery is really dead, & the spirit of caste is banished, they may arise & be equal to the colored people.[33]

The Roman Catholic Sisters of St. Joseph and the Protestant American Missionary Association teachers and clergy also shared a common weakness in trying to attract African Americans to their respective ministries. Both were confounded by the style of worship most blacks practiced. In despair, Mother Sidonie wrote of the difficulties in competing with the African American churches in Jacksonville. Some AMA missionaries

33. E. B. Eveleth, Jacksonville, to S. S. Jocelyn, New York, February 4, 1865, ARC.

had a similarly horrified view of black services.[34] This inability to relate to African American culture was a major factor in limiting the success of both the Catholic and AMA efforts. With the end of Reconstruction in 1877, the AMA suffered a loss of contributions. Northern philanthropic societies and mission committees in evangelical churches grew tired of supporting the AMA's missions in the South. Although the AMA work continued its work there, it had "lost its momentum" by 1880, and the AMA's prominence as a rival to the Sisters of St. Joseph was superseded by the Episcopal Church.[35]

Among the Protestants, the Episcopal Church came the closest to providing the same sort of worship experience the Catholic Church offered. It, too, was liturgical and employed ritual. Like the Catholic Church, the Episcopal Church expected its form of worship to attract blacks. Their optimism was tied to the expanded opportunities for education that were available to the freedmen. The 1877 *Diocesan Journal* for the Diocese of Florida predicted, "With their [the blacks'] present and daily increasing ability to read, with their natural and great love of music, with the pleasure it gives them to join in a responsive service, the Liturgy and the chants and psalms of the Church would doubtless take hold upon them and influence them as in past years."[36]

In spite of its similarities with the Catholic form of worship, like other Protestant denominations, the Episcopal Church was alarmed at the prospect that blacks would be drawn to the Catholic Church. Likewise, Catholics and mainstream Protestant denominations shared an abhorrence of the African American denominations that were rapidly proliferating during the Reconstruction period. Reports of the state of the Episcopal Church in Florida urged greater outreach to blacks, for, it warned, "if the

34. Letter no. 31, Mother Sidonie, Jacksonville to Mother Le Superieur, Le Puy, December 18, 1872, ASSJSA; Richardson, *Christian Reconstruction*, 144.

35. Richardson, *Christian Reconstruction*, 259.

36. *Diocesan Journal*, 1877, 41–43; quoted in Cushman, *A Goodly Heritage*, 138.

Church neglects them [the blacks] a few will be hurried into Romanism, and the rest carried away with the forms of emotionalism which foster the feeling of animal rather than spiritual life of true goodness."[37]

The leaders of the Episcopal Church in the Diocese of Florida recognized that one of the major appeals of the African American churches was the opportunity they offered blacks to be preachers and to rise to positions of authority. As early as 1869, Bishop John Freeman Young ordained Richard R. Love, from the British West Indies (the Bahamas), and sent him to Jacksonville. Nothing is known of his ministry, however, and no mention of him appears in the *Diocesan Journals* after 1870. Twelve years later, Bishop Young ordained another black man, Jacob R. Ballard, "to start a mission for his race," but Ballard's level of success in Jacksonville to establish a mission was dismal also. Discouraged, Ballard left Jacksonville to head the Florida Negro Normal School in Tallahassee (now Florida Agricultural and Mechanical University) and was able to establish a congregation there.[38]

Ballard was succeeded in Jacksonville by the Reverend Brooke G. White. White was admitted to the Episcopal deaconate on December 19, 1883, and ordained a priest in 1884, specifically to serve a black congregation. An indication of the sensitivity afforded the black members of his flock is the name of the church, St. Philip's Protestant Episcopal Church. A white congregation in East Jacksonville had been established with that same name a short time before. At the request of Bishop Young, the white congregation gave up its name so it could be used by the newly established black mission and assumed the name St. Andrew's instead. The name change was made in consideration of "the peculiar significance St. Philip had for the colored race."[39]

37. *Diocesan Journal*, 1877, 43; quoted in Cushman, *A Goodly Heritage*, 139.
38. Cushman, *A Goodly Heritage*, 139–40.
39. Works Progress Administration, Survey of Church Records, Mss. on file in the

Under Father White's leadership, St. Philip's Church thrived. In 1885, the church ran an industrial school with seventy-five students and had plans to establish a parochial school. White was among the many clergymen who ministered to yellow fever victims in Jacksonville during the great epidemic in 1888. He served the church intermittently: 1883–88, 1895–97, 1900–1904, and 1906–9. The WPA Church Records show that most of the clergy that served at St. Philip's until 1927 were white, but from 1927 to 1935 (the last year covered by the records), the clergy serving the church were black.[40]

The Episcopal Diocese of Florida had recognized the need for separate black parishes with the establishment of St. Philip's Mission in Jacksonville in 1869, but the congregation did not achieve the status of a parish with its own black pastor until 1882. In St. Augustine, black Episcopalians remained a part of Trinity Episcopal Church, founded in 1763 during Florida's British Period, until 1891, when St. Cyprian's Protestant Episcopal Church was founded. According to the WPA Church Records, Julia Jackson, "a negress from Nassau, who came to St. Augustine during the latter part of 1890, [saw] no place for negroes to worship." For ten years black Episcopalians met in a private home on Washington Street (in the black Lincolnville area of St. Augustine). In 1901, a winter visitor, Miss Emma White, had a church building constructed for them as a gift.[41] St. Cyprian's continues to use this building.

Elsewhere in Florida, the Episcopal Church's efforts competed with those of the Sisters of St. Joseph in Fernandina, where in 1884, black Episcopalians were given the use of the old building used by the white congregation of St. Peter's Church,

Florida Collection, State Library of Florida, Tallahassee, Florida. Hereafter cited as WPA Church Records. Acts 8:26–39 relates that the Apostle Philip preached the gospel to an Ethiopian eunuch, an official in the court of Candace, queen of the Ethiopians, resulting in the black official's desire to be baptized.

40. WPA Church Records.

41. WPA Church Records.

THE COMPETITION FOR BLACK SOULS AND MINDS

and in Palatka, where a new St. Mark's Church was built for them in 1883. In addition to churches, Bishop Young also envisioned schools for the blacks in his diocese, and black children from St. Philip's Mission in Fernandina attended an Episcopal parochial school.[42]

In their letters back to their motherhouse in Le Puy from 1866 to 1875, the Sisters of St. Joseph most often mentioned the opposition they encountered from the northern Protestant missionaries and, later, the local Episcopalians. Their greatest challenge in strengthening Catholicism among Florida freedmen outside of St. Augustine, however, came from the blacks themselves. Although their schools fared well, the efforts of the sisters, and, indeed, those of the AMA missionaries and of the Episcopal Church in Florida, all paled in comparison to the successes achieved by the independent black denominations that sprang up throughout the state after the Civil War and into the twentieth century. The African Methodist Episcopal (AME) Church was particularly strong in Jacksonville after Elder Charles H. Pearce arrived in February 1866. Such was not the case, however, in St. Augustine. "To the south at St. Augustine, Roman Catholicism remained a formidable barrier to African Methodism and other Protestant churches. As one local missionary put it, 'this is a Catholic city.'"[43]

The experiences of Mrs. Hamie Williams-Jordan dramatically show that the Baptists also found the influences of Roman Catholicism to be quite strong in St. Augustine. In 1874, at the age of sixteen or seventeen, she had gone to Lincolnville. She noticed how few Protestant churches there were in St. Augustine.

On a second trip to St. Augustine, while living with a Catholic family, she joined the efforts of a Protestant preacher from

42. Cushman, *A Goodly Heritage*, 83–84, 140, 187.
43. Larry Eugene Rivers and Canter Brown Jr., *Laborers in the Vineyard of the Lord: The Beginnings of the AME Church in Florida, 1865–1895* (Gainesville: University Press of Florida, 2001), 35.

Jacksonville, Ivey Barnes, who also tried to establish a church in Lincolnville. They were greatly hampered by strong Catholic hostility to their efforts. There was too much fear to even organize a Sunday School. Because of Williams-Jordan's persistence in trying to organize a Baptist Sunday School, the Catholics with whom she was staying no longer welcomed her in their home, and another Catholic family gave her lodging.

When Williams-Jordan went door to door in the neighborhood looking for children to attend her Sunday School, the first mother she approached informed her that black people "don't know about conducting Sunday School; only the whites know." Nevertheless, Williams-Jordan managed to recruit ten students, mostly Catholic children. They started meeting in a house at the corner of St. Benedict and Francis streets, and when she added an organ and singing to the meetings, participants flocked to the gatherings. Her Sunday School thrived. The Catholics became alarmed, and as Williams-Jordan recalled,

One night, fourteen banded themselves to destroy "Jordan and Barnes" for they believed that if we were destroyed the idea of establishing a Protestant Church there [the church] would be destroyed. At that time, the city gates opened only one way so that seven got on one side and seven on the other side of the gates and waited for us to come from prayer meeting—they had threatened to take us to the outskirts and beat us to death. Just before we came to the city gate something touched me and said: "Go this way" and we turned and went around by the Abbey House; we had never been that way before, but I obeyed what I later and now believe was the spirit.

The next night some of those who had intended to attack them came to ask her forgiveness. One even came back the next night and expressed a desire to be baptized and to join the Baptist Church. Despite the fears of the pastor, a public baptism was held. She recalled, "The day of the baptism came—it was held in the pond 'all were properly dressed and a great crowd of

THE COMPETITION FOR BLACK SOULS AND MINDS

Catholics followed us down to the pond and threw stones at Reverend Barnes; they threw dogs in the boats and did many things to try to stop us, but the baptism went on to the finish.... After that we got other Catholics in and baptized them." Even in the face of the violent Catholic opposition, St. Augustine's First Baptist Church was established in 1874.[44]

Despite the gloomy portrayal of Protestant prospects in St. Augustine, a survey of church records conducted by the Works Progress Administration during the Depression shows that at least thirteen Protestant black churches of various denominations were founded in or near St. Augustine in the late nineteenth and early twentieth centuries and were still functioning in the 1930s. Unless noted otherwise, all listed here were located in St. Augustine. They are, with their date of foundation: St. Paul AME (1873), First Baptist (1874), St. Mary's Baptist (1875), Mather Perit Memorial Presbyterian (1876), Zion Baptist (1881), North City Baptist (1886), St. Luke's AME (1888), St. Cyprian's Protestant Episcopal (1891), St. James Baptist (1898), Dawson Chapel, Colored ME (1908), Friendship Baptist in Elkton/Armstrong (1910), St. Mary's AME in Armstrong (1914), and Hurst Chapel AME (1918).[45]

Unless they were already Catholics, most blacks chose to join the rising number of independent black denominations. Both the American Missionary Association and Catholic Church had "failed to recognize the richness and vitality of black culture and institutions and only belatedly to comprehend black insistence on self-determination."[46] The 1890 census shows that black denominations continued to grow. The mainline white Protestants in Duval and St. Johns counties counted 339 Southern Baptists, compared to 1,972 black "Regular Baptists," and

---

44. "Beginnings of First Baptist Church," interview for the Federal Writers' Project, WPA, accessed online at http://www.drbronsontours.com/firstbaptist.htm.

45. WPA Church Records. Many of these churches are still in existence.

46. Richardson, *Christian Reconstruction*, ix.

1018 Methodist Episcopalians compared to 4,133 black Methodist Episcopalians (African Methodist Episcopalians, African Methodists Episcopalians Zion, and Colored Methodist Episcopalians).[47] The Catholic population of Florida in 1908 was about 30,000, of which only 1,750 were blacks. Concerning African Americans, the *Catholic Encyclopedia* of 1910 reported:

Reliable religious statistics of the coloured people are difficult to obtain owing to multiplicity of organizations and mobility of religious temperament. Five distinct branches of Methodists report 635 preachers, 400 churches, and 7,470 members. Baptist organizations approximate the Methodists in strength, while the coloured membership of other denominations is very small.[48]

It is notable that it was not until 1911, in the second decade of the twentieth century, that a separate parish for black Catholics was established in St. Augustine. Unlike the Protestants, Catholics could not act independently of their clergy, and priests could not disobey their bishops. The Catholic Church claimed apostolic succession through its bishops, leading back to St. Peter, the first bishop of Rome. The succession depended upon consecrations by bishops who had received their own "laying on of hands" from others who were directly "descended" from St. Peter. As a result, in the Catholic Church there was no rapid exodus by blacks from the "mother church" to create their own new denominations. After the Civil War, therefore, most Catholic blacks remained in their parishes even though they were forced to sit in segregated areas and were often excluded from activities of the wider church.

The discrimination against black Catholics in St. Augustine was, indeed, long-standing. Since 1565, black Catholics in St. Augustine had attended the cathedral along with whites, though

47. Henry K. Carroll, *Report on the Statistics of Churches in the United States at the Eleventh Census: 1890* (Washington, D.C.: Government Printing Office, 1894).

48. *Catholic Encyclopedia*, 1910 ed., s.v. "Florida," subsection "Other Religious Denominations," online at http://www.newadvent.org/cathen/06115b.htm.

they were relegated to a separate gallery. On January 5, 1867, the *St. Augustine Examiner* reported that the cathedral's black members had held a fair to raise funds to enlarge their gallery. They had raised close to $350. The paper directed its praise, however, toward the whites who had contributed:

This is indeed good—nay, very good in a small place like St. Augustine and it bespeaks highly the generosity of the people of the Ancient City. All went nobly to the Fair for the good cause, setting aside all prejudices, and wishing to sympathize with the colored people in an object so laudable as the extension of Church accommodations. The Fair was liberally patronized by all classes of society and the amount raised proves it sufficiently as indeed the scarcity of money in the South is a fact which requires no demonstration ... ought to go far to prove what some people in the North have so much difficultly to understand, that in the South are yet to be found the best friends of the colored people who are willing to get their hands into their pockets and make sacrifices to come to their assistance.

The fair netted enough to cover the cost of "neat and comfortable pews in the place of the wretched benches they [the blacks] have had hitherto."[49] The whites' support of black Catholics was indeed vital to improving the blacks' situation, but their assistance to them was paternalistic and did not represent a desire to truly accept blacks. Their more sincere motive may have been to impress Northerners with their "generosity." The gallery at the cathedral, with all its paternalistic and condescending overtones, served the needs of St. Augustine's black Catholics until 1911.

The success of St. Cecilia's School, the school built on DeHaven Street for the Sisters of St. Joseph's instruction of blacks in 1898, spawned the need and desire of St. Augustine's black Catholics to have a church of their own. Bishop Moore had intended to build a separate church for the blacks at the cathedral and laid out a plan for such in 1898. Describing the land that

49. *Examiner*, January 5, 1867.

had been donated to the diocese, he revealed that, in addition to the school building that was completed in 1898, Moore hoped "as soon as possible to build a separate church for colored people and a house for the priests who will attend them. There are 105 Catholic colored families in St. Augustine, as good Catholics on the average as can be found anywhere. I am anxious to do my best for them and implore the help of the Commission to enable me to do so."[50]

Bishop Moore died in 1901 and never got to see his hope fulfilled, but eight years later, on September 19, 1909, his successor, Bishop William J. Kenny, laid the cornerstone for the first separate black church in the Diocese of St. Augustine, named St. Benedict the Moor. For St. Augustine's black Catholics to have their own church was to see a dream long deferred finally realized. As was recalled during the Jubilee celebration of the church's founding, "For some time there existed, on the part of many, the desire for a separate place of worship, as they believed they could develop better as a separate unit, with their own parish activities to engage in, and their own parish burdens to shoulder."[51] The blacks worked diligently to raise the necessary funds. The church was completed in early 1911, and a grand dedication ceremony was held on February 5, heralded by the headline, "St. Augustine Proud of First Catholic Church Exclusively for Negroes—Impressive Dedication." After the dedication, the first High Mass was sung, and Bishop Kenny delivered the sermon. Adding to the solemnity and joy of the occasion, the "colored choir rendered excellent music.... At High Mass they sang Farmer's Mass in B," under the direction of their organist and conductor.[52]

50. McGoldrick, *Beyond the Call*, 309–10. The Commission Moore referred to was probably the Commission for Catholic Missions among Colored People and the Indians, established by the Third Plenary Council of Bishops that met in 1884; Stephen J. Ochs, *Desegregating the Altar: The Josephites and the Struggle for Black Priests, 1871–1960* (Baton Rouge: Louisiana State University Press, 1990), 62.

51. "St. Benedict the Moor," *Brief History*, 26–27.

52. "Negro Catholic Church Dedicated by Dr. Kenny," *Florida Times-Union*, February 6, 1911, 3.

The dedication of the state's first Catholic church for blacks brought great joy to the Catholic Church in Florida, for it was a positive sign in the midst of an otherwise dismal record of success among African Americans. In 1912, Father Maurice P. Foley, the rector of the cathedral, wrote to his superiors:

Your Graces: The accompanying report of work among our Colored Brethren of this diocese shows that notwithstanding the utmost care and attention on the part of our priests and Sisters comparatively little progress is made in the way of conversions. What few converts we have made during the past year is due principally to the influences of the colored schools. The Protestant churches, the Methodists and Baptists especially, are working actively and perseveringly among them and Winter visitors contribute large sums yearly to the aid of the Protestant churches.

He went on to say that the Presbyterians had established a parochial industrial school that provided day care for the young children of working parents. "This appeals to the colored people and some few of our Catholics send their children to them."[53] Against this grim background, he was indeed happy to report on the growing attendance at the new St. Benedict the Moor Church.

The members of St. Benedict the Moor remained under the pastoral care of the clergy at the cathedral until 1914. Bishop Michael J. Curley, Kenny's successor, further strengthened the diocese's commitment to black Catholics by inviting Josephite priests from Baltimore to assume oversight of St. Benedict's. The Josephites were members of an order founded in 1866 as St. Joseph's Society of the Sacred Heart for Foreign Missions in Mill Hill, England, by the Reverend Herbert Vaughan, to missionize the poor, particularly "Negroes." The first group of Josephite fathers came to the United States in 1871 to preserve

53. Maurice P. Foley, Rector, Cathedral, St. Augustine, to Your Graces [1912]; typed manuscript 3R12 in Records of the Diocese of St. Augustine, on microfilm at P. K. Yonge Library, University of Florida, Gainesville.

black Catholic faith and to convert unchurched and Protestant blacks.[54]

The Josephites worked primarily in the South, where most African Americans lived, but church policy frustrated many of their efforts. Although their early intent was to train blacks for the priesthood, over the next five decades only three American black men were ordained: Charles Randolph Uncles in 1891, John Henry Dorsey in 1902, and John J. Plantevigne in 1907. All three were ordained in Baltimore, Maryland, the center of Catholicism in the United States; no black priests were ordained elsewhere in the South because of resistance from the Southern bishops. Only when a separate seminary for blacks was established in Mississippi in 1923 were blacks able to study for the priesthood in the South, and it was not until the 1930s that any appreciable numbers of blacks in the region received ordination.[55]

At the Fourth Black Catholic Congress, a gathering of Catholic laymen in Chicago in 1893, the head of the Josephite fathers in the United States had expressed his frustration: "Is not the Catholic church in America to be blamed for lack of zeal? I answer with an unhesitating Yes. After all Protestantism has done something to Christianize the blacks; but we have done, I may say, nothing." He then cited the Protestant expenditure of $35 million on evangelism among blacks, the establishment of 130 institutions, and the education of 25,000 scholars "of whom one thousand are preparing for the Protestant ministry."[56] In 1914, therefore, Bishop Curley's best option to meet the needs of the African American members of his fold was to invite the Josephite fathers to take over the priestly duties at St. Benedict's.

The black Catholics of St. Augustine thrived once they had

54. Ochs, *Desegregating the Altar*, 3–6.
55. Ochs, *Desegregating the Altar*, 3–6, 456.
56. Cyprian Davis, OSB, *The History of Black Catholics in the United States* (New York: Crossroad, 1991), 184.

their own church. During World War I, St. Benedict the Moor had its own Local War Council, organized at a meeting held at St. Benedict the Moor School on April 30, 1918. Their pastor, a Josephite father, was the president, but the other officers were members of the congregation. Committees included finance, men's society, women's society, publicity, chaplain's aid, and historical records. The council was affiliated with the National Catholic War Council. Its purpose was to "render aid spiritual or temporal that might tend to bring solace, cheer and comfort to those who are fighting their country's cause, and to co-operate with the National War Council in furnishing records of war activities engaged in by our people [particularly black servicemen]." Activities of St. Benedict's members included working with the Red Cross, leading the knitting and sewing efforts of the Lincolnville Auxiliary Red Cross, providing "pious articles to the boys in camp," and organizing drills for the children. They reported, "Our first great accomplishment was the farewell given to forty colored members of St. Johns County draft now at Camp Johnston. They were entertained at our school hall [St. Benedict the Moor School] and served cigars and icecream. The occasion was indeed pleasing to all."[57]

In 1919, perhaps inspired by St. Benedict the Moor Church, the first black parish in Jacksonville, St. Pius V, was begun. Jacksonville's black Catholics had been members of the Church of the Immaculate Conception but had experienced the typical "second class" status afforded blacks: separate seating and limited participation. They raised enough money over a period of three years to prompt Bishop Curley to invite Josephite fathers to start a black parish for them. Josephite father Michael

57. War Activities, St. Benedict's Parish, St. Augustine, Florida [ca. April 30, 1918], typed manuscript 4(B)T2 from the Records of the Diocese of St. Augustine, on microfilm at P. K. Yonge Library, University of Florida, Gainesville. The officers were: president: Rev. J. J. Lyons; vice president: Louis Plummer Sr.; treasurer: Miss Lydia Papino; secretary: Louis Plummer Jr.; rec. secretary: M. N. Fleming.

Gumbleton celebrated the congregation's first Mass in the schoolhouse located behind Immaculate Conception. He described the parish's first Christmas Mass: "This is the first time in the history of this city that the Black congregation has had the privilege of seeing their own boys in cassock and surplice assisting the priest at the altar. The first time they hear the voices of their own parishioners singing in the choir." The congregation grew steadily, and after using a series of successively larger facilities, a church building was finally completed for St. Pius V and dedicated by Bishop Curley on February 27, 1921. Describing the occasion, Father Gumbleton wrote:

It was one that was looked forward to with much expectancy by the whole parish for a year or more, and an occasion long to be remembered by the Colored People, Catholic and non-Catholic alike; for it was the first time in the enterprising city of Jacksonville that the Right Reverend Bishop Curley of this diocese was called upon to dedicate a church for the Catholic people of the Negro Race. Interest was manifested on every side, for the Colored People of this city felt that there was something to see worth seeing, something to hear worth hearing, and they were not going to miss it.[58]

It was a firm foundation for a congregation that continued to grow and that still ministers to the needs of Jacksonville's black Catholics.

By 1923, St. Pius's sister parish, St. Benedict the Moor Church, had about 270 members, and the school averaged about 100 students, most of whom were not Catholic. The effort to gain converts, however, was still a struggle. The goal put forth in the account of St. Benedict's Church history, written in 1923, was that they might at least reach the level of membership reported by Father Henry P. Clavreul, who had worked with Bishop Verot, in 1858: "Of the nine hundred 'colored people' in

58. St. Pius V website, online at http://www.stpiusvjax.org/parhist.htm.

St Augustine fully one half are Catholic.'"[59] Sixty-five years had passed since Clavreul's cheerful report, however, and the rise of firmly established black denominations had since provided a way for blacks to affirm their dignity and independence in a society that was otherwise controlled by whites. Although the blacks happily benefited from the educational opportunities offered by the church through the Sisters of St. Joseph, most chose to attend a black church under black leadership.

Why did the Catholic Church fail to promote the ordination of black priests when the effectiveness of using indigenous clergy was so obvious? In his study *Desegregating the Altar: The Josephites and the Struggle for Black Priests, 1871–1960*, Stephen Ochs delineates the major reasons few blacks joined the Catholic Church and some abandoned the faith; all relate to the status of the Catholic Church in America and prevailing attitudes of the American Catholic hierarchy and/or white Catholic membership. First, the Catholic Church was a minority religion in the overwhelmingly Protestant United States. This was especially true in the South. Second, because of the great influx of Catholic immigrants, beginning in the mid-nineteenth century, Catholics experienced great hostility, and the church hierarchy did not want to risk greater disfavor by upsetting the status quo. For the same reason, the church had not taken a political stand on slavery before the Civil War. Third, the church leaders also feared the disapproval of white Catholics who were indifferent or even hostile to the idea of reaching out to blacks. Fourth, part of the status quo in predominantly white Catholic churches was the practice of segregating blacks in parish life, relegating blacks to separate seating areas and requiring them to take Communion only after the white members had finished. The issue of providing separate seating or separate churches was one discussed at the Second Plenary Council of Catholic Bishops

59. "St. Benedict the Moor," *Brief History*, 28.

in Baltimore in 1866. Fifth, blacks were also often barred from any leadership positions among the lay groups of such congregations. Sixth, and probably the most detrimental factor in the efforts to maintain black membership in the Catholic Church, was the almost complete absence of black clergy. This was no accident, but a conscious decision of Catholic leadership based on racial biases. Most Catholics considered African Americans to be unfit to hold any leadership position. They believed their priests to be far more than preachers; they were the "mediators between God and humanity" and "messengers of God and dispensers of His mysteries." In the Catholic mind, such a role could never be fulfilled by men whom they considered to be their racial inferiors, both intellectually and morally.[60]

Similar attitudes were held concerning the establishment of orders for black women religious. Three black orders of sisters were founded between 1829 and 1916, primarily to educate black youth. The first order, founded by Elizabeth Clarisse Lange (known in religious life as Sister Mary Elizabeth Lange) and the Rev. James Hector Joubert, SS, for free women of color, regardless of prior servitude, was the Oblate Sisters of Providence, established in Baltimore in 1828 by Haitian refugees. In 1842, Henriette Delille and Juliette Gaudin founded the Sisters of the Holy Family in New Orleans. To gain the support of the white community, members were required to be free-born (that is, not former slaves), wealthy, and fair-skinned. Even meeting those requirements, local officials did not allow them to wear their habit in public until 1872. The third order was created in 1916 in response to the Georgia legislature's proposed law to prohibit whites from teaching blacks, a policy that was sweeping the South at that time. Finding little support in Savannah, where they began, the sisters moved to Harlem in 1922. In 1930 the Handmaids affiliated with the Franciscan Third Order and

60. Ochs, *Desegregating the Altar*, 2 10–11; Davis, *History of Black Catholics*, 120.

became the Franciscan Handmaids of the Most Pure Heart of Mary. They remain active in Harlem.[61]

In the long run, neither the AMA nor the Catholic Church was successful in developing a strong membership among unchurched freedmen. The Sisters of St. Joseph were successful among those who were already Catholics, especially in St. Augustine. Otherwise, however, the black community was more drawn to the rising African American denominations than they were the elaborate ritualism of Roman Catholicism or the subdued traditionalism of white Protestantism. In their own churches, blacks were able to express their emotions freely and enjoyed leadership from among their own ranks. In spite of the strength of the Catholic Church in St. Augustine, African Americans had established nine Protestant black churches in that city by 1898. Even today, the American Catholic Church has an extremely small number of black members, due in large part to the church's failure to train and raise up appreciable numbers of black priests and bishops.[62] One might conclude that the Sisters of St. Joseph were faced with a losing battle, forced upon them by the Catholic hierarchy. One might also conclude, however, that, in spite of their adverse circumstances, they succeeded in nurturing St. Augustine's black Catholics who, though relatively few in number when compared to the numbers of Protestants, remain a vibrant part of the black community in the Ancient City and, along with black Catholics in other parts of Florida, contribute to the well-being of the state.

61. Diane Batts Morrow, *Persons of Color and Religious at the Same Time: The Oblate Sisters of Providence, 1828–1860* (Chapel Hill: University of North Carolina Press), 117–18, 192; Juliann Dossantos, "Franciscan Handmaids of Mary Begin Second Century of Service," *Catholic New York*, E-edition, https://www.cny.org/stories/franciscan-handmaids-of-mary-begin-second-century-of-service,14611, posted October 26, 2016.

62. In 2002, the *Chicago Tribune* reported that in the United States, the Roman Catholic Church, with a membership of about sixty million, had only thirteen black bishops and 350 black priests; Tom McCann in the *Chicago Tribune*, September 2, 2002; cited in Louie Crew, "Black Priests in the Episcopal Church," online at http://www.rci.rutgers.edu/~lcrew/blkpr.html.

Chapter 4

Sisters Facing the Yellow Jack
in 1877 and 1888

⌐

The deadliest events encountered by the Sisters of St. Joseph during the pioneer days were two yellow fever epidemics that struck northeast Florida in the late nineteenth century. Although three Sisters of St. Joseph lost their lives from the disease, the epidemics benefitted the order and the cause of Catholicism in the South.

On July 28, 1888, R. D. McCormick, a traveler from the Tampa area, arrived in Jacksonville, Florida, and shortly after entering his room at the Grand Union Hotel became ill. Dr. Neal Mitchell, the president of the Duval County Board of Health, who lived nearby, was summoned. His initial diagnosis of McCormick's condition was yellow fever, but before making such a dire pronouncement he sought confirmation from other doctors. He called the city health officer and Dr. Joseph Porter, who happened to be visiting him from Key West, to examine McCormick the next morning. Porter was acknowledged as the leading expert on yellow fever in the state, and his confirmation that the transient was suffering from the dreaded yellow fever was alarming. They transferred McCormick by ambulance to the Sand Hills Hospital, located north of town.[1] So began the worst yellow fever epidemic in Florida history.

The fear of yellow fever was well founded. Its origins were as yet not understood, but it was known to decimate entire communities, and quarantines imposed against towns to stop the disease could cripple their economies. Where did it come from? Yellow fever probably originated in West Africa and was brought to the New World through the slave trade. The first recorded epidemics in the New World occurred in the Yucatan (1648) and Cuba (1649). In the 1700s it also struck in the United States as far north as New York, Boston, Philadelphia, and Charleston. Outbreaks in Florida occurred nearly every two years from 1764 until 1905. After 1825, there were few outbreaks in the North, but the South continued to be gripped by the scourge every summer, though only occasionally did it reach epidemic proportions.[2]

The South also experienced similar but less harsh maladies, such as bilious fever, remittent fever, and malaria. These "summer complaints" were expected from June to November, and those who could afford to do so simply left for cooler, higher climes, such as North Carolina, to avoid the nuisance of dealing with them. The deadly yellow fever was a different matter, however, and its presence was dreaded. A diagnosis of the disease was never lightly made.

Not until 1905 did epidemiologists discover the cause of yellow fever in humans. The disease is caused by a virus that is contracted by humans through the bite of a female *Aëdes aegypti* mosquito; male mosquitoes do not bite. Females become carriers

1. Richard A. Martin, *The City Makers* (Jacksonville: Convention Press, 1972), 222–23.

2. William L. Pond, "This Is Yellow Fever," *Journal of the Florida Medical Association* 58 (August 1971): 8; Khaled J. Bloom, *The Mississippi Valley's Great Yellow Fever Epidemic of 1878* (Baton Rouge: Louisiana State University Press, 1993), 2–3; William M. Straight, "The Yellow Jack," *Journal of the Florida Medical Association* 8 (August 1971): 43; Barbara Elizabeth Miller, "Tallahassee and the 1841 Yellow Fever Epidemic" (unpublished masters' thesis, Florida State University, 1976), 17.

by biting an infected person. Once the mosquito is infected, at least twelve days must pass before it can communicate the virus, which can be transmitted only by a bite from the infected female; it is not passed on to her offspring or from human to human. The two hosts of the organism, an infected *Aëdes aegypti* mosquito and a susceptible human being, therefore, must be available. From the time a bite by a fever-carrying mosquito is received, there is a three- to six-day incubation period before symptoms appear in the victim. If no symptoms are manifested within that time, the person is immune to the disease. A virus that remains in its human host dies after ten or eleven days. The natural life of a mosquito is approximately two months after breeding, so even if a breeding area such as stagnant water or water in artificial containers is eliminated, an infected mosquito may remain an active carrier of the disease. An epidemic, therefore, will end naturally only if all susceptible hosts are eliminated by death, removed from the area, or become immune through a mild contraction of the disease or if the infected mosquitoes are eliminated through eradication, freezing temperatures, or expiration of their two-month life span.[3]

A number of factors contributed to the yellow fever epidemic in Florida. Yellow fever is more prevalent in cities than in rural areas because the higher concentration of people provides plenty of hosts for the virus, particularly among adults. Cases among young children are usually so mild that they are often not detected, but children can serve as carriers. The atmospheric temperature range for breeding is 72 to 101.5 degrees Fahrenheit; higher temperatures adversely affect the mosquito's breeding capacity, but these temperatures must exist over an extended period of time to end the reproduction cycle. Indoor containers of water, such as vases, found commonly in homes provide

---

3. Miller, "Tallahassee and the 1841 Epidemic," 19–20. In areas near jungles, monkeys can become hosts.

the optimal breeding condition for this type of mosquito and remain within the temperature range for breeding for longer periods. Bilges of ships are an excellent breeding environment and can transport infected mosquitoes from yellow fever regions of the Caribbean to many of America's port cities.

Since at least the seventeenth century it was commonly believed that black people were immune to yellow fever, but by the late nineteenth century, scientists realized that they are just as susceptible as any other race to infection but rarely die from the disease. Yellow fever is believed to have originated in West Africa, and the relative immunity of persons of West African descent may be a result of generations of exposure to the disease.[4]

In the nineteenth century, people were unaware of these factors in the spread of yellow fever. To them, the disease mysteriously broke out in the summer and disappeared after a few frosts. Populated areas near marshy lowlands were most affected. Exposure at night was considered extremely dangerous, precluding sleeping in the open air or traveling about after sundown. One belief was that fog or mists from marshes caused fever. No sound explanation for the disease existed at that time, and it seemed to strike randomly without regard to class or moral character. Because the spread of yellow fever cannot be stopped until all necessary factors are eliminated, nineteenth-century efforts to clean cities and establish sanitation laws, while certainly beneficial for the general health of a community, no matter how enthusiastically applied, could not curb the disease.

Before 1905, the origins of yellow fever were a disturbing mystery; its symptoms, in severe cases, were terrifying. The virus

4. Miller, "Tallahassee and the 1841 Epidemic," 20–21; Bloom, *Mississippi Valley's Epidemic*, 10–11; George M. Sternburg, M.D., *Report on the Etiology and Prevention of Yellow Fever* (Washington, D.C.: Government Printing Office, 1890), 51–53, http://books.google.com/books?id=qZ-Od89oQyoC&printsec=titlepage&dq=Yellow+fever+suscep. Yellow fever is endemic in Africa between 15°N and 10°S of the equator, an area that includes West Africa. It is also endemic in the Caribbean and parts of South America.

attacks the liver, kidneys, and heart and can produce harrowing physical manifestations. The first indications of the fever were the victim's feelings of heaviness and oppression, loss of appetite, and a slight headache, all of which were often disregarded. Violent symptoms usually followed within twenty-four hours. These could include sudden faintness, giddiness, and chilling followed by a fever of 103 to 104 degrees. Sharp, darting pains leaped in the back or cut across the forehead. A victim's pulse went from very weak to pounding, flushing and swelling the face and neck. The victim's eyes sometimes protruded and became extremely red. An intense burning occurred in the stomach, followed by violent heaving of bilious matter that was dark and sometimes bloody. Jaundice, yellowing of the skin, usually appeared on or after the third day. These symptoms continued for one to four days and then suddenly stopped, only to resume just as suddenly, bringing death in a few hours. A doctor in 1841 reported, "Occasionally, the fatal moment takes place in a convulsive fit. Toward the closing scene the saliva becomes thick, and is easily disengaged and ejected to a distance, and the patient seems as if amusing himself spitting against the wall." "Walking cases" of yellow fever developed very slowly, remaining undetected from two to ten or fifteen days, finally manifesting themselves in one great paroxysm with the heaving of black vomit. In the nineteeth century, after the appearance of this bloody substance, which looked much like coffee grounds, there was little hope of recovery.[5]

Such was the extent of the understanding of the people of Jacksonville in 1888 and was why the doctors hoped that Mc-Cormick's yellow fever was an isolated case and that they had detected it in time to stop its spreading. On August 8, however, eleven days after the presence of the disease was first discovered,

5. Miller, "Tallahassee and the 1841 Epidemic," 27–28. For a thorough descripton of the physical manifestations of yellow fever, see Bloom, *Mississippi Valley's Epidemic*, 4–10.

four more cases were reported. Two days later, the local board of health announced that yellow fever had begun to assume epidemic proportions. People had already started to leave Jacksonville, but with that announcement, panic struck, and citizens used every mode of transportation available to flee the city. All outgoing boats and trains were filled to capacity, and roads were jammed with people in vehicles or on foot. Nearly half of Jacksonville's 25,000 inhabitants fled. The majority who left were whites, most blacks being too poor to evacuate.[6]

When officials in Tallahassee learned of the fever in Jacksonville they declared a quarantine against the city. Other Florida municipalities followed suit, including nearby Palatka and St. Augustine. Fernandina, which had suffered a yellow fever epidemic in 1877, barred all trains from Jacksonville from entering Nassau County, and steamers from Jacksonville were denied entry at Charleston's harbor. Soon, cities across the Southeast and others in states as far north as Kentucky and Tennessee joined in quarantining anyone from Jacksonville. Jacksonville established a cordon around the city to keep people from coming and going. This shotgun quarantine required citizens who had left to have passes to return, a common request from businessmen wishing to check on their establishments.[7]

Those who remained in the city sought ways to protect themselves from the disease, to prevent it from spreading, and to treat those already stricken. The mayor of Jacksonville was away when the epidemic struck and, because of the quarantines, was unable to return. On August 10, Acting Mayor J. W. Archibald

6. T. Frederick Davis, *History of Jacksonville, Florida and Vicinity, 1513 to 1924*, a facsimile reproduction of the 1925 edition (Gainesville: University Press of Florida, 1964), 180; Webster Merritt, *A Century of Medicine in Jacksonville and Duval County* (Gainesville: University Press of Florida, 1949), 149; Charles S. Adams, ed., *Report of the Jacksonville Auxiliary Sanitary Association of Jacksonville, Florida, Covering the Work of the Association During the Yellow Fever Epidemic of 1888* (Jacksonville, 1889), 34; hereafter cited as *JASA*.

7. Incoming Correspondence of Dr. Jos. Y. Porter, Record Group 894, Series 868. Florida State Archives, Tallahassee; hereafter cited as Incoming Correspondence. Letters to Porter are full of such requests.

met with representatives from the board of trade, the city and county boards of health, the city council, and the county commission. At this meeting, a citizens committee was formed to coordinate efforts to deal with the crisis. The official mission of this committee, named the Jacksonville Auxiliary Sanitary Association (JASA), was to preserve lives, to protect the public health, to prevent the introduction and spread of disease, and to provide for the relief of the destitute.

On August 16, Florida's U.S. senators Wilkinson Call from Jacksonville and Samuel Pasco from Monticello and Representative Charles Dougherty from Port Orange sought speedy passage of a relief bill to assist the people of Jacksonville. According to *JASA*, the prospect of federal funds drew "hundreds of colored people from various places ... attracted by hopes of free rations and money."[8] Reports of problems with "unruly colored people" appeared in northern papers, prompting the creation of a Colored Auxiliary Bureau (CAB).

The CAB, formed by Jacksonville's leading black citizens on August 29, sought to aid the JASA and to provide assistance and employment to the city's black citizens and to speak in their defense. They wrote a resolution "couched in strong and unmistakable language, in refutation of the falsehoods reported in the Northern papers with reference to the colored people here." Their resolution condemned the negative reports in the press that had claimed "the colored citizens of Jacksonville ... [were] being organized into bands, breaking into stores and dwellings, and committing other depredations" and published it in the *Boston Journal*, *New York World*, and *Philadelphia Press*. It read,

Resolved, that we ... representing from fifteen to twenty law-abiding citizens, do emphatically denounce the slanders referred to as being entirely false in every particular, and without the least shadow of truth, and that the authors are not our friends. Further, we are prepared to

8. *JASA*, 17 and 21.

prove that the city was never so quiet and orderly as it is now, and has been since the yellow fever began. The truth is that the unemployed colored citizens are doing now just what they did during the [Civil] war—nursing the sick, burying the dead, and guarding the deserted houses and property of the whites who have fled.[9]

On September 10, the CAB organized four relief committees: finance, conference, labor, and information. The board worked well. An example of its efforts was its provision of soup for the sick. It also set large numbers of idle and needy laborers to work improving streets, rather than simply giving them free rations. African Americans also served as guards in the cordons around the city. Black clergymen showed great courage and leadership during the crisis. Several were members of the CAB. Some, such as the African Methodist Episcopal ministers Thomas Higginbotham, William W. Sampson, and William P. Ross, who chose to stay in the stricken city to assist their congregants, died from the fever.[10]

After Governor E. A. Perry appealed for federal aid, the city received aid from the Surgeon General's Office of the United States Marine Hospital Service (MHS), a predecessor of the United States Public Health Service. Joseph Y. Porter, the doctor who confirmed the presence of yellow fever in Jacksonville, was made the Surgeon in Charge of Government Relief Measures. He was to oversee the operation of the quarantines, fumigation, disinfecting, federal aid for operating refugee camps, distribution of free medicine, and the selection and supervision of medical personnel paid with federal funds.

One of the first actions of the JASA was to establish a program to clean up Jacksonville. The executive committee ordered citizens to remove refuse around their houses and keep their

9. *Florida Times Union*, August 30, 1888.
10. *Florida Times Union*, September 11, 1888; *JASA*, 41; *Florida Times Union*, October 27, 1888; Rivers and Brown, *Laborers in the Vineyard*, 164.

yards clean. Sanitary agents inspected houses daily, and privies were either cleaned or burned down. Disinfecting crews spread lime on tree trunks, posts, hydrants, curbs, and sidewalks. They also burned down some buildings where fever had occurred, then covered the site with the disinfectant. Fumigation brigades treated anything thought to carry yellow fever. Countless mattresses and pillows and upholstered furniture pieces from buildings where yellow fever was found were burned and the edifices marked with a yellow flag (a yellow jack) to warn others to keep away. Outgoing mail was fumigated as well. Letters were placed in a railroad car that was divided by a partition in the middle. One end contained wire shelves, where the mail was opened. A small mallet with sharp spikes was used to perforate the mail to create holes to allow fumigating fumes to impregnate the paper. The letters were then placed on the shelves. A large tin boiler with legs about six inches long and filled with sulfur was then set in the shelf end of the car. The sulfur was lighted and the door closed to create an almost air tight space. After about six hours in the fumes, the mail was removed and sent on to its intended recipients.[11]

Some citizens burned bonfires and kept cauldrons of tar smoldering to "smother the microbes," and others fired five cannons at night, hoping the concussion caused by the explosions would make the microbes collide, thus destroying them. People were to stay indoors at night and to keep their windows and doors shut or covered with curtains. Those who remained in the city must have suffered through the long, hot summer nights, sweltering in their shut-up houses, listening to continuous explosions accompanied by the sound of breaking glass, the silence between explosions filled with the clatter of ambulances as the stricken were taken to hospitals, or the sound of death carts as the

11. *Florida Times Union*, August 20, 1888. Evidence of this procedure is visible in punctured letters in the Porter Collection at the Florida State Archives, Tallahassee, and letters at the Archives of the Sisters of St. Joseph in Le Puy, France.

bodies of those who had perished were gathered. All forms of the senses were assaulted as the sights, sounds, smells, tastes, feelings, and the resulting fears gripped the inhabitants of Jacksonville.

By September 2, there had been 259 cases resulting in thirty-four deaths. A census taken September 5 showed 13,757 remaining in the city, either unwilling or unable to evacuate. Of those, 9,812 were black and 3,945 were white. The head of St. Joseph's Academy in Jacksonville, the convent school operated by the Sisters of St. Joseph, wrote to her superiors in Le Puy on September 14:

As you know it is a month and nine days that yellow fever is ravishing Jacksonville, every day making rapid progress, new cases are 50 to 70 a day, already a thousand persons prostrated, and of this number, nearly a hundred have died. They are hastening to depopulate the town, without which action, doctors say that soon there will be a hundred cases daily. Judge then, dear Father, the general terror.[12]

By September 18, the total was 1,203 cases and 156 deaths. People who remained in Jacksonville were at great risk, and the federal, state, and local officials had, indeed, concluded total evacuation of the city was the only way to stop the spread of the fever. For those who desired to leave, but could not afford to go far, the JASA established three refuge camps outside of the city, assisted with federal aid. Refugees had to wait out a ten-day period before they were allowed to leave the Jacksonville area. If they remained healthy, they were free to leave to seek asylum elsewhere. The camps had very few cases of the fever and remained healthy refuges for the citizens of Jacksonville. There reportedly was only one death in the camps, for whenever inmates showed any symptoms, they were immediately transferred to one of the hospitals in Jacksonville for treatment.[13]

12. Mother Claverie, St. Joseph's Academy, Jacksonville, to Mr. Bonhomme, Canon of Cathedral in Le Puy, September 14, 1888, ASSJSA.

13. Martin, *City Makers*, 229–30; *JASA*,191; *Florida Times Union*, August 24, 1888;

By the end of the nineteenth century most of the harsh treatments of the early 1800s, such as heavy doses of quinine and calomel, had been abandoned, and more attention was given to making patients comfortable. During the 1888 epidemic, the board of health recommended the following treatment:

Give a hot mustard foot bath with the patient in a chair under a blanket for 15 minutes. After drying under the blanket place the patient in bed with hot water bottles. Give five grains of calomel to adults and one-half this amount to a child. After 3 or 4 hours give a dose of castor oil or salts, later warm drinks of orange leaf tea. After the medicine acts, give 1/2 teaspoonful of Nitre in cool water every 2 hours, and an enema if necessary. Give a little brandy, whiskey or champagne if the patient is very weak. Give 3 tablespoonfuls of beef or chicken broth or gruel and discourage efforts to vomit.[14]

Such was the treatment given at the two main hospitals in Jacksonville: the Sand Hills Hospital, a public facility established in 1883, and St. Luke's Hospital, a private hospital established in 1871 to meet the needs of transients. During the early stages of the epidemic, the Sand Hills Hospital, located about four miles north of town, received all of the yellow fever cases.[15]

In the late nineteenth century most of the sick received care at home, and only in the most dire circumstances was a patient taken to a hospital, for hospitals were considered places to die. However, R. D. McCormick, whose yellow fever was declared the source of the epidemic, recovered at the Sand Hills Hospital. Upon his discharge, he cheerfully reported his satisfaction with the care he received there: "Mr. McCormick said the fear which many people have of going to the Sand-Hills hospital is entirely without reason, as the place is high, dry, and reasonably

Margaret C. Fairlie, "The Yellow Fever Epidemic of 1888 in Jacksonville," *Florida Historical Quarterly* 19, no. 2 (October 1940): 100.

14. Merritt, *Century of Medicine*, 155.

15. *Florida Times Union*, August 9, 1888; Merritt, *Century of Medicine*, 149; Martin, *City Makers*, 294fn5.

comfortable; the air is pure, patients are provided with comfortable beds, and the best of fare and attention. The patients are carefully nursed and visited by a physician twice a day."[16]

St. Luke's Hospital was located on Palmetto Street in East Jacksonville. Because of its accessibility within the city limits, as the epidemic continued the most critical cases were taken there. As a result, patients were often already dying upon their arrival, giving the hospital an abnormally high death record. Adding to their difficulties was the fact that their regular resident physician was out of town during the epidemic, causing a hardship and creating a state of panic. The matron of the hospital recounted the experience to a reporter:

I shall never forget the horrors of those first two weeks. . . . Our resident physician was called North just at the outbreak of the fever, while we had a virulent case of yellow fever in the house, though at the time of her departure it had not been so conceded.

When it was known in the house that the case was considered suspicious, my help became completely demoralized and most of them fled panic-stricken, leaving me with the violent case of yellow fever, among fourteen other sufferers from other diseases, who all, together with those of us who were well, had been exposed to and were of course liable to become victims of the fever. . . . As soon as the physicians decided upon the case, we were immediately quarantined, which made matters still worse, and for a time we were sorely distressed.

She went on to tell how the physician substituting for the absent doctor fell ill himself, and one of the nurses died. It was during that time that "all those pitiful dying cases" were sent to St. Luke's. She recalled, "One poor soul was covered with black vomit from head to foot when brought in, and only lived twenty minutes. . . . Others lived longer, but their cases were aggravated, and their sufferings [made] more acute by being moved when in such a critical condition, and the air was filled with their dying

16. *Florida Times Union*, August 13, 1888, and August 17, 1888.

shrieks and groans." Once the hospital stopped receiving all the terminal patients, St. Luke's death rate compared favorably with the rate realized in private homes, and by late October, St. Luke's enjoyed a good reputation.[17] In addition to these public hospitals, there were some private organizations that provided medical care for their employees or members.

Not long after the epidemic started, it became clear that the local physicians and nurses were not able to meet all the city's medical needs. The JASA sent out a call across the nation for doctors and nurses to come assist the local effort, and on September 5, the city issued its own public appeal for financial aid. Responses came from all over the country and even from overseas. On September 6, some of the funds were used by the JASA to establish a Committee on Nurses and Medical Attention. Dr. Porter was in charge of the selection and oversight of the doctors and nurses who would be paid with federal relief funds.

Because the city's hotels and boardinghouses were closed, the committee supplied food and lodging for the visiting or "foreign" doctors and nurses who either worked at the hospitals or were dispatched to private homes. In addition to eleven local doctors, eighteen physicians came from other Florida cities, Missouri, Mississippi, Texas, Ohio, Kentucky, Alabama, South Carolina, Alabama, and Georgia. Many became sick themselves; five died.[18] In addition to hiring doctors, Porter also received all applications for nurses. The main qualification sought was immunity to yellow fever, but training was also desirable. Organized, trained nursing was an emerging profession for women at the end of the nineteenth century. Nurses, black and white, performed services, usually under strict oversight by a physician. Typical duties included applying plasters, giving carbolic acid

17. *Florida Times Union*, August 21, 1888, and October 27, 1888.
18. *JASA*, 132–39; *Florida Times Union*, September 29, 1888; Martin, *City Makers*, 243.

gargles and enemas, administering rectal feedings, cupping, and leeching. Nurses were not permitted to answer patients' questions about their condition and were required to refer them to their doctors. A primary qualification for nurses was the ability to obey orders.[19]

Some of the most effective nurses in the nineteenth century were Catholic nuns. Doctors often preferred them, based largely on the service they had provided during the Civil War. They had shown themselves to be "generally capable of following directions with discretion but who were also experienced in initiating independent judgment and managing institutions when necessary" and were "disciplined, organized and would calmly volunteer for the dirtiest, most difficult tasks."[20]

The Sisters of St. Joseph probably were acquinted with caring for the sick, because their rule of life required them to help care for the sick poor in hospitals or to visit them, to make them soups, and to "prepare the medical remedies ordered by the physicians." They also nursed each other; if a sister died, they sometimes helped to prepare her body for burial.[21] Given their rule of life and their own sympathy for the afflicted, the Sisters of St. Joseph, particularly those from St. Augustine and from Jacksonville, were among the first who volunteered their aid during the epidemic. Their help was immediately accepted, probably based on the service they had rendered during the yellow fever epidemic in Fernandina, Florida, in 1877.

19. Darlene Clark Hine, *Black Women in White: Racial Conflict and Cooperation in the Nursing Profession, 1890–1950* (Bloomington and Indianapolis: Indiana University Press, 1989), 9; Josephine A. Dolan, *Nursing in Society: A Historical Perspective* (Philadelphia: W. B. Saunders, 1978), 193–94, 211.

20. Christopher J. Kauffman, *Ministry and Meaning: A Religious History of Catholic Health Care in the United States* (New York: Crossroad, 1995), 83; John J. Fialka, *Sisters: Catholic Nuns and the Making of America* (New York: St. Martin's, 2003), 60–61.

21. *Constitutions of the Congregations of the Sisters of St. Joseph* (New York: O'Shea, 1884), 22, 28–29. Concerning the longtime practice of the medical arts by women religious, especially the Sisters of Charity, see Martha M. Libster, *Herbal Diplomats: The Contribution of Early American Nurses (1830–1860) to Nineteenth-Century Health Care Reform and the Botanical Medical Movement* (Wauwatosa, Wisc.: Golden Apple Healing Arts), 191–229.

According to a special report to the *Catholic Mirror*, a national publication, yellow fever had entered Fernandina by way of sailors whose ship from the West Indies had entered the port there in August 1877. For some reason, the crew was not quarantined, and the sailors had freely gone ashore. The epidemic began slowly and at first was not recognized, perhaps out of ignorance, or perhaps out of an effort to preserve the healthy reputation of the city. Nevertheless, between August 28 and September 8, yellow fever struck down four in a single family. The sickness in the Bordeaux family began with the father, who was a cabinet maker, and his twelve-year-old son, Leon. The two had been frequently aboard a ship in the port, working on a job both day and night. Leon fell ill on August 25 and died on August 29. His father showed signs of the fever on August 28 and succumbed on September 3. The Bordeaux mother and another of their children then fell ill and died within the week. According to the *Catholic Mirror*, the Bordeaux family died "in great agony with symptoms of virulent yellow fever." The fever continued to spread throughout the city, especially in Old Town Fernandina, an area near the river.[22]

Although most people who were able had fled Fernandina in terror, abandoning the stricken, the Bordeux family had not died alone, for Catholic Sisters of St. Joseph were with them. Bishop Moore informed the sisters, who were gathered at the motherhouse in St. Augustine from their various communities in Fernandina, Jacksonville, Mandarin, and Palatka, for their

22. "Yellow Fever, Description of the Plague at Fernandina: How the Priests and Sisters Devoted Themselves to the Noble Work of Ministering to the Stricken," Special Report for the *Catholic Mirror* [1877]; hereafter cited as *Catholic Mirror*. A copy of this article was inserted in a letter copybook held at the Archives of the Sisters of St. Joseph, Le Puy, France (ASSJLP). See also the article in the *Weekly Florida Union* (Jacksonville), October 13, 1877, which lists the deaths of only three Bordeuxs: Leon, Mr. J. B., and Gaston; and C. W. Horsey, M.D., "Report of the Epidemic of Yellow Fever at Fernandina, Florida, August, September and October, 1877," *Proceedings of the Florida Medical Association, Session of 1878* (Jacksonville: Union Book and Job Rooms, 1878), 72, which provides an additional contemporary account of the epidemic.

annual retreat, of Fernandina's urgent need. He asked them, "Are the Sisters ready to go to assist the sufferers?"[23] The four sisters who were based in Fernandina returned to the stricken city about September 1. They were Mother Célenie, superior of the house, Sister Marie de Sales, Sister Xavier, and Sister Mary Louise. They found Fernandina desolated, with empty homes and businesses and deserted streets. A peculiar odor filled the air, perhaps from fumigation efforts. They went immediately to the bedsides of the fever victims, remaining with them and nursing them, taking turns around the clock. They also cared for the bodies in death, preparing them for burial themselves, as everyone else was too terrified to assist them.[24]

The sisters assisted Protestants and Catholics alike and were greatly appreciated and admired. One Protestant doctor said, "You have, my Sisters, more courage than a soldier on the battlefield: this one goes to his death on the road to glory, pushed by the prestige of ambition and honor, but you, you go to it by way of the greatest test, and standing up to the most horrible in nature, to fly to the assistance of suffering humanity! Oh, noble ladies!"[25]

Mother Célenie, though sick herself, continued to nurse another victim. On the night of September 16 to 17, the other sisters took her back to the community house in Fernandina, where Sister Marie de Sales had just died. Three sisters from the Jacksonville house arrived in time to be there when Mother Célenie died within eight hours of Sister de Sales's death. Two other sisters came, Mother Julie Roussel from the Mandarin house and Sister Augustine Verot from St. Augustine, but arrived too late, and could only assist at the funerals. In retrospect, sisters recalled Mother Célenie's and Sister de Sales's behavior

23. Records, Sisters of St. Joseph, St. Augustine, 1866–1937, MS680, ASSJSA.

24. *Weekly Florida Union* (Jacksonville), September 15, 1877.

25. Congrégation de Saint-Joseph Du Puy, *Religieuses Décédées*, Depuis le mois de Juillet 1877 jusqu'au de Janvier 1878, ASSJLP.

at the retreat they were attending in St. Augustine when they learned of the epidemic in Fernandina. Of Mother Célenie, they said, "There was something celestial about her." She had told Mother Sidonie, superior of the house in St. Augustine, "I feel that I will not see you again." Sister de Sales had said, "Mother, bless me, I am going to my death. So long, until Heaven!"[26] Three sisters from the other houses in Jacksonville and St. Augustine went to Fernandina to replace Sister Marie and Mother Célenie: Sisters Jane Francis, Helen, and Mary Ann. All told, five of the additional sisters contracted the disease, but all recovered by October 23.[27]

Fernandina's yellow fever epidemic ended after the first frost of the season appeared on November 30. The city's population was about 3,100: about 1,300 whites and 1,700–1,800 blacks. Approximately 1,100 whites remained in Fernandina during the summer, but many of them fled at the onset of the epidemic. At the height of the sickness, there were 518 whites and 1,014 blacks remaining in the city. Among the whites there was a 16 percent mortality rate. Among the blacks there was only a 2 percent death rate. As reported in the *Catholic Mirror*, "The sisters and priests are more justly appreciated in Fernandina since the epidemic than they had been before. All classes and creeds benefited from their labors and sufferings, and all now join in their praise."[28] So it was after Catholic sisters nursed soldiers during the Civil War, and so it would be in Jacksonville in 1888.

The 1888 epidemic broke out in Jacksonville shortly after the Sisters of St. Joseph's annual August retreat. On August 21, the

26. Congrégation de Saint-Joseph Du Puy, *Religieuses Décédées*.
27. *Catholic Mirror*.
28. *Weekly Florida Union* (Jacksonville), December 3, 1877; Horsey, "Fernandina Epidemic Report," 72. Statistics concerning the epidemic vary. In his 1971 article, William Straight reported that Fernandina had a population of 3,000 and suffered 1,612 cases of the fever, resulting in 95 deaths, a mortality rate of 5.9 percent; Straight, "Yellow Jack," 45. Two priests also served: Fernandina's Father Augustine Spandonari, until he fell ill, and Father J. L. Hugon from Tallahassee, who replaced him; *Catholic Mirror*.

Times-Union reported that Sisters of Charity (actually four Sisters of St. Joseph of St. Augustine from the motherhouse) had volunteered their services to care for the female ward at the Sand Hills Hospital after Bishop John Moore told them of the city's plight, just as he had eleven years before when Fernandina was struck. The JASA ordered the construction of a house for them adjoining the hospital.

Sisters from the Jacksonville community served at St. Luke's Hospital and visited the sick in the city. Among the Jacksonville sisters were Sister Mary Ann, who had nursed during the Fernandina epidemic, and Sister Rose de Lima, a native of France, who worked at St. Luke's, "putting up prescriptions." Before the end of the month, on August 28, after three days of sickness, Rose de Lima was dead. Her loss was a shock to the sisters. Mother Claverie, the superior at St. Joseph's Academy in Jacksonville, wrote to the Canon of the Cathedral in Le Puy of Rose de Lima's death and lamented that, after her death, five other sisters, as well as an orphan living at the convent in Jacksonville, had "fallen under the clutches of that malignant fever." Trying to reconcile herself to the ongoing tragedy, she wrote, "I try to resign myself to the holy will of the good God, Father, . . . I do not consider our dear sick ones out of danger. We can say only 'Fiat.' If only we were together there would be some consolation; but no, we are all scattered." It was some comfort that Bishop Moore also went to Jacksonville to minister to the needy. Mother Claverie wrote, "The Bishop is tireless and his goodness toward the sick poor is admirable; how edifying it is to see a Bishop alone, on foot, going to the dying to bring Last Sacraments."[29]

Bishop Moore bore witness to the tireless work and sacrifices performed by the Sisters of St. Joseph and himself in a letter he wrote from Jacksonville in the midst of the epidemic:

29. Mother Claverie, St. Joseph's Academy, Jacksonville, to Mr. Bonhomme, Canon of Cathedral in Le Puy, September 14, 1888, ASSJSA.

This city is now one yellow fever hospital.... We have plenty to do. There is a hospital at the Sand Hills nearly four miles from the city.... We have three Sisters there doing well. We also had three Sisters in St. Luke's hospital but Sr. Rose de Lima died of the fever and Sr. Jane Francis is now down with it, but is doing well so far; we have however some fear for her as she is not strong. Sister Marie Louise is there doing heroic [?] work; she is strongly and compactly built and is thoroughly healthy, she bosses [?] the patients and the[y] all want to have her around them.... Eight orphans [at St. Mary's Home, an orphanage in Jacksonville established by Sister Mary Ann] have gotten the fever.... Sister Mary Ann was in bed for two days from over work but had no fever. She is every where hunting up the sick and doing all she can for them. She gets plenty of work for Father Duffo [Dufau, a priest assisting the Bishop] and myself.[30]

Less than a week later, on September 23, Sister Joséphine, who had come to serve at the Sand Hills Hospital, was stricken. She received last rites, but recovered. She returned to St. Augustine on Christmas Eve.[31] Thus the sisters and bishop courageously nursed and ministered to the people of Jacksonville throughout the epidemic.

Just as the Sisters of St. Joseph had been praised for their work during the Fernandina epidemic, the sisters who nursed patients at the Sand Hills Hospital were lauded. In his report, Dr. Sollace Mitchell, administrator of the hospital, declared, "I must name those devoted Sisters of St. Joseph who have worked so nobly night and day for these many weeks, refusing pay. The many Sand Hills patients will not soon forget Sister Josephine, Sister Elizabeth, Sister Gerasim and Sister Agatha, and I wish to give them my personal thanks."[32]

30. Bishop John Moore, Jacksonville, to Dr. Pace, Philadelphia, September 12, 1888, Diocese of St. Augustine Papers, Microfilm Reel 2, on file at the P. K. Yonge Library, University of Florida, Gainesville.
31. McGoldrick, *Beyond the Call*, 251.
32. Elihu Burritt, *Jacksonville, Florida: Experiences in a Stricken City* (Jacksonville: Riverside, 1888), 4. Sister Gerasim probably should be Sister Gertrude, per Sister Thomas Joseph, Archivist, Sisters of St. Joseph of St. Augustine, email correspondence, February 25, 2008.

The Sisters of St. Joseph were welcomed and lauded for their work, but some of the "foreign" nurses who came to Jacksonville caused considerable problems, and their legacy stands in stark contrast to that of the sisters. One set was a group sent by Harry Miner, a theatrical manager from New York. Miner had offered to send trained nurses and to pay for their salaries and transportation, only asking if they could be provided accommodations and how many were required. The JASA accepted the offer and asked for ten nurses. Nine men and one woman came and set to work. Because the agreement was based on Miner's offer to pay the nurses, they were not placed on the government payroll. Soon, the nurses applied for aid, for Miner refused to pay them, pointing to an agreement they had signed in New York to provide free services. After protracted negotiations, the JASA paid the nurses, even though, with two exceptions, all were "sick with the fever, and averaged but a few days of actual service apiece." Problems in settling the issue remained long after the epidemic.[33]

Even more vexing were Red Cross nurses who came to assist the stricken city. Clara Barton, president of the American Red Cross Association, offered to establish a Red Cross headquarters in Jacksonville, and the surgeon general strongly recommended that the offer be accepted. The American Red Cross Association, which had been created only seven years before, had assisted people suffering from forest fires, floods, cyclones, and famine, but had never dealt with an epidemic before. The Old Howard Association in New Orleans united with the Red Cross with the express purpose of providing nurses for the yellow fever victims. Barton accordingly offered the surgeon general of the Marine Hospital Service "all nurses that could be required, even to hundreds, all experienced and organized for immediate action." Barton's own lack of immunity and prior commitments

33. *JASA*, 146–48.

precluded her going to Jacksonville herself, so she called upon an old associate, Colonel F. R. Southmayd, to raise a group of nurses to go to Jacksonville. Thirty, including both women and men, white and black, volunteered. Many had had experience with yellow fever before.[34]

The quality of the Red Cross nurses, however, was generally very unsatisfactory, and some were found to lack moral character, their selection seemingly based solely on their immunity to the fever. Scandals among some of them abounded: thievery, assault of one against a doctor, dereliction of duty, and drunkenness, and several were "branded as prostitutes and ordered to leave town."[35] Although there were difficulties with the Harry Miner nurses and the Red Cross, most nurses during the epidemic did noble service, but the problems with a few overshadowed their good work.[36]

The long-awaited frost finally came on November 25, 1888, and the last recorded death occurred December 5. By December 8, only one yellow fever patient remained at St. Luke's Hospital. On December 12, the epidemic was officially declared over, five and a half months after it began, and the quarantine of Jacksonville was lifted on the fifteenth. After the city was fumigated, those who had fled joyfully returned. Those arriving at the railroad depot were greeted by other citizens with banners reading, "Welcome Home," "Jacksonville Greets You," and "No Microbes on Us," and by a full brass band playing such tunes as "Dixie," "Annie Laurie," and "Johnnie Get Your Gun."[37]

The 1888 Jacksonville yellow fever epidemic was a major catastrophe for the city. Although the fever was widespread

34. *JASA*, 143–44; *Florida Times Union*, September 9, 1888; Clara Barton, *The Red Cross in Peace and War* (Meriden, Conn.: American Historical Press, 1899), 107–15, 136, 148.

35. W. H. H. Hutton to J. Y. Porter, October 15, 1888, incoming correspondence; Elizabeth Brown Pryor, *Clara Barton: Professional Angel* (Philadelphia: University of Pennsylvania Press, 1987), 255–56.

36. *JASA*, 147; Pryor, *Clara Barton*, 256–57.

37. Martin, *City Makers*, 250–51.

across the South that year, Jacksonville, Florida's leading industrial city and a rising resort, suffered the most, with at least 4,696 cases, resulting in 430 deaths. Jacksonville's population fell from 25,000 in 1888 to 17,201 in 1890 and did not recover its pre-epidemic level until 1900. Many of Jacksonville's most capable leaders died in the epidemic. Economic losses resulting from the quarantine and deaths of businessmen were heavy.[38]

Although Jacksonville had suffered yellow fever epidemics in 1857 and 1877, neither of those approached the magnitude of the 1888 epidemic. Fortunately, 1888 was the last year Jacksonville suffered from yellow fever; the last major epidemic in the country was in 1905. Concerted efforts to eradicate the mosquito vector and the development of a vaccine in 1938 finally eliminated yellow fever as an annual scourge in the United States.

Yellow fever struck across most of the Southeast in 1888, but the news of the epidemic in Jacksonville had gripped the nation. Disaster relief efforts had been massive, and citizens from as far away as New York and Ohio had sent monetary aid and supplies or had come themselves. The unfortunate experience with some of the Red Cross nurses left its mark on the association, tarnishing its reputation and causing Clara Barton to resolve never again to entrust a major relief effort to anyone but herself. Her refusal to delegate authority hindered the development of the American Red Cross until her death. The mark of the 1888 experience on the Red Cross remained on Jacksonville, too. During the Spanish American War, two Red Cross nurses assigned to Jacksonville were not allowed to work under the association's badge because the locals still considered Red Cross nurses to be disreputable.[39]

38. Straight, "Yellow Jack," 45; Martin, *City Makers*, 251. According to Davis, *History of Jacksonville*, 185, there were 4,704 cases, with 427 deaths (324 white, 103 black). The count is uncertain, and could have been as high as 5,000 cases, with 500 deaths; Martin, *City Makers*, 297, fn76.

39. Pryor, *Clara Barton*, 256.

There were, however, positive results, too. Dr. Joseph Y. Porter emerged a hero. Mr. D. W. Onley, president of the CAB and leader of Jacksonville's black community, was also commended for his work, and it was hoped that a new era of better racial relations would follow. Not long after the epidemic, newly elected governor Francis P. Fleming convened a special session of the Florida legislature to establish a state board of health; Porter was its first director. In 1897, the Marine Hospital Service modeled refugee camps in New Orleans and Mobile after Jacksonville's camps.[40]

Despite the problems cited with a few medical personnel in 1888, the doctors and nurses who served during the epidemic were heroic. Among the most lauded were the Sisters of St. Joseph, who lost three sisters to yellow fever during the 1877 and 1888 epidemics. Their sacrificial ministries to care for the stricken, black or white, Protestant or Catholic, did much to gain them the esteem and appreciation of the people who lived in Fernandina and Jacksonville, both largely Protestant communities. The good will their efforts engendered would serve the Catholic Church well in later years, when promoters of anti-Catholicism would seek to undermine the church's work in Florida.

40. All these and several others were commemorated in *Ye Heroes of Ye Epidemic* by One of Ye Heroes, T. O. S. (Jacksonville: DeCosta, 1888); Straight, "Yellow Jack," 42; Bloom, *Mississippi Valley's Epidemic*, 250.

Chapter 5

The End of the Nineteenth Century

The yellow fever epidemics were crises that broke into otherwise calm days as the Sisters of St. Joseph pursued their primary missions of education and helping the needy in the last decades of the nineteenth century. One exception was when the normal pattern of classes was briefly interrupted in 1887 by the arrival of Apache Indians from Arizona and New Mexico. They were held as prisoners of war by the federal government at St. Augustine's Castillo de San Marcos, which at that time was called Fort Marion. Their arrival afforded the Sisters of St. Joseph another opportunity to reach out to the needy and the outcast.

At the end of the Mexican War in 1848, the United States took over the lands that the Apaches had occupied. After the Civil War, the United States turned its attention toward subjugating the native peoples of the area, forcing them onto reservations. As more and more settlers moved to the West, the reservation lands became steadily smaller, generating tensions among the tribes and the whites who were encroaching upon them. Some bands of Apaches attacked the white settlers. The fiercest and most well-known of these bands was led by Geronimo. Some Apaches cooperated with the U.S. government and served as scouts to track Geronimo's bands. After Geronimo's capture, the Chiricahua tribe, many of whom served as scouts, and Warm Spring Apaches who had obediently stayed on their reservations, were sent by train out of the volatile situation to Florida for safe-keeping. On October 25, 1886, fifteen Apache men were delivered to Fort Pickens near Pensacola, while their women, children, and young men were sent on to Fort Marion in St. Augustine.

The conditions at Fort Marion were horrible. The commandant felt he had room for 150 prisoners, not the 400–500 men, women, and children who arrived. He set up a tent city on the flat roof of the fort. There, about 130 tents were crowded, with hardly any room for cooking fires. Removed from their home in the arid West to a dank fort only slightly above sea level, the Indians had little to do and suffered from homesickness. Field Representative C. J. Ryper commented on the conditions:

There are 447 of these Apache Indians held as prisoners of war in the old Spanish fort at St. Augustine, Florida. They are idle, and cannot be otherwise. They spend their time foolishly, or worse, as idle people always do. As I looked upon these men, women and children, crowded together like cattle in a pen, I wondered if our Government were making the wisest use of these Apaches in holding them in this confinement, that must result in increased viciousness. A Christian lady, after looking at these Indians, said: "Why, the very sight makes me blush for my country!"[1]

The federal government finally decided to establish schools for the Apaches in an effort to counter the boredom and to "civilize" them and arranged for two groups to be taught. For the adults, Miss Sarah A. Mather led two other teachers in instructing the Apaches in English, arithmetic, spelling, and religion. Miss Mather had been an American Missionary Association (AMA) teacher from October 1872 to December 1878, teaching Cheyenne, Arapahoe, Kiowa, and Comanche individuals who

1. C. J. Ryper, "Notes in the Saddle," *American Missionary* 41, no. 4 (April 1887): 111, http://cdl.library.cornell.edu/cgi-bin/moa/moa-cgi?notisid=ABK5794-0041-69.

had been confined at Fort Marion in the 1870s. Before that, she had spent many years in St. Augustine as headmistress of Miss Mather's School for Young Women.[2]

The second group was the Sisters of St. Joseph of St. Augustine, who had a contract from the United States government to teach the children. The agreement between the U.S. commissioner of Indian Affairs and the Bureau of Catholic Indian Missions was dated January 1, 1887. Its terms called for the sisters to run a day school five days a week, except on legal holidays, for six months. They were to teach at least fifteen pupils, but no more than sixty-eight, ages six to eighteen. They were also responsible for providing schoolbooks and supplies and submitting regular reports on their work. The curriculum was to include "the ordinary branches of an English education" (basic reading, writing, and arithmetic). For this, they were to receive seven dollars and fifty cents ($7.50) per pupil per quarter, for a total of no more than $900.[3]

The Bureau of Catholic Indian Missions was created in 1874 to protect and promote Catholic missionary efforts among the Indians by facilitating the necessary interactions with the U.S. Indian agents who had control over the various tribes. In 1874, under President Ulysses S. Grant's Indian Peace Policy, much of the government's work with the Indians had been turned over to the Christian mission organizations, but out of seventy-two Indian agencies, only eight were given over to Catholic missionaries, the rest to Protestants. The bureau, based in Washington, D.C., was created to negotiate better arrangements for Catholic efforts. The Indian Peace Policy was in force from 1874 to 1882, but the bureau continued its work after that time.[4]

2. Amistad Research Center, American Missionary Association Correspondence Index, http://www.tulane.edu/~amistad/ama-corres.htm; Sally Jenkins, *The Real All Americans: The Team that Changed a Game, a People, a Nation* (New York: Doubleday, 2007), 52.

3. Quinn, *Story of a Nun*, Appendix I, 405–6.

4. William Ketcham, "Bureau of Catholic Indian Missions," *The Catholic Encyclopedia* (New York: Robert Appleton, 1910), http://www.newadvent.org/cathen/07745a.htm.

Father Joseph A. Stephan, the director of the bureau, wrote the Sisters of St. Joseph on January 24, 1887, to warn them to be careful, for "strong efforts were made by parties up to the time this contract was secured to have these children placed under other auspices than yours, and as a consequence your work will be watched with jealous eyes, eager to find some excuse to criticise your management of the children."[5] The sisters had already begun teaching at the fort on January 12 under the supervision of Sister Alypius Laurent, who had come from Le Puy in September 1879. Sister Jane Francis and Sister Alypius taught classes from 9 o'clock in the morning until noon. The children soon learned to read, write, draw, and sing, while Sister Alypius soon learned their language. Herbert Welsh, the corresponding secretary of the Indian Rights Association, wrote a full report on the treatment of the Apaches at Fort Marion. After visiting Miss Mather's and the sisters' classes he had nothing but high praise for the ladies' efforts. Of the sisters, he reported, "I heard the children singing and in their recitations, and I was entirely pleased with all that I heard and saw. The sisters are ladies of cultivation and refinement, and, from all that I could learn during my brief visit, are well fitted to perform the task assigned them."[6]

The Apaches' confinement at the fort was not strict. The women and children were free to go where they pleased, and groups of the men were sometimes allowed to go into the town of St. Augustine. Expanding beyond their contract, the sisters obtained permission from the fort commandant and Bishop Moore to visit the Apaches and to give them medicines, "and notwithstanding their surly looks and many rebuffs received,

5. Father Joseph A. Stephan, director of the Bureau of Catholic Indian Missions, Washington, D.C., to Mother [Superior Lazarus L'hostal], Sisters of St. Joseph, St. Augustine, January 24, 1887, in Quinn, *Story of a Nun*, 124–25.

6. Herbert Welsh, *The Apache Prisoners in Fort Marion, St. Augustine, Florida* (Philadelphia: Office of the Indian Rights Association, 1887), 12–13.

they finally gained their good will."[7] It was not long before some of the young Apache men were attracted to the sisters' classes, and twenty-five enrolled. One amusing incident shows the regard with which the sisters were held. One day Sister Jane Francis was sick, so a postulant, new to the convent and still to receive her habit, was sent as Sister Jane Francis's substitute. According to the account,

When the Indian braves saw their new teacher, they betook themselves to the remotest corner of the class room, turned their backs toward her, and with loud voices, in their own dialect, expressed their disapproval of the substitute imposed on them. Occasionally they looked fiercely at her and pointed menacingly to the door. In vain did the poor postulant with trembling hand lift the pointer toward the chart, endeavoring to interest the pupils in "Mr. Dog" and "Mr. Cat." Angry growls were the only response.

To the relief of the young postulant, Sister Alypius arrived. When she asked what was going on, "in one voice the savage yell came 'We no want that lady for teacher; we like a Sister.'"[8]

The conditions at Fort Marion were so crowded that the Indian Rights Association, based on Welsh's report, strongly recommended that the Apaches be moved to a larger facility. The Apaches remained in St. Augustine only until April 27, 1887, when they were transferred to Mount Vernon Barracks in Alabama. From the Sisters of St. Joseph the Apaches had acquired a foundation in English and basic skills, but they had also developed dear friendships, and "wept bitterly when leaving the sisters."[9] The sisters had honored their contract well, living up to Father Stephan's expectations and fulfilling their mission to reach out to their neighbor, and in doing so continued to

7. Sister Mary Alberta, "Study of the Schools," 16.

8. Sister Mary Alberta, "Study of the Schools," 18. The traumatic experience was not enough to deter the young postulant, for this story was related to Sister Mary Alberta by then Sister Euphemia, the postulant who had been Sister Jane Francis's replacement.

9. Sister Mary Alberta, "Study of the Schools," 18.

build on the good will their works engendered among non-Catholics.

Meanwhile, the sisters' academies and schools for poor whites and for blacks that dotted the northern half of the diocese were thriving. In 1905, the Sisters of St. Joseph established St. Catherine's Academy and a convent in Miami; it was their tenth foundation. In St. Augustine, the free schools the sisters had established in the early days had become part of the public-school system in 1878. St. Agnes School, an extension of St. Joseph's Academy, was established in North City, a suburb of the Ancient City just north of the City Gates and Castillo in 1889. St. Benedict the Moor School for African Americans in St. Augustine's Lincolnville area was completed in 1898. The sisters began offering annual teacher training institutes in 1890. The free schools and academies in Mandarin, Jacksonville, Fernandina, Palatka, Elkton (southwest of St. Augustine), Orlando, and Ybor City were going strong.

In 1889, under the direction of Sister Margaret Mary, the students at St. Joseph's Academy in St. Augustine began publishing *Pascua Florida*, a cross between a newspaper and a magazine. It remained in publication through 1908. It included news of the students' and sisters' comings and goings, compositions, historical sketches, excerpts from other Catholic publications, and reports on special events. *Pascua Florida* provides a window into daily life at the convent school for the girls who boarded there and for the girls and boys who attended the day school. In giving his permission for the publication of the magazine, Bishop Moore wrote to Sister Margaret Mary, the principal of the academy:

I heartily approve your purpose of permitting the pupils of your Academy to publish periodically their own juvenile compositions. I trust that the undertaking will produce all the good results you expect from it. Your scholars should be stimulated to take greater care with their tasks, by the foreknowledge of the fact that they are to be printed, and thereby exposed to the criticisms, even though indulgent, of their friends and of the public, who will read them.[10]

The compositions in *Pascua Florida* display a high quality of writing and an advanced level of maturity in thought and expression developed through the students' Saturday task of writing an essay in an hour and a half. An essay by Florida Latimer expresses one student's views on who should have the right to vote. Her "Should Voting Be Made Compulsory?" decried the enfranchisement of the uneducated and then went on to discuss whether women should vote:

I think a lady's place is at home, and not running around on election day, to the poles, as the men do; they spend the day there. Suppose the women would do the same. I most decidedly think that a woman has no business voting. Now, just let me ask you one question—What would become of the babies at home if all the women would get that crazy notion into their heads? Yes, I know few have but don't judge all by a few. Now, would it not look nice to have a lady president, and all the senators and representatives women, not but that some would make as good public officers as the men, still I am afraid that they would think more of the fashion than they would the good of the nation. [In Europe] they say that this [American government] is a very good government; but the reason it is so good is because it is run by the American women, as all men are influenced by the women. Let us women keep that power of influence by the keenness of our judgment and the nobility of our lives and let the men do the voting.[11]

Impressive, too, are the topics that were debated in formal competitions that were often judged by the cathedral priests. Arguments presented in the debates were sometimes printed in *Pascua Florida*. Examples are: Should Woman Ride a Bicycle?

10. *Pascua Florida* 4, no. 1 (October 1892), 1. The "Bishop's Approbation" was printed on the first page of each issue.
11. Florida Latimer, "Should Voting Be Made Compulsory?" *Pascua Florida* 14, no. 3 (December 1902), 3.

Have Savages a Right to the Soil? Which Is More Important, the Army or the Navy, Inventor or Discoverer? Who was the Better General, Washington or Napoleon? Which is More Useful, the Printing Press or the Steam Engine? Such exercises served to develop critical thinking among the students. The magazine also included pieces on the merits of Catholic education, emphasizing its attention to the whole person, intellectual, physical, and spiritual, and articles with patriotic themes, especially regarding the Columbian Exposition and the Spanish-American War.

Under nineteenth- and early twentieth-century religious rules of decorum, women religious were not to call attention to themselves; bishops were the mouthpiece for the Catholic Church on public matters. Although *Pascua Florida* was a student magazine, in a way it provided a voice for the otherwise "voiceless" Sisters of St. Joseph. The magazine's articles, many of which addressed ideals such as appreciation for nature, care for the poor, and social responsibility, were prepared under the watchful eyes of the sisters and show the influence these women religious had in shaping the thinking of future adults who would be able to influence public policy.

Throughout *Pascua Florida*, whether in formal essays or chatty comments on the latest news, the students at St. Joseph's Academy displayed an ease with adults; the students and sisters shared warmth and respect for each other. Part of the high regard for the sisters was perhaps a result of the students' exposure to them in daily life and the students' participation in the ceremonies at which young women entered the convent as postulants or took their vows as novices or professed sisters. *Pascua Florida* regularly reported on such events. An impressive ceremony for the reception of novices, those who had completed their initial trial period as postulants, took place on April 24, 1892. The service began at 6:30 a.m. in the candlelit chapel decorated with flowers and plants. As the Wedding March was played, three students dressed as bridesmaids processed down the aisle toward the altar, led by another student carrying a processional cross. Following the bridesmaids, in order, were the novices, the professed sisters, and the two young women who were to make their profession. Those two were distinguished by their white veils laced with orange blossoms. Last came the mother superior and her assistant. The bishop then delivered a short inspirational talk to the new novices. After two years, a novice in the Sisters of St. Joseph could be considered for acceptance as a sister and make temporary vows; perpetual vows were taken some years later.[12]

Sisters, as a rule, did not actively recruit their students for the sisterhood. Indeed, many of their students were not even Catholic. Nevertheless, including students in such milestone ceremonies in the life of the sisters was intentional. The bishop directed his homily toward the newly professed women, but his words also fell on the ears of the students. His verbal encouragement and the visual beauty of the ceremony surely made a strong impression on some of the girls, as revealed by a student reporter of one such ceremony. After giving the names of the "aspirants for the holy habit" (postulants) and the novices who made their profession of vows, she wrote, "The ceremony was impressive throughout, and the address of the Rt. Rev. Bishop on the occasion was well calculated to inspire a spirit of love and esteem for the religious life."[13] Although the convent schools were, indeed, a major source of young women to enter the religious life, the sisters sought only those who felt truly called to God's service and did not seek young women who were carried away by romantic ideas inspired by impressive ceremonies.

12. *Pascua Florida* 2, no. 7 (November 1890), 4, no. 7 (April 24, 1892); Quinn, *Story of a Nun*, 175–78. Quinn provides a detailed description of the profession ceremony at which a novice took her temporary vows. See also Vermeersch, "Religious Profession," in *Catholic Encyclopedia*, 1911.
13. *Pascua Florida* 10, no. 1 (October 1898), 10.

Most girls who went to convent schools graduated and went on to be married and raise families; occasionally, however, some entered the religious life, while some went on to attain exceptional achievement in the wider world. The lives of three alumnae from St. Joseph's Academy serve as examples of the impact the sisters' training could have in molding exceptional lives.

Cora L. Bostick was the editor of *Pascua Florida*, and in 1892, she won the gold medal for her essay "The Valiant Woman." After providing a historical review of women in ancient times, she asserted that women had always been noble, but Christianity brought that nobility to light. She acknowledged the greatness and nobility of men, but held that

the courage and nobility of woman holds a stronger power over the destinies of life, than that of man. Man and woman cannot be judged by the same rules; there are many radical differences in their natures. Man is the creature of interest and ambition; his nature leads him forth into the bustle of the great world, there he can figure in many ways; but woman's whole life is a history of those gentler qualities which she needs must practice at home.... Thus we find that the kind and elevating influence of the valiant woman, is ordained by Omnipotence, to conquer rebel natures when everything else has failed. We find her on the battle-field, we meet her in the prisoner's gloomy cell; and often her gentle acts of charity and patience, are the only light which sheds its effulgence upon youth, and throws a halo around old age. Her happy influences in many cases, glorifies the present by the light cast backwards, and brightens the future by the gleams sent forward.[14]

Cora's essay reflects the traditional ideals of domesticity held up before women in nineteenth-century America. In May 1895, three years after her graduation, Cora wrote her friends at the academy that she was shortly to become a novice of the Order of the Precious Blood, a cloistered order dedicated to prayer

14. *Pascua Florida* 3, no. 10 (July 1892).

in Brooklyn, New York. In October 1896, *Pascua Florida* reported that she had made her perpetual vows.[15]

Jeanie Gordon Brown presents a slightly different example. She was born September 7, 1886, into a "well-to-do upper class family" in Scotland. Her mother had died from complications after the birth of Jeanie's sister, Nony, in 1889, four days after Jeanie's third birthday. Jeanie attended a private school for girls in Scotland. In 1894, her father left to establish a new home for them in Hypoluxo, Palm Beach County, Florida. He sent for his sons to join him in Florida in 1897, leaving eleven-year-old Jeanie and eight-year-old Nony with their tutors and nannies in Scotland. He brought his daughters to Florida after he had remarried in September 1902. Jeanie was sixteen years old, Nony thirteen. The girls lived for a short time in Hypoluxo, but because of the rustic conditions and inadequate schooling available there, Brown sent his daughters to attend boarding school at St. Joseph's Academy in St. Augustine. Jeanie attended from 1903 until 1906. In 1904 Nony, who had always been frail, had to leave school and died that year.[16]

Jeanie felt "safe and well taken care of" at the convent, finding comfort in the restrictions and rules enforced by the sisters. One of her classmates described her as being "always intent upon reading, and [having] genial, lady-like ways. Contentment and happiness are written on her face, which is in striking contrast to the dreamy, melancholy expression of another of our boarders."[17] Jeanie was greatly drawn to the sisters' Catholic faith and way of life, and they were impressed with her. Much to her Protestant family's disapproval, she converted to Catholicism and was baptized on March 18, 1907. She taught in public school in Palm Valley, a small community in St. Johns County, north of St. Augustine, until she was twenty-one, for at that age she

15. *Pascua Florida* 7, no. 8 (May 1895), 9, and 8, no. 1 (October 1896).
16. Quinn, *Story of a Nun*, 28–30, 35, 41, 44, 61, 66.
17. Quinn, *Story of a Nun*, 71.

could legally enter the convent without her father's permission. On March 19, 1908, Jeanie Gordon Brown received the veil and her religious name, Sister Theresa Joseph.

Over the years, Sister Theresa Joseph taught at several of the sisters' schools, beginning at the academy in Jacksonville. Having already been sent to summer school at Catholic University from 1915 to 1919, in 1925 she was among the first group of Sisters of St. Joseph from the Diocese of St. Augustine who earned bachelor's degrees in education from the University of Florida. That same year she obtained a Florida teacher's certificate. She was a respected teacher and administrator. In 1927, Theresa Joseph was made principal at St. Joseph's Academy in St. Augustine, and in 1931, she was sent to Orlando, where she was principal of St. James School and the superior of its associated convent. Two years later, on May 3, 1933, she became an American citizen.

Jeanie Brown, a Presbyterian boarding student at St. Joseph's Academy in St. Augustine who converted to Catholicism and became a nun, steadily rose in the ranks of the Sisters of St. Joseph of St. Augustine and was elected mother superior of the statewide congregation in 1937. She held the post until 1945, when she returned to teaching, this time at the academy in Coral Gables (near Miami). While there, she earned a master's degree at the University of Miami in administration and supervision in 1952, at the age of sixty-five. She was the first member of a religious order to complete that degree at the University of Miami. Her academic pursuits demonstrated the growing willingness of the Catholic Church to invest in women religious by giving them opportunities to gain professional credentials. In 1959, Sister Theresa Joseph fell ill. She died from colon cancer on August 19, 1960.

Sister Theresa Joseph Brown was a rising star among the Sisters of St. Joseph, but the alumna of St. Joseph's Academy who was probably the most well-known to Floridians was May Mann Jennings. May was born in New Jersey in 1872, and in

1874, her family moved to Crystal River, Florida. Her father, Austin Shuey Mann, became a state senator and exposed his eldest daughter to the exciting world of politics at an early age.[18]

May's mother died in 1882 from tuberculosis and, some felt, also from the grief of the death of two of her youngest children. Austin Mann was left a widower with two older boys, with May, age ten, and another sickly daughter, Gracie, age three. Unable to care for the girls, their father enrolled them into St. Joseph's Academy in St. Augustine in 1883. Like some other students, they were not Catholic, and they retained their Baptist affiliation. Sister Lazarus L'hostal was the mother superior of the convent, and Sister Margaret Mary was the principal of the academy. They became "May's mentors and counselors" and maintained a relationship with her for many years.[19]

Life at the convent school was strict, but the sisters were mild and parental in their discipline, emphasizing good morals and proper behavior. The prospectus of St. Joseph's Academy described the sisters' standards: "strict adherence to correct and refined language, polite deportment, gentle and engaging manners at all times, mandatory attendance at all public exercises, the observance of silence except in the hours of recreation, no visits home during the entire year, the subjection of letters and packages to inspection, and the prohibition of private friendships." Such a restrictive atmosphere perhaps sounds oppressive by today's standards but was consistent with what was expected at a school for fine young ladies, and for many, such as Jeanie Brown, it created boundaries that provided a measure of security and comfort.[20]

Besides academics, the boarders received lessons in plain sewing, embroidery, and other kinds of needlework, including

18. Linda D. Vance, *May Mann Jennings: Florida's Genteel Activist* (Gainesville: University Press of Florida, 1985), 6.

19. Vance, *May Mann Jennings*, 7–10.

20. Vance, *May Mann Jennings*, 10, 12. Although the prospectus called for "no visits home the entire year," May went home on holidays and over the summers.

French lace making. The making of bobbin lace, a special skill the French sisters brought with them from Le Puy, was one of the ways the sisters supported themselves in the early days of the Florida mission. The lace was very popular with St. Augustine's winter visitors, and its sale to them provided a fair income. Some of the students took up the intricate skill. The *Pascua Florida* reported that one apparently very patient girl was "progressing rapidly with her French lace. She averages an inch every two weeks."[21] In later years, May was known for her fine needlework, including lace making. The girls were not confined to the convent, but enjoyed picnics, hikes to North City, and occasional trips to the beach and the St. Augustine lighthouse. For those who embraced the experience of convent life, their days at St. Joseph's Academy produced many fond memories.

May was one of the most outstanding students ever to attend St. Joseph's Academy. She was consistently listed on the monthly honor roll. This was no small accomplishment, requiring a score of 100 percent in all studies, conduct, and neatness and attendance at all exercises.[22] May excelled in music, piano, voice, art, English composition, and French and received gold medals at the end of her junior and senior years. The range of courses May studied at the academy was comprehensive, embracing the major fields of religion (catechism and church history), English (etymology, rhetoric, grammar, logic, literature, composition, mental philosophy, and classics), social sciences (geography, ancient history, Middle Ages history, modern history, and civic government), science (science, chemistry, botany, geology, and astronomy), and mathematics (mental and practical arithmetic, algebra, and bookkeeping).[23] With such a curriculum, many academy graduates were broad in their views and articulate in expressing them. Later in life, May credited

21. *Pascua Florida* 1, no. 2 (1889), 10.
22. *Pascua Florida* 8, no. 1 (October 1896).
23. Vance, *May Mann Jennings*, 14.

her wide-ranging interests and capabilities to her days at St. Joseph's: "I was educated in a convent and I look at life through much broader glasses than the average person does."[24]

May spent six years at St. Joseph's Academy, from ages eleven to seventeen, and graduated in 1889, the valedictorian of her class. After one year of postgraduate work there, she returned home to Brooksville in 1890 to assist her father with his political career. It was he who introduced her to William Sherman Jennings, a Brooksville lawyer and judge with political aspirations. Jennings and May were married on May 12, 1891. The event was announced in the *Pascua Florida*: "Our esteemed friend and scoolmate, Miss May Mann, was married on the 13 ult. [*sic*] in Tallahassee, Fla., to Judge Jennings, a well known and prominent lawyer of Brooksville."[25]

For the next ten years, May, William, and their son led a genteel life in Brooksville together, actively supporting their Baptist church at local and statewide levels. William developed a highly successful law practice and engaged in profitable business dealings. In 1892 and 1894, he was elected to the state legislature, where he rose in popularity and esteem among his fellow legislators. In 1898, he was chairman of the Democratic state convention. For her part, May became involved in the woman's club movement and worked to improve the Brooksville community. In 1899, she helped Jennings in his campaign to be elected governor. Her natural talents, honed to highly effective tools of persuasion at St. Joseph's Academy, served her and her husband well, for as one newspaper put it, "There is little doubt that the rise of young Jennings was promoted by his marriage to May Mann, a lady of great charm [who] inherited much of her

24. May Jennings to Carrie McCollum, April 30, 1915, in May Mann Jennings papers, box 5, quoted in Vance, *May Mann Jennings*, 10; May Mann Jennings papers, P. K. Yonge Library, University of Florida, Gainesville; hereafter cited as MMJ papers. I was unable to locate this letter.

25. *Pascua Florida* 2, no. 14 (June 1891), 10.

father's political ability. She was just such a person who would impress all those who came in contact with her, just such a one as would prove a most fitting helpmeet to a husband who had both ability and political ambitions."[26] Jennings won the gubernatorial election and took the oath of office on January 8, 1901.

The Sisters of St. Joseph were duly proud of May. The day after the inauguration, Sister Margaret Mary, May's principal at St. Joseph's Academy, wrote the new governor's wife:

You have no idea of the degree of laudable pride which fills my heart for the happiness which is yours. I am happy to think that others look upon you as I do, that others know you as I do, and that your merits, becoming known [to] others, esteem you as I do. May God bless you dear child and may you continue to give honor to the Academy which gave you the Christian education which you enjoy. Always bear in mind while carrying your honors that charity to the poor will entail a blessing on your household, and that while honors are conferred upon you, you must refer them all to God who is the author of all.... Never neglect to thank God for the blessing which He has given you, and daily beg Him for new favors; lead a life worthy of a true woman, and thus while you glorify God you will be a credit to yourself and an honor to [illegible word].[27]

May heeded Sister Margaret Mary's advice and did support the poor and needy personally or through her growing work with woman's clubs. Her papers are full of requests for assistance. May graciously, but carefully, responded to such letters. She often helped people through her influence, but usually refrained from supplying money directly.

In a more public role, May was a leader in the woman's club movement and tackled major issues such as conservation, social welfare, and women's rights. In 1914, she was unanimously elected the president of the Florida Federation of Women's Clubs

26. Vance, *May Mann Jennings*, 24.
27. Sr. Margaret Mary, St. Joseph's Academy, Jacksonville, to Mrs. W. S. Jennings [Tallahassee], January 9, 1901, MMJ papers, box 1.

and played an important role in the establishment of the Florida Park Service, the Florida Forestry Service, and Everglades National Park. In 1924, she was a candidate for president of the General Federation of Women's Clubs, the national organization. Much as candidates running for political office, May promulgated statements of her stands on various domestic and international issues, many of which are still of concern in the twenty-first century.[28] She was very clear concerning women's rights. Although she supported the woman's right to vote, she was "unalterably opposed" to the federal constitutional amendment, known as the "Blanket Amendment," which said, "Men and women shall have equal rights throughout the United States, and every place subject to its jurisdiction." In May's opinion, "[The amendment] would either repeal or make inoperative all special and Federal legislation for the protection of women and children, sponsored by women, [and] organizations covering a period of many years work, and would be of exceedingly doubtful benefit otherwise."[29] One can easily imagine such topics being debated in *Pascua Florida*.

The training May received at St. Joseph's Academy admirably prepared her for her life of leadership. Comments by her contemporaries or biographers describe someone who embodied the core ideals promulgated by the sisters: "Her popularity was enhanced by her unfailing gentility and decorum," or "Mrs. Jennings shows a marked degree of disregard of cliques.... In fact fairness is one of the attributes that has been most salient in all that she has done. She is approachable at all times."[30] May's biographer, Linda Vance, sums it up best: "May's education at St. Joseph's fitted her for a public career; it reinforced her protective attitude and strengthened the sense of public duty that she had received

28. For a detailed discussion of Jennings's club work and positions on issues, see the previously cited biography by Linda D. Vance, *May Mann Jennings*.
29. "Mrs. Jennings' Stand on the Most Important National Issues," MMJ papers, box 23.
30. Vance, *May Mann Jennings*, 63, 71.

Sister Mary Ann Hoare, SSJ.
Courtesy of the Archives of the Sisters of St. Joseph
of St. Augustine, St. Augustine, Florida.

from her father. The genteel but sound academic training and the moral and emotional stability she received at the school inculcated characteristics important to her future."[31] May Mann Jennings died in 1963, at the age of 90, having heeded Sister Margaret Mary's exhortation to "lead a life worthy of a true woman."

Thus, the Sisters of St. Joseph's academy work contributed to the development of women who were willing and equipped to take places of leadership. One of the brightest lights for the Catholic Church in Florida at the turn of the twentieth century, however, was not an academy graduate, but a simple nun who had led her entire life of devotion in Florida: Sister Mary Ann. She was one of the Sisters of Mercy who came to Florida in 1859, the first group of women religious who came to the state. She was a "true woman" of a different sort.

31. Vance, *May Mann Jennings*, 143.

Born in Ireland in 1828, Ellen Hoare, like so many other young Irish women who were caught in the dire poverty brought about by the potato famine, arrived in the United States in 1848. She came to New York City to join an uncle and his family, only to find they were moving to the West and had no room for her. Destitute and alone, she was able to get work as a maid. Although abandoned by her uncle, by chance she found her sister, who had come to the United States a few years before. Together, they practiced their Catholic devotions at daily Mass. Ellen was engaged to be married, the date was set, and all preparations had been made, when she felt God's call to become a nun.[32] Determined to follow the call, Ellen went to New Haven, Connecticut, where she attended night school at the convent of the Sisters of Mercy. Her cheerful disposition and devotion soon showed her to be an ideal candidate for entry into the religious community. In 1858, she entered the convent of the Sisters of Mercy as a novice.

It was at about this time that Bishop Augustin Verot asked the Sisters of Mercy from the Diocese of Hartford to send sisters to teach in St. Augustine. Ellen was among the Sisters of Mercy who arrived in the Ancient City on April 1, 1859. She was still a novice, but after completing her novitiate she publicly professed the traditional vows and received her veil as a Sister of Mercy from Bishop Verot at the Cathedral in St. Augustine on August 15, 1861. Along with the veil, she received the religious name of Mary Ann. Because of her limited education, Sister Mary Ann was admitted as a lay sister to perform domestic duties and ministries to the poor and the sick, rather than to teach.[33]

During the Civil War, she helped care for soldiers, both

---

32. Keuchel, "Sister Mary Ann," 97–99; Sister St. Andrew McLaughlin, SSJ, ed., "Jacksonville's Angel of Mercy: Sister Mary Ann and an Abridged Account of St. Mary's Home, Jacksonville, Florida" (unpublished manuscript, ca.1940), unpaginated [5–9].

33. For a description of the clothing ceremony for the Sisters of Mercy, see Fialka, Sisters, 40–41.

Union and Confederate. She tended them at the hospital in Savannah and after the Battle of Olustee, which took place near Lake City, Florida. According to Edward Keuchel, there is no documentation that Sister Mary Ann was at Olustee or Andersonville, but all accounts at the time of her death mention her work at these sites. Further support for the veracity of these claims is the recognition Sister Mary Ann received from the United Daughters of the Confederacy.[34]

When the Sisters of St. Joseph arrived from France, they depended on the Sisters of Mercy as they adjusted to their new surroundings and tried to learn English. Sister Mary Ann's duties included doing the laundry every week for both the Sisters of Mercy and Sisters of St. Joseph. She had begun a special relationship with the French sisters during the early days after their arrival, when they were eating their meals with the Sisters of Mercy. Unaccustomed to Southern food, they often left the table hungry. In later years she would tell "how she watched the Sisters of St. Joseph ... with the greatest sympathy; she instinctively felt that they were hungry, as they really were; she often went to the pantry and carried bread to them, which they gladly accepted."[35]

In 1869, when the Sisters of Mercy left St. Augustine, Bishop Verot asked Sister Mary Ann to remain to assist the French sisters. It was to be only for a year, but at the end of that time, Verot decided she should not only remain in Florida but also become a Sister of St. Joseph. Obediently, Sister Mary Ann permanently transferred to the Sisters of St. Joseph on August 15, 1869; it was the eighth anniversary of her entry into the Sisters of Mercy. Although she had a warm relationship with the Sisters

34. McLaughlin, "Jacksonville's Angel of Mercy" [21]; Edward F. Keuchel to Sister Mary Denis Maher, CSA, Ursuline College, Pepper Pike, Ohio, November 29, 1989; copy of letter held by Edward Keuchel.

35. McLaughlin, "Jacksonville's Angel of Mercy" [29]; Letter no. 16, Mtr. Sidonie, St. Augustine, to Mtr. Léocadie Broc, Le Puy, November 5, 1866, ASSJSA.

of St. Joseph, it pained her deeply to leave her beloved Sisters of Mercy.[36]

On November 15, 1869, Sister Mary Ann was among the Sisters of St. Joseph who left St. Augustine to establish a new community in Jacksonville, where she spent the rest of her life ministering to the poor and needy. Her energy seemed endless as she nursed victims during the yellow fever epidemics in 1877 and 1888, contracting the disease herself; provided meals, clothing, spiritual comfort, and simple friendship to the condemned prisoners in the Duval County jail; and prepared holiday meals and distributions of provisions to the poor. In 1898, during the Spanish-American War, Tampa was a major staging area for sending troops to Cuba. The Sisters of St. Joseph in Ybor City assisted soldiers who were stationed or hospitalized in the Tampa area. Jacksonville was the site of Camp Libre. Soldiers from the camp, many of whom were suffering from typhoid, were hospitalized at the sisters' beach house at Pablo Beach, near Jacksonville. A visitor to the hospital, who later wrote a history of the New Jersey military units, reported finding "three cheerful faced Sisters of Charity [St. Joseph] in the kitchen, headed by Sister Mary Ann, . . . cooking delicacies and nourishing soups for the sick boys of the Second New Jersey [Volunteers]."[37]

Sister Mary Ann's greatest and longest-lasting accomplishment, however, was the establishment of St. Mary's Home for orphaned girls. In 1885, on one of her visits to the county hospital, a little girl whose mother had recently died clung to Sister Mary Ann, begging her to take her home with her. The result was the establishment of an orphanage for girls, long one

36. Sister Mary Albert, SSJ, Archivist, Sisters of St. Joseph of St. Augustine, to Edward F. Keuchel, November 14, 1986; McLaughlin, "Jacksonville's Angel of Mercy" [28–29].

37. Harry L. Harris and John T. Hilton, eds., *A History of the Second Regiment, N.G.N.J., Second N.J. Volunteers (Spanish War), Fifth New Jersey Infantry, Together with a Short Review Covering Early Military Life in the State of New Jersey* (Patterson, N.J.: Call Printing and Publishing, 1908), 144.

of Sister Mary Ann's dreams. When others learned of the proposed orphanage, contributions poured in, due in large part to the good will and trust Sister Mary Ann had developed among those who knew of her other good works. In 1886, one of the local newspapers included this testimony of the mark she had made on Jacksonville:

Every city, every town, and . . . locality, points with pardonable pride to its greatest philanthropist. Many great communities cannot boast of these personages, but Jacksonville comes conspicuously to the front in this respect, and "Bears away the palm." No city can point to a nobler or more benevolent woman, or one who has accomplished any greater good than Sister Mary Ann. No Protestant in Jacksonville will deny that she has in thousands of homes, been a ministering angel. Everybody knows this most remarkable woman, and no little boy or little girl lives in this city who has not heard of the noble deeds of the good Sister Mary Ann, as she is effectionately [sic] called.... The writer, although a Protestant[,] could fill volumes with her benevolent deeds.... Little wonder that everybody loves her.[38]

St. Mary's Home opened on August 15, 1886, an auspicious day in several ways, for besides being the feast of the Assumption of the Blessed Virgin Mary, it was the anniversary of Sister Mary Ann's profession as a Sister of Mercy and of her transfer to the Sisters of St. Joseph. The facility was a modest, wood-frame, two-story house. There were five little girls in residence. In 1890, supporters provided a three-story brick building, with room for twenty-five orphans. There, the girls were taught basic academic subjects, catechism, and a skill that would enable them to support themselves. One little girl, for example, stayed at St. Mary's Home for twelve years, leaving in 1897 with an education and skills in dressmaking. She married and had a family. Sister Mary Ann enjoyed preparing meals for the girls and taking them on

38. McLaughlin, "Jacksonville's Angel of Mercy" [39–40]. A reference in the larger quote indicates this probably appeared in the *Metropolis*.

picnics. The girls affectionately called her "Grandma." The Jacksonville *Florida Times-Union* delighted in reporting on these and Sister Mary Ann's other works of charity, and the home received support from Protestants as well as Catholics. The paper often included Sister Mary Ann's detailed accounting of the donations she had received; such a report was a front-page story even in the midst of the 1888 epidemic.

Although a "lay sister" and never the superior of St. Mary's Home, it is clear she carried much authority. In 1899, she traveled to the North to raise money to expand the home. Her successes there provided enough funds to construct a new wing.[39] Much of Sister Mary Ann's work had been accomplished trudging the unpaved streets of Jacksonville. In 1906, when she was seventy-eight years old and beginning to slow down, the mayor of Jacksonville gave her a new horse and buggy to assist her in her work. No one wanted her to wear herself out, for her services were too valuable.

In her eightieth year, Sister Mary Ann celebrated her Golden Jubilee, fifty years of life as a professed sister. The celebration on August 15, 1911, also commemorated the founding of the St. Mary's Home, the only orphanage in the diocese at that time. It was a grand event, with a Pontifical Mass celebrated by Bishop Kenny, assisted by numerous members of the clergy from around the state. Sisters from various convents throughout Florida, as well as the public, were also in attendance. A reception at St. Mary's Home filled the building with guests. The county gave Sister Mary Ann a purse of over $1,600, with more to come, to express the community's appreciation of her work. After the reception, the girls from St. Mary's presented an entertainment that featured instrumental and choral music, dance, and recitations, a demonstration of the fruits of Sister Mary Ann's labors.

39. "For the Orphans," *Florida Times-Union*, September 2, 1888, 1; McLaughlin, "Jacksonville's Angel of Mercy" [52].

One of the girls recited, "To Sister Mary Ann," a poem that summed up Sister Mary Ann's life:

> Fifty years since first you made
> The vows which bind your heart to Him—
> To One who died on bitter cross
> To save all people from their sin.
>
> Fifty-long, devoted years,
> In service of the sick and poor!
> And never one in all that time
> That went unaided from our door.
>
> O woman, of the loving heart,
> And of the gentle helping hand!
> Those fifty golden years of yours
> Have been a blessing to our Land.
>
> The poor and sinful, with your aid,
> Have risen to a higher life;
> The orphans, in St. Mary's Home
> Are shielded from the world's hard strife.
>
> The sick will ever bless your name
> Because of your devoted love;
> All sick and well and rich and poor—
> Will blessings crave from God above.
>
> May all your future days be fair
> Until you lay life's burden down;
> And then the One you've served so well
> Will change the cross for glorious crown.[40]

Not long after this grand celebration, Sister Mary Ann's strength began to fade. From November through December of 1913, she was unable to leave her room. She received the last rites and gradually faded until she died on January 14, 1914, in

40. McLaughlin, "Jacksonville's Angel of Mercy" [78–81].

her eighty-sixth year. Her body lay in the chapel at the home for three days. The funeral held the next day was a sung Requiem Mass held at the Church of the Immaculate Conception, a large building that was "filled to its utmost capacity." Once again, clergy and sisters gathered from around the state, joining the mourning citizens of Jacksonville and Duval County. Also in attendance was a delegation from the United Daughters of the Confederacy, who came to acknowledge Sister Mary Ann's work during the Civil War.[41] Sister Mary Ann had been faithful to her vows as a Sister of St. Joseph, but had always remained a Sister of Mercy at heart. In accordance with her wishes, it is believed she was buried in St. Mary's Cemetery dressed in the habit she had worn as a Sister of Mercy.[42]

Sister Mary Ann truly had a charitable heart. At a time when caring for the poor was becoming a profession or the pet projects of women's groups, Sister Mary Ann simply continued to do what she had always done—where there was suffering, she attempted to alleviate it, regardless of the color, creed, or supposed worthiness of the recipient. This is most clearly seen in her ministries to the condemned prisoners at the county jail who were awaiting their executions. She treated all people with dignity, faithful to her motto, "When you do charity, do it [in] a charitable way."[43]

Through her truly good works, Sister Mary Ann won the hearts of the people of Jacksonville, both Protestant and

41. McLaughlin, "Jacksonville's Angel of Mercy" [84–85].

42. Edward F. Keuchel, Florida State University, to Sister Mary Denis Maher, CSA, Ursuline College, Pepper Pike, Ohio, January 29, 1990; copy held by author. It is more likely that Sister Mary Ann's Sisters of Mercy habit was destroyed in the Great Fire of 1901.

43. Keuchel, "Sister Mary Ann," 109. For a discussion of the concepts of the worthy versus unworthy poor and the professionalization of charity work, see Nathan Irvin Huggins, *Protestants against Poverty: Boston's Charities 1870–1900* (Westport, Conn.: Greenwood, 1971). The Rev. William Byrne spoke out against the Boston plan for charitable work in 1880, giving the official Catholic view by citing "undue concern that relief go only to the worthy poor," saying it was "'not only unchristian but inhuman'"; see Mary J. Oates, *The Catholic Philanthropic Tradition in America* (Bloomington: Indiana University Press, 1995), 51.

Catholic. Gone were the strident exchanges between Protestant and Catholic missionaries of the 1870s, replaced with seemingly unbounded adulation for a "little Catholic nun" who cared for people with joy and abandon. It was perhaps because of Sister Mary Ann's legacy in Jacksonville that the Sisters of St. Joseph there were not assailed when the forces of anti-Catholicism that began to sweep across Florida struck the Sisters in St. Augustine two years later.

Chapter 6

The End of the French
Mission to Florida

By the late 1800s, the Sisters of St. Joseph were well established
in northeast Florida. Their schools, black and white, were highly regarded, and they were even paid by some county school
boards to teach in public schools. The care of yellow fever victims during the 1877 and 1888 epidemics gained them the respect
and gratitude of Protestants and Catholics, blacks and whites.
Sister Mary Ann's ministrations to orphans, prisoners, and the
poor of the city earned her the moniker "Jacksonville's Angel of
Mercy." The days of public ridicule and whispers of "nigger Sister" were gone, for the most part. The sisters had lived through
those days, and the work among the blacks for whom they had
been sent by the motherhouse in Le Puy was largely a success, at
least with black Catholics. It was in the midst of these positive
ministries that tumultuous change came to the Sisters of St. Joseph. The public was unaware of the strife that was tearing the
sisters apart.

The sisters had gained the respect of the people of Florida,
but women religious in general during this time also enjoyed increased respect within the Catholic Church. On December 17,

1890, Pope Leo XIII promulgated a decree, *Quemadmodum*, intended to protect members of religious communities, male and female, from superiors who pried into the consciences of those who were subject to their authority. Although religious could grow in their efforts toward spiritual perfection by voluntarily discussing their thoughts with their superiors, unsolicited inquiries concerning those thoughts were solely the responsibility and prerogative of a religious's designated confessor and were to be made within the confines of the Sacrament of Confession or Penance. The decree was directed against superiors who abused their authority by forcing or pressuring their subordinates to discuss matters of conscience, sometimes even taking it upon themselves to prevent or limit the subordinates' access to Holy Communion. Pope Leo ordered all such misuse of authority to cease, no matter how long it may have been a common practice within a congregation. He was emphatic, forbidding "absolutely such Superiors, Male and Female, no matter what may be their rank and eminence, from endeavoring, directly or indirectly, by command, counsel, fear, threats or blandishments, to induce their subjects to make them any such manifestations of conscience, and he commands these subjects on their part to denounce the higher Superiors such as done to induce them to make such manifestations." Failure to follow this decree subjected the superiors themselves to incur papal excommunication. The pope ordered that the decree be translated into the vernacular, incorporated into organizations' constitutions, and read at least once a year at a stated time in each house, at a full gathering of the body "in a loud and intelligible voice."[1]

In 1895 or 1896, Bishop Moore set October 15, the Feast of St. Teresa of Avila, as the day the decree was to be read annually in each religious community in his diocese. As it turned out,

1. D. I. Lanslots, OSB, *Handbook of Canon Law for Congregations of Women under Simple Vows*, 8th ed. (New York and Cincinnati: Frederick Pustet, 1919), 277, 279.

that day was already filled with other activities at the St. Augustine house of the Sisters of St. Joseph, which made it difficult to gather everyone together. Mother Lazarus L'hostal, the provincial superior who had been the superior in St. Augustine, asked Moore if the reading could be postponed and suggested the Feast of the Holy Name of Jesus in January of each year as an alternative. Moore agreed, saying, "Provided that it be read once a year, that suffices." It later became the regular practice for the priest who led the sisters' annual retreat in August to read the decree and explain it to all in the congregation.[2] This decree became a major factor in the history of the Sisters of Joseph's Florida mission.

With their past accomplishments having opened the way for further successes, little prepared the sisters for the devastating blows they received in the fall of 1899. On the morning of November 14, Bishop Moore sent a note to Mother Lazarus in St. Augustine that he would be coming to the convent at three o'clock to speak to the entire community. Mother Lazarus and he had always had a warm, cordial relationship, and he usually let her, as the provincial superior, know the nature of his visits. This time he did not. At three o'clock, Bishop Moore and the chaplain at the cathedral came to the convent chapel and prepared for the meeting, still without giving any explanation to Mother Lazarus. Once everyone was assembled in the chapel, Bishop Moore formally read from a large paper:

I had given orders to Mother Lazarus that the Decree of the Holy Father [*Quemadmodum*] was to be read every year to the Community on the Feast of St. Teresa. This order has not been carried out. Mother Lazarus has not read the Decree of the Pope: she is disobedient. In the presence of all the community she is deposed from her position and

2. Sister M. Lazarus L'hostal, Fall River, Massachusetts, to Rev. Mother, Le Puy, September 28, 1908; hereafter cited as Lazarus, 1908, ASSJSA. Mother Lazarus wrote this account at the request of her superior nine years after the events, when she was seventy-four years old.

she is excommunicated by the disobedience to orders from the Pope. She will no longer fill any position in the community. I appoint Sister Eulalia Ryan in her place. Again I claim and it is ordered, as before, that the Decree be read each year to the community on the Feast Day of St. Teresa under pain of papal excommunication.[3]

With no further comment, the bishop and priest then left the chapel. Stunned by this totally unexpected pronouncement, Mother Lazarus followed them out, and on her knees, asked Bishop Moore if she would be barred from receiving the sacraments. He replied that she would be denied them but told her to go to confession and to obey whatever her confessor told her to do to repent sufficiently. As a result of her removal from office, Mother Lazarus was ordered to present all the community's money before Bishop Moore and turn it over to her successor, Sister Eulalia.

Ten days later, Mother Lazarus was summoned to the convent parlor, where Bishop Moore furthered the devastation by announcing to her that all ties between the Sisters of St. Joseph in the Diocese of St. Augustine and their motherhouse in Le Puy were severed and that she should tell the other French sisters of the new arrangement. Moore did not order her to go back to France or to leave the diocese, but he did require her to leave St. Augustine. Her request to go to the Mandarin community, near Jacksonville, was denied. She was ordered, instead, to go to Ybor City, over two hundred miles away. It was the furthest house from St. Augustine and the one with the most challenging ministries.[4]

Mother Lazarus left for Ybor City on November 24, 1899, with direct orders not to visit any of the other Sisters of St. Joseph communities along the way. In her new position, she was a

3. Lazarus, 1908, ASSJSA.
4. Lazarus, 1908, ASSJSA. See chapter 2, "Notre Chère Mission d'Amerique," regarding the Ybor City Mission.

teacher for the youngest children in the Ybor City mission. The recorder for the Ybor City community wrote, "[Mother Lazarus] bears her heavy cross with a patience that is truly remarkable, but we are all a little embarrassed with her. Having looked up to her so long as our Superior, it is very difficult to treat her as a simple Sister. There is an unavoidable constraint in our intercourse."[5]

Although Mother Lazarus graciously and humbly accepted her situation and enjoyed her new assignment, which was free from the responsibilities of leadership, she was greatly torn as to what she should do—should she stay in the diocese she had served for thirty-two years or return to the welcoming and comforting arms of the superiors at the motherhouse in Le Puy? Mother Eulalia, her appointed successor, implored Mother Lazarus to stay in Florida for at least another year; at the same time, the mother general in Le Puy was inviting her to return "home." The situation was tearing all the sisters apart. What effect would her leaving have on the Florida mission? Would other French sisters who held the positions of leadership leave, too? Would it damage the sisters' reputation among the communities and with the public or destroy the foundations they had worked so hard for thirty-three years to establish?

Mother Lazarus sought the advice of priests, but few ventured to give her any definitive direction. Her inner turmoil finally ended when she learned that Bishop Moore felt it best, because of the divided loyalties that were emerging among the communities, for her to return to France. That confirmation was all she needed. She said, "From that moment all my doubts and perplexities were calmed in thinking I was doing Holy Obedience. It is a great consolation in religious life to be directed by Superiors."[6]

5. Annals of the Sisters of St. Joseph in Ybor City, 45, ASSJSA.
6. Lazarus, 1908, ASSJSA.

Plans for the return to France commenced. On April 27, 1900, Mother Eulalia, the sister thrust into the middle of the controversy when Bishop Moore appointed her to replace Mother Lazarus, wrote the mother general in Le Puy. She said:

It is needless for me to say that I am sorely grieved at parting with our good and devoted religious. They have been long our models and their example and virtue will be missed by us, as long as life lasts.... It is truly heartrending for us to be forced to separate from our beloved Sisters and Superiors with whom we spent many happy years in true religious affection.[7]

On May 3, 1900, Mother Lazarus and four other French sisters left the Florida Mission to go to Le Puy. Three were superiors of communities: Mother Louise Claverie Chambouvet, Mother Louise Thérèse Romeyer, and Mother Marie Joséphine Deleage; Sister Constance Degeorges was the fourth. On July 19, 1900, Sisters Onésime Vedrine and Octavie Fabre also departed for Le Puy. The recorder for the sisters' house in Jacksonville described the departure of the French sisters with a note of resignation and finality: "They will leave Fernandina [where they had gathered from houses around the state] for New York on May 3d, thence to France never to return."[8] Other French sisters followed suit over the years. Of the twenty-two French sisters in the Florida Mission in 1899, eleven returned to France.[9]

In the confusion wrought by these events, some of the remaining French sisters considered the possibility of establishing a new foundation in a different diocese. Several bishops had requested their services, but the one that seemed most promising was in Fall River, Massachusetts, an industrial town with a large French-Canadian population. In May 1902, Sister Louise

7. Sister M. Eulalie, St. Joseph Academy, St. Augustine, to Very Rev. Mother, Le Puy, April 27, 1900, ASSJSA.
8. Record Book, Jacksonville, p. 35, quoted in Quinn, *Story of a Nun*, 83.
9. McGoldrick, *Beyond the Call*, 344.

Antonia Marconnet, the superior over the community in Fernandina, and Sister Eusebie Bouchet, the superior in Mandarin, went to Fall River to explore the suitability of this new mission field. Mother Antonia wrote Mother Pélagie Boyer in Le Puy enthusiastically:

I really cannot enumerate all the ways in which the arrangements are just great; it is simply incredible what this good father [Father Giguere, the priest who had invited them to come to Fall River] has accomplished in the three years only that this parish is in existence.

Father wants everything to be in French and they are doing their best to conserve it in this way, but the state law requires that English be taught and that is why he has asked you for one or two Sisters with the English language.... I would never be able to tell you how well we have been received. It is plain to see they love the French.[10]

Mother Joséphine went to Fall River in September 1903. At some point, she returned to her birthplace, St. Sigolène, France, where she died at the age of eighty-two on February 26, 1912. Mother Lazarus died in Fall River on November 29, 1916, at the age of seventy-four, and is buried there in Notre Dame Cemetery. Fall River promised to be a fertile field for gaining new subjects. The needs of Fall River were great, more than the Sisters in Le Puy could handle, but it was a successful mission for many years. The last French sister went from Le Puy to Fall River in 1903 and died in 1966.[11]

Although the Fall River mission was a blessing to the Sisters of St. Joseph, one must ask how the tumultuous break between the Florida mission and the motherhouse in Le Puy came to be. As stated before, the work of the sisters was progressing well when the heretofore fatherly Bishop John Moore suddenly turned on Mother Lazarus. Years after these events,

10. Sister Louise Antonia, Providence, R.I., to Madame Pélagie [Rev. Mother Pélagie Boyer], Le Puy, May 2, 1902, ASSJSA.
11. Table of Sisters of St. Joseph, Sisters of St. Joseph Archives, Le Puy; copy at ASSJSA. The Sisters of St. Joseph still serve in Fall River.

Mother Lazarus was still confounded by the bishop's change in attitude toward her, saying, "Monseigneur Moore had been a good and devoted Father to us; in my difficulties I used to go to him without fear; he was my support."[12] The best explanation for the bishop's radical change is that he had suffered a stroke on or about September 7, 1899, in Wilkes-Barre, Pennsylvania, while on a "begging tour" in the North. He was partially paralyzed and spent the next six weeks at a hospital in Baltimore, returning to St. Augustine on October 22.[13] Moore continued to lead the diocese, but the stroke had "had a devastating effect on his energy and personality."[14] Three weeks later, on November 14, he humiliated and deposed Mother Lazarus from her position as provincial superior for the Sisters of St. Joseph throughout the diocese, and nine days after that he severed the sisters' ties to their motherhouse in Le Puy.

Moore wrote Mother Pélagie Boyer on November 23, declaring to her that the relationship with Le Puy was ended. Mother Pélagie responded on December 14, 1899:

I have the honor of acknowledging your letter of 23 November in which Your Excellency informs me that henceforth all connections are broken between the Community of St. Joseph in Florida and the Motherhouse in Le Puy.

The blow which strikes us is assuredly very unforeseen; nevertheless we are accepting it with an entire submission to the designs of Divine Providence.

The consequence of the action you have judged appropriate to take is that our French Religious may return to France, if they wish.

Another consequence seems to us equally required of your justice, Monseigneur, the expenses of returning to their homeland should be

12. Lazarus, 1908, ASSJSA.

13. *Florida Times-Union and Citizen*, September 8 and 11, October 18 and 22, 1899.

14. There are varying dates and places given for the stroke: Michael J. McNally, *Catholic Parish Life on Florida's West Coast, 1860–1968* (St. Petersburg: Catholic Media Ministries, 1996), 163; Charles Gallagher, Ph.D., *Cross and Crozier: The History of the Diocese of St. Augustine* (n.p.: Editions du Signe, 1999), 49. The *Florida Times-Union and Citizen* provides clarification. See note 16.

the obligation of the Florida mission [that is, the Diocese of St. Augustine]. That is, moreover, the opinion of our ecclesiastic Superior here.[15]

Mother Pélagie's response brought this reply from Bishop Moore:

I wish to inform you that I do not acknowledge any obligation to furnish the Sisters who want to return to France either the costs of the journey or of apparel, and much less [to furnish] dowries or provisions for those who have served the diocese for many years.

I am not dismissing them; they are all free to remain. Many of them had expressed the intention of remaining, but I am told lately that almost all have changed their mind as a result of encouragement which you wrote to them, and they want now to go away.[16]

Bishop Moore was clearly peeved by the sisters' desires to leave, something he apparently had not expected and that he felt were prompted by Mother Boyer's letters to them. In the same letter, he revealed the underlying reason for his desire to be rid of the French leadership. Besides Mother Lazarus's alleged flagrant act of disobedience regarding reading the papal decree, *Quemadmodum*, he asserted that the French superiors, as far back as Mother Sidonie Rascle, the original founding superior in St. Augustine, had not been unquestioningly obedient to him and cited his experiences with them during the yellow fever epidemics of 1877 and 1888. He wrote:

In 1888, when yellow fever was epidemic in Jacksonville, the Mayor of the City and many doctors telegraphed me for Sisters to care for the sick in hospitals. In my simplicity, I thought I had only to notify Mother Lazarus to be obeyed immediately. What was my surprise when she refused, saying she ought to have the right to be consulted [to have something to say on the point]. I returned home all disturbed and disappointed. I was about to telegraph to New Orleans for some

15. Sister Pélagie Boyer, superior general, Motherhouse in Le Puy, to Bishop Moore, St. Augustine, December 14, 1899, ASSJSA.

16. John Moore, D.D., Episcopal Residence, St. Augustine, to Reverend Mother, Le Puy, January 31, 1900, ASSJSA.

Sisters when a little girl arrived from the convent to say that some Sisters would be sent to Jacksonville.

In 1877 [during the epidemic in Fernandina] Mother Sidonie had made the same refusal to venerable Father Dufau. As Mother Lazarus did, Mother Sidonie soon repented (had a second thought) and sent some Sisters to care for the sick.

How is this! I said to myself, in France the Sisters are evicted from hospitals [referring to a wave of anti-clericalism in France at the time] and in America when the authorities ask for them, the Superior of the French Sisters refuse. I am sure it is only in the Diocese of St. Augustine that any Sisters even hesitated to give their assistance in times of an epidemic.... I repeat, I want Sisters who obey me like their Bishop; and who are not in any manner subject to orders of a Superior in another distant country.[17]

Bishop Moore's displeasure with Mother Lazarus did, indeed, begin with her response during the 1888 yellow fever epidemic in Jacksonville. Shortly after the end of the epidemic, Sister M. Madeleine, a sister at St. Joseph's Academy in St. Augustine, wrote Mother Léocadie Broc in Le Puy:

My dear Mother, I don't want to end without telling you a word about our dear Bishop so that you'll pray to St. Joseph that he may change his ideas. Up to now he has been very good to us but lately he has changed. It seems that [way?] ever since our Mother [Lazarus] didn't seem to wish to send Sisters to Jacksonville to take care of the sick during the epidemic. She did not refuse but she let him know it was hard for her to do. The same day, though, she sent three and a few days later, two more.

If this man turns against us, I don't know how we will manage.[18]

Little did Sister Madeleine know how her words foreshadowed the events that followed.

17. John Moore, D.D., St. Augustine, to Rev. Mother Pélagie Boyer, Le Puy, January 31, 1900, ASSJSA; see also McGoldrick, *Beyond the Call*, 319–21. Mtr. Sidonie Rascle returned to France in 1878 and died in Le Puy on April 24, 1889; McGoldrick, *Beyond the Call*, 278.

18. Letter no. 10, Sr. M. Madeleine, St. Augustine, to Rev. Mother Léocadie [Broc], Le Puy, December 2, 1888, ASSJSA.

Moore's desire to have sisters directly and solely under his authority was not unusual for bishops in America at the time. Bishop William Gross, the prelate over the Diocese of Savannah, had brought an even more abrupt separation of the Sisters of St. Joseph of Georgia from the Le Puy motherhouse in 1874.[19] Gross gave the sisters in Savannah twenty-four hours to accept diocesan status, which would put them directly under his control, or leave the Diocese of Savannah. Rather than break with the motherhouse, Mother Joséphine Deleage, the superior over the Savannah community, returned to Florida and helped to establish the house in Palatka. The bishop's desire to have complete authority over religious men and women certainly and understandably was not unusual.

What was unusual concerning the Sisters of St. Joseph of St. Augustine was that even after they came to Florida they continued to maintain their ties to the motherhouse in Le Puy. Their coming to Florida without going under the authority of the local bishop was arranged by Bishop Augustin Verot despite the Sisters of St. Joseph's constitution (Holy Rule), which stipulated that all Sisters of St. Joseph communities would be diocesan, under the control of the local bishop.[20] It is not clear why Verot made such an arrangement, especially since he would have been the one given authority over the sisters. Perhaps this was a condition that persuaded the French superiors to accept and support a mission in the United States.

At the very beginning, the arrangement seemed to function well. Pope Pius IX had sent the founding sisters his personal blessing before they left Le Puy in 1866. In 1885, an obviously pleased Bishop Moore wrote Mother Lazarus of his audience with Pope Leo XIII, to whom Moore had reported on the fine work the sisters were doing: "He was delighted to hear all the

19. This is described fully in chapter 8.
20. Sister Marie Julie [Roussel], St. Joseph Convent, Mandarin, Florida, to an unnamed Sister, March 28, 1886, ASSJSA.

good things I had to tell him about my good Sisters and their work.... I gave the Holy Father a good account of you all, and he was so pleased that he took a big pinch of snuff on the head of it, and sent you a big blessing from the bottom of his heart."[21] Bishop Moore seemingly continued to support the unusual arrangement until the calamitous events in 1899. The *Florida Times-Union and Citizen* reported:

Mother Lazarus, who for twenty years had been in charge of St. Joseph's Convent and Academy in this city, has resigned as Superioress on account of failing health, and will go to France. At an election recently held by the Sisters of St. Joseph, Sister Eulalia was elected to fill the important office of mother Superior. The resignation of Mother Lazarus was keenly felt by the Sisters, who had learned to love her dearly during her many years of active work.[22]

This report disagrees with the account later provided by Mother Lazarus in several important points. She stated that she did not resign but was deposed and that, although she eventually returned to France in May 1900, she was ordered to leave St. Augustine and go to Ybor City at first. In addition, Mother Lazarus stated that Sister Eulalia, who replaced her, was not elected, but was appointed by Bishop Moore. Mother Lazarus was, indeed, dearly loved by the sisters, and her departure was keenly felt. No mention is made of the separation from the motherhouse in France.

Bishop Moore died in St. Augustine on July 30, 1901, nearly two years after the break with France. The pain of the sudden break was still palpable. No further sisters from Le Puy went to the Florida mission. Instead, the communities in Florida relied increasingly on subjects from Ireland and Canada. As Jane Quinn points out, the growing power of Irish Catholicism was

21. John Moore, D.D., bishop of St. Augustine, Rome to Mother Lazarus, St. Augustine, April 13, 1885.
22. *Florida Times-Union and Citizen*, December 3, 1899.

a trend throughout the church in America. The French domination of the Sisters of St. Joseph of St. Augustine in the nineteenth century gave way to Irish hegemony in the first half of the twentieth century.[23] The new arrangement eliminated the difficulties of dealing with sisters who did not know English and of trying to obtain sisters from a motherhouse in France that had its own responsibilities to meet and was faced with an anticlerical government that was making it more difficult to function.[24]

Although the logic behind severing the bureaucratic ties with Le Puy is understandable and Bishop Moore's actions were fully within the bounds provided by the Constitutions of the Sisters of St. Joseph, the way in which the break was accomplished was unnecessarily harsh, and the treatment Mother Lazarus received was incomprehensible, even in the mind of Bishop Kenny, Moore's successor. Two years after Bishop Moore's death, Kenny told Sister Louise Antonio, who was still the mother superior over the house in Fernandina, that "he would never have thought that what was done two years ago [the deposition of Mother Lazarus and the break with France], would have had such consequences," and told her, "I am far from approving what was done, but it cannot be undone." Mother Louise Antonia wrote to the mother general in Le Puy, saying she felt that if all could be done over, the break would not have been made, at least in the same manner.[25]

The following introductory words of the *Quemadmodem* decree are ironic in light of Bishop Moore's actions: "Just as it

23. Quinn, *Story of a Nun*, 83.
24. Under the Third Republic, established in 1871 after France's defeat in the Franco-Prussian War, anticlerical forces came to power in 1877. A series of laws passed in the 1880s made primary education in France "free, obligatory, and secular." Teaching sisters were barred from the public schools in 1886. Even more aggressive laws against teaching orders, threatening their very existence, were passed between 1901 and 1904; Sarah A. Curtis, *Educating the Faithful: Religion, Schooling, and Society in Nineteenth-Century France* (DeKalb: Northern Illinois University Press, 2000), 107 and 146.
25. Mother Louise Antonia, Fernandina, to Rev. Mother, Le Puy, August 15, 1903, as quoted in McGoldrick, *Beyond the Call*, 360.

Mother Lazarus L'hostal, SSJ.
Courtesy of the Archives of the Sisters of St. Joseph of
St. Augustine, St. Augustine, Florida.

Bishop John Moore.
Courtesy of the Archives of the Sisters of St. Joseph of
St. Augustine, St. Augustine, Florida.

is the fate of human things, how praiseworthy and holy soever they may be in themselves, even so is it of laws wisely enacted, to be liable to be misused and perverted to purposes opposed and foreign to their nature."[26] How true these words are for Mother Lazarus, who was deposed and excommunicated through her bishop's interpretation of this decree, the very purpose of which was to protect subordinates from abuse.

The ministries of the Sisters of St. Joseph continued under Irish leadership, but the Florida mission of the Sisters of St. Joseph from Le Puy came to an end. Eventually, the ties between Le Puy and St. Augustine were forgotten. Not until 1977, through the efforts of Sister Thomas Joseph McGoldrick, who was then the provincial general of the Sisters in St. Augustine, were the loving bonds with the Sisters in Le Puy renewed.[27]

---

26. Lanslot, *Handbook of Canon Law*, 275.
27. McGoldrick, *Beyond the Call*, 425–39.

Chapter 7

The Politics of
Anti-Catholicism and Racism in Early
Twentieth-Century Florida

⌒

When the first Sisters of St. Joseph arrived in St. Augustine in September 1866 to teach the recently freed slaves, they had no idea that fifty years later their benevolent actions would be considered criminal and lead to the arrest of three sisters. By the 1910s, however, anti-Catholicism, along with racism and anti-Semitism, rested as a pall over the South. Anti-Catholicism had been present in America since the colonial period, when Catholics were persecuted and were limited to a few colonies. In the 1830s, convents were the targets of raging mobs and the subject of fabricated tales of bizarre, sordid activities. In 1839, the American Bible Society made it a goal to have the Bible, specifically the Protestants' King James Version, read in every classroom. Most Americans considered the United States to be a Protestant nation, and all other forms of religion, including Catholicism, were classified as sects. As such, Catholic schools were ineligible for public funds. In the mid-nineteenth century, the Know Nothings led the nativist charge as immigrants from Ireland and Germany, many of them Catholic, poured into the United States.

Concerned by the influx of so many Catholics, in 1874, U.S. Senator James G. Blaine of Maine proposed an amendment to the U.S. Constitution that said, "No money raised by taxation in any State for the support of public schools, or derived from any public source, nor any public lands devoted thereto, shall ever be under the control of any religious sect, nor shall any money so raised or land so devoted be divided between religious sects or denominations." The proposal was defeated in 1875 but lived on as the inspiration for the adoption of "Blaine Amendments" in thirty-four state constitutions over the next thirty years. Among them was the 1885 Florida State Constitution.

The United States experienced another wave of immigrants in the late nineteenth century, this time from Southern Europe. Like the earlier Irish and German immigrants, most of the newcomers went to urban areas in the Northeast and Midwest, and among them were Catholics. They, too, were met by the anti-Catholic sentiments of avowedly Protestant Americans. Catholic parochial schools became a target of anti-Catholic rhetoric, especially after the American Catholic bishops, at their Third Plenary Council, held in Baltimore in 1884, required the establishment of Catholic parish schools. The bishops' action was in response to what they considered persecution of Catholic students in the public schools, such as the forced use of the King James Version of the Bible and McGuffey readers that contained blatantly anti-Catholic language. The American Protective Association, founded by Henry Bowers in 1887, sought to oust Catholics from political power and to attack Catholic institutions, especially parochial schools. Anti-Catholics targeted the Catholic schools because they said the parochial institutions undermined the American public-school system, which was "the foundation of the nation's character and development" and a source of national unity.[1] They believed that if Catholics weakened the

1. Justin Nordstrom, *Danger on the Doorstep: Anti-Catholicism and American Print*

public-school system they could more easily realize their alleged goal of taking over the country for the pope. One of their major complaints was that tax dollars were being used to support parochial schools despite the Blaine amendments.

Unlike these earlier manifestations of anti-Catholicism in America, the anti-Catholic movement of the 1910s did not spring from the urban North, but from the rural South. Several historians have attributed the Progressive-Era war against Romanism to the disappointments of the failed Populist movement and the rapid social changes that were occurring at the time. Modernism, the result of such forces as industrialization, the advent of the automobile, the growing power of big business, Darwinism's undermining of traditional biblical beliefs, and changing social mores prompted a strong reaction. Such changes were seen by leaders in many smaller communities in rural areas as a threat to the balance of power and the small-town "way of life."[2]

The ferocity with which anti-Catholicism swept through the South was largely due to the vitriolic writings of Tom Watson, the Populist politician from rural Thomson, Georgia, and Wilbur Franklin Phelps, a printer/newspaperman from Aurora, Missouri. Watson began publishing diatribes against the Catholic Church in a series of articles in his *Jeffersonian Magazine* from 1910 to 1917. He promulgated the old nineteenth-century ideas of the supposed immoralities of Catholicism, but focused chiefly on the claim that Catholics, loyal to the pope, had plans to turn the United States over to the papacy. Furthermore, he claimed that Roman Catholics blindly followed the directions of the pope and his priests, a thought seemingly substantiated by the Catholic Church's 1870 adoption of the dogma of papal

Culture in the Progressive Era (Notre Dame, Ind.: University of Notre Dame Press, 2006), 110, 112; Donald L. Kinzer, *An Episode in Anti-Catholicism: The American Protective Association* (Seattle: University of Washington Press, 1964), 5.

2. Robert B. Rackleff, "Anti-Catholicism and the Florida Legislature, 1911–1919," *Florida Historical Quarterly* 50, no. 4 (April 1972): 354; Nordstrom, *Danger on the Doorstep*, 57, 66.

infallibility. Their "blind loyalty" to the Roman Church, Watson claimed, made Catholics incapable of the independent thinking that was a necessary aspect of American democracy; Catholics, therefore, were dangerous to the United States. Phelps published *The Menace*, which was by far the most widely distributed of the anti-Catholic newspapers. He was particularly opposed to urbanism and believed his paper was needed to counter the city newspapers, which he insisted spread "modernism and Catholic lies."[3]

In his study of the anti-Catholic journals during the Progressive Era, Justin Nordstrom aptly describes Watson's, Phelps's, and other anti-Catholic writers' approach: "Using the rhetoric of patriotic militarism, anti-Catholic writers, editors and publishers lambasted their Romanist opponents as disloyal, backward-thinking, and intellectually stunted conspirators whose dedication to a corrupt priestly hierarchy rendered them unable to grasp or appreciate the tenets of American liberties, and, thus unworthy of national belonging or citizenship."[4] Concerning schools, Watson exclaimed, "Look how the Catholics refuse to send their children to our public schools, and yet have the audacity to ask the government to support their parochial schools, which are simply training camps for Popish perversion of the coming generations."[5] Catholic teachers in public schools were also viewed with great suspicion, for nativists feared the "duplicitous Catholic teachers" would indoctrinate their Protestant students. Nordstrom further says that Catholicism was "to a large degree, scapegoat for excesses of modernity," and that "this blending of familiar anti-Catholic diatribes with new accusations that speak directly to Progressive-Era concerns is what made anti-Catholic literature such a prevalent cultural force in the mid 1910s."[6]

3. Nordstrom, *Danger on the Doorstep*, 87.
4. Nordstrom, *Danger on the Doorstep*, 3.
5. Tom Watson, *Watson's Magazine*, August 1912, 279, quoted in Nordstrom, *Danger on the Doorstep*, 112.
6. Nordstrom, *Danger on the Doorstep*, 4.

Several historians have described the very different nature of the anti-Catholicism that in the 1910s so suddenly and strongly spread across the rural South, where there were relatively few Catholics. John Higham points primarily to xenophobia that saw Catholic immigrants who were settling in urban centers as a threat to the country. He argues that by the early 1910s, nativism in cities had become more secular than religious, and the better-educated urbanites no longer focused on Catholicism but on Progressive-Era issues, such as health, urban planning, and fighting corrupt government. He says, "What had issued from Boston, New York, and Philadelphia in the 1840s radiated from the smaller cities of the Middle West in the 1880s and finally found its most valiant champions among the hicks and hillbillies."[7]

Justin Nordstrom, however, argues that far from being the province of backward "hicks and hillbillies," the anti-Catholicism of the 1910s was part of mainstream American culture. His study of anti-Catholic journals from the period shows that in 1915, *Watson's Magazine* had a circulation of 80,000, while copies of *The Menace* reached 1,469,400 subscribers. These statistics show that more than two million Americans bought anti-Catholic newspapers each week. Their circulation statistics rivaled those of the mainstream media of the day.[8]

Watson's and Phelps's influential publications were particularly popular in the rural parts of the South,[9] and their writings helped shape the politics of Florida during the mid-1910s. From 1913 to 1917, the Florida legislature considered and sometimes passed a number of anti-Catholic bills, and fear of papists was a major factor in the gubernatorial and senatorial elections of 1916. Several historians, some of whose work is now

7. Higham, *Strangers in the Land*, 181.
8. Nordstrom, *Danger on the Doorstep*, 56–57, 63.
9. C. Vann Woodward, *Tom Watson: Agrarian Rebel*, 2nd ed. (1938; Savannah, Ga.: Beehive, 1973), 362, 103–4.

thirty to sixty years old, have written about this brief season of anti-Catholicism in Florida. Two issues have received the most attention: the employment of Catholic sisters in some of Florida's public-school systems and the more well-known controversy over the instruction of African Americans by Sisters of St. Joseph in their segregated parochial schools. The oft-quoted sources for accounts of these events are master's theses written by Sisters of St. Joseph of St. Augustine. They perhaps relied too heavily upon oral histories provided by their fellow sisters, which give a narrow view and limited understanding of the surrounding events that led to the sisters' withdrawal from the public-school system and later arrest. Additional research now sheds more light on those events.

The 1913, 1915, and 1917 legislative sessions saw a rash of anti-Catholic bills.[10] The 1913 legislative session especially impacted the Sisters of St. Joseph and other Catholic religious orders teaching in Florida. One of the pieces of proposed legislation, House Bill no. 577, was "An Act Prohibiting the Wearing of the Garb or Insignia of Religious Societies by Public School Teachers While Performing Their Duties as Such," which had been introduced by Representative Samuel H. Strom of Gadsden County. According to the *Tampa Morning Tribune*, a Catholic-friendly newspaper, Strom introduced the bill at the request of some St. Johns County citizens; the bill was a "direct attack on the Catholic Sisters who are engaged in school work."

10. The obviously anti-Catholic bills included measures to: authorize the inspection of convents, parochial schools, and other private institutions ("Convent Inspection Bill"); prohibit the carrying or drinking of intoxicating liquors at churches (including sacramental wine) and other public gatherings; bar teachers from wearing religious clothing or insignia while teaching in public schools ("Anti-Garb Bill"); authorize the taxation of church property; allow Bible reading (King James Version) and prayer in public schools; and authorize the compulsory attendance of children in public schools. All but the inspection bill were defeated. The "Convent Inspection Bill" was never enforced and was repealed in 1935; see Rackleff, "Anti-Catholicism and the Florida Legislature," 356–64; David P. Page, "Bishop Michael J. Curley and Anti-Catholic Nativism in Florida," *Florida Historical Quarterly* 45, no. 2 (October 1966): 115–16; and Dennis Michael McCarron, "Catholic Schools in Florida, 1866–1992" (Ph.D. diss., Florida State University, 1993), 88–96.

Edwin Spencer, a representative from Marion County and the Speaker *pro tempore*, also spoke against the bill, saying,

It is the most vicious piece of legislation that could be enacted into law, because it is a strike at the religious liberty of the Roman Catholic Church. Secondly, it is an attempt to bring a local fight into the Legislature, and have this House settle a matter that the people of the counties affected have not the courage to settle among themselves. Furthermore, under this bill a school teacher is debarred from wearing an Epworth League pin or a B.Y.P.U. pin. It will make a criminal practically of every school teacher in the state.[11]

Representative Otis R. Parker from St. Lucie County denounced it as "the worst of all the freak bills that had been 'thrust upon' the present Legislature." Representative Glenn Terrell of Sumter County, however, spoke in favor of the bill, saying it would be in support of the "fundamental principle in the constitution, … the separation, complete divorcement, of the church and state, and that the bill sought this simply and nothing more." Terrell, who would later serve on the Florida Supreme Court from 1923 to 1964, three times as the chief justice, carried the day. The bill passed the House by a vote of 49 to 11 and was sent to the Senate.[12] On June 6, 1913, the *Tallahassee Semi-Weekly True Democrat* reported that the House had passed the measure and that the true intent of the bill was "for the relief of" Duval, St. Johns, and Pasco counties, where public-school funds were being used to support denominational schools. The paper explained, "The effect of this bill is to keep the public school neutral ground religiously, and to prevent the appropriation of public-school funds for denominational purposes." Although the bill passed in the

11. *Journal of the Florida House of Representatives* (Tallahassee: T. J. Appleyard, 1913), 2064. The Epworth League, founded in 1889, was a Methodist association for young adults ages eighteen to thirty-five; the Baptist Young People's Union [B.Y.P.U.], organized in 1891, still exists.

12. "Religious Garb Bill Starts Row," *Tampa Morning Tribune*, May 31, 1913, 3.

House, it failed in the Senate.[13] Sister Mary Alberta, in her 1940 thesis on schools operated by the Sisters of St. Joseph of St. Augustine, cites the 1913 Anti-Garb bill as a factor in the sisters' decision to relinquish their positions as public-school teachers, posts they had held since 1878 when Bishop John Moore was able to realize Bishop Verot's dream of having the sisters' schools in St. Johns County and elsewhere in Florida included in the public-school systems. She wrote that the sisters would have laid aside their habits, but because Catholic patrons could support them and good schools were then available to non-Catholics, "the Sisters quietly surrendered their public schools."[14]

The *St. Augustine Evening Record* provides a fuller account of how the change transpired. On July 14, 1913, several citizens of St. Augustine complained to Governor Park Trammell that St. Johns County was in violation of Article XII, Section 13 of the state constitution of 1885. This "Blaine amendment" provided that "no law shall be enacted authorizing the diversion or the lending of any County or District School Funds, or the appropriation of any part of the permanent or available school fund to any other than school purposes; nor shall the same, or any part thereof, be appropriated or used for the support of any sectarian school." Their letter was signed by S. J. Baker, pastor of the Baptist church, and cosigned by: E. E. Boyce, ex-mayor; L. Orin Larson, real estate agent; C.M. Fuller, vice president of Greenleaf and Crosby Co.; C. D. Vanaman, master mechanic, Florida East Coast Railway Company; A. R. Dale, president of the Law and Order League; E. H. Reynolds, ex-school superintendent; Alfred S. Badger, pastor of Flagler Memorial Presbyterian Church; L. Fitz-James Hindry, rector of Trinity Episcopal

13. "Religious Robes in Public Schools of This State," *Semi-Weekly True Democrat*, June 6, 1913.

14. Bishop Verot was first successful in establishing Catholic free schools as part of a public-school system in Savannah, Georgia. For a detailed discussion of the concept and the negotiations that brought that about, see chapter 7, "The Catholic Public School," in Gannon, *Rebel Bishop*; Sister Mary Alberta, "Study of the Schools," 42.

Church; the Rev. W. G. Fletcher, pastor of the First Methodist Episcopal Church, South; and J. H. Martin, pastor of Grace Methodist Episcopal Church.[15]

The intent of the parties was to demonstrate that the free schools taught by the Sisters of St. Joseph of St. Augustine in St. Johns County, Public School no. 12 in St. Augustine, and Public School no. 13 in Moccasin Branch were in fact sectarian schools and that Trammell, as president of the State Board of Education, should put a stop to the misappropriation of public-school funds used for the support of those schools. They supported their case by pointing out that (1) checks to the teachers were made out, not to individuals who happened to be members of the Sisters of St. Joseph, but to the "Sisters of St. Joseph," a Roman Catholic organization; (2) a list of county teachers gave the name of the teachers at schools 12 and 13 as "sister this or that" and pointed out that School no. 12 was a building on the grounds of St. Joseph's Convent and therefore was owned by the Roman Catholic Church; (3) only Sisters of St. Joseph taught at Schools 12 and 13; (4) Roman Catholic catechism was taught, admittedly not during school hours, but in the building used for public-school purposes and taught by teachers who were paid out of public-school funds. (They also noted that public funds were being used for sectarian purposes in Duval and Pasco counties); (5) the children at these public schools were taught to observe Roman Catholic saints' days and were given those days off from school "contrary to law"; (6) twice a week the children were taken to their school auditorium to sing Roman Catholic hymns; (7) while teaching, the Roman Catholic sisters wore the religious garb and insignia of their orders (although the Anti-Garb Bill of 1913 failed, the sisters' use of their habits bolstered the arguments that their schools were sectarian); (8) the

15. "School Question before Governor," *St. Augustine Evening Record*, August 22, 1913, 2. The *St. Augustine Evening Record* is hereafter cited as *SAER*.

fact that the Catholic bishop, William J. Kenny, "approved" Public Schools 12 and 13 "branded" them as sectarian institutions; and (9) the complainants pointed out that the county's Public School no. 1 in St. Augustine was large enough to accommodate the students at Public School no. 12, and the school on the convent grounds (no. 12) was therefore unnecessary. In closing, they said, "We confidently appeal to you for your help. Our lovely state is yet American rather than sectarian. We appeal to you to help us to preserve it such."[16] Their final pleas may have been alluding to the anti-Catholic charge that the pope's aim was to take over control of the United States through the schools.

On July 25, the governor wrote L. A. Colee, chairman of the St. Johns County School Board, sending him a copy of the complaint and asking him to advise him. On July 29, the board replied, after conferring with Sister Mary Louise, the mother superior of the Sisters of St. Joseph of St. Augustine, and Sister Agnita, the principal of School no. 12. There were no disputes with the complainants' assertions except on a few points. They clarified that School no. 12, located on the convent grounds, was owned by the sisters, not by the Roman Catholic Church. They confirmed that the catechism was taught, but the religious instruction was given outside of regular school hours and the students were not forced to learn it. The catechism was not taught in School no. 13 at all, but in a separate building distinct from the school. At no. 12, on Holy Days of Obligation, only two or three days per year, students were dismissed from their studies, but the time was made up by opening the school year one week earlier than the other public schools. On Friday mornings, the children at no. 12 went to the convent auditorium, where with "ample musical instruments, they were taught not only Roman Catholic hymns, but also patriotic hymns and airs." Sisters did,

16. "School Question before Governor," *SAER*, August 22, 1913, 1–3; Florida State Constitution of 1885 online at http://www.law.fsu.edu/crc/conhist/1885con.html.

indeed, wear their habits and a cross or crucifix. Concerning the suggestion to combine the students of School no. 12 with those at the commodious School no. 1, the board pointed out that because there were so many children in the lower grades at no. 12, it would be too crowded for the youngest students at School no. 1 if the classes were combined.[17]

The school board further explained that the Sisters of St. Joseph of St. Augustine had been teaching in the public schools of St. Johns County for over forty years and referred to Bishop Moore's 1878 agreement with the county. Furthermore, they said that the first public-school teachers' institute ever held in the state to train teachers was held on the sisters' convent grounds under then state Superintendent of Public Instruction A. J. Russell.[18] The board had never intended to make Public Schools 12 and 13 sectarian, and the sixteen or eighteen Protestant students out of the 109 who attended the schools were never forced to practice Catholic rites. Never before had there been a complaint

17. "School Question before Governor," *SAER*, August 22, 1913, 1–3.

18. St. Johns County held a teachers' institute in St. Augustine on September 1, 1890. It was not, however, the first institute held in the state. In an effort to obtain a higher-caliber teaching force, state superintendent of public instruction William P. Haisley organized the first teachers' institute in 1879 and established institutes to provide instruction for teachers in "Duval, Hernando, Marion, Nassau, Orange, Santa Rosa, Suwannee, Washington and other counties." The legislature provided $1,000 to support the institutes in 1883, but funding was not consistent. Succeeding superintendents Foster and Russell promoted the institutes also and personally organized some of them. The legislature did not fund state institutes in 1890, but many counties held their own, for two months in Alachua and Polk counties and for one month in Hillsborough, Marion, Putnam, Washington, Levy, Jefferson, and St. Johns counties; W. N. Sheats, *Biennial Report of the Superintendent of Public Instruction* (1895), 40; Thomas Everette Cochran, *Public School Education in Florida* (Lancaster, Pa.: New Era, 1921),75–76; George Gary Bush, *History of Education in Florida*, Bureau of Education Circular of Information no. 7 (Washington, D.C.: Government Printing Office, 1889), 27. St. Johns' was attended by teachers from St. Johns County as well as some from neighboring counties. Among the attendees were Sisters of St. Joseph of St. Augustine: Sisters Clotilde, Jones, and Ambrose from Moccasin Branch; Sisters Theresa Hernandez, Gertrude Capo, Lucy Dellon, and Ignatius Morrell from St. Augustine; and Sisters Sidonia McCarthy and Aloysia Andrew of New Augustine; "The Teachers' Institute: A Big Gathering of the 'Schoolmarms' of St. Johns County," *Florida Times-Union*, September 2, 1890, 2. The official record of the Sisters of St. Joseph for September 1, 1890, confirms the location, noting the "first Teacher Institute held at Public School Building. 7 Srs. attended all passed exams."

about the board's employment of the Sisters of St. Joseph, nor had there ever been an assertion that the board was using public-school funds illegally.[19]

On August 8, Governor Trammell asked the school board for further information: Did the sisters who taught in Public Schools 12 and 13 hold teaching certificates? Why were only Catholics used to teach at those schools? Were there other schools where the teachers belonged to only one denomination? What were the purpose and the object of the corporation known as the "Sisters of St. Joseph"? Did the board maintain any other schools in St. Augustine that were "separate and apart" from the high school?

Colee responded on August 14. He provided a list of the teaching sisters by name, giving the number of each one's certificate and the date it was issued. As to why only Catholics were employed at the schools, he referred to the 1878 correspondence between Bishop Moore and Thomas T. Russell, who was then the superintendent of schools for St. Johns County. In his letter to the board, Moore pointed out that the Catholics of St. Augustine had educated their own children, both black and white, amounting to about 330 students, each year. They had done this without any financial support from the state or county, "there being, it is believed, a want of harmony between the religious principles upon which Catholic schools are conducted and the State law on education, as that law now stands on the statue [sic] book." Because Catholics paid most of the taxes in the county, he proposed a plan that would give them the "benefit of the school fund without violating either the spirit or the letter of the State law on education." Moore then put forth a seven-part plan: (1) Catholic schools would be under the school board as public schools and subject to the board's disciplinary rules; (2) the Sisters of St. Joseph would take teacher examinations and be certified just

19. "School Question before Governor," *SAER*, August 22, 1913, 2.

as other public-school teachers were; (3) the Catholic schools would be subject to inspection, just as other public schools were; (4) the Catholic schools would use the same textbooks as those used in the public schools; (5) the sisters would be paid salaries, based on their level of certification, just as public teachers were paid; (6) religious instruction would take place outside regular school hours; and (7) the schoolrooms and furniture used in the Catholic schools were offered to the board for its use. On August 27, 1878, the school board unanimously agreed to adopt the bishop's proposal with the hope "that the schools will be conducted in a spirit of harmony and brotherly love." Governor Trammell turned all the information over to Attorney General Thomas F. West and asked for his advice on the matter.[20]

As the citizens of St. Augustine awaited the attorney general's opinion, preparations for the new school year continued. The Sisters of St. Joseph planned to open their free schools for the poor on Monday, September 15, and their tuition-funded St. Joseph's Academy the next Monday. In the meantime, a meeting was held at the academy auditorium on the Sunday afternoon before the school opening to talk about the formation of a Catholic School Association. With great optimism the newspaper claimed, "While the schools taught by the Sisters have always held an enviable reputation as institutions of learning the future holds a promise of greater achievement than ever in the past and the co-operation of the entire Catholic community is requested and expected." The public schools opened that same Monday with an equally bright outlook and, like the Catholics, claimed record high enrollments.[21]

20. "School Funds Cannot Be Paid to Sisters of St. Joseph," *SAER*, September 5, 1913.
21. "Sisters' Schools to Open Next Monday in This City," *SAER*, September 8, 1913, 1; "Public Schools Will Open for Term Monday Morning," *SAER*, September 11, 1913, 1; "Public Schools Will Open for New Year Next Monday" and "Catholic Schools Open Monday—Meeting Tomorrow," *SAER*, September 13, 1913, 1; "With Splendid Attendance Parochial Schools Are Open," *SAER*, September 15, 1913; "With a Record Attendance St. Joseph's Academy Opens," *SAER*, September 22, 1913.

On September 23, the Catholics met again to discuss the future of their parochial schools. Father John O'Brien, the rector of the cathedral, emphasized the need to provide training for their youth. He said that, while secular education was "essential and necessary," a thought contrary to the widespread anti-Catholic belief that the Roman Church saw secular schools as evil, it was the responsibility of the Catholics to provide religious instruction for their children, and that was possible only in their own parochial schools.[22] The association was then formed, with O'Brien elected president and treasurer and Clarence R. Rogero, a layman, secretary. The assembly also elected a twenty-member executive committee to serve as an educational board. There was an outpouring of financial support, with members enthusiastically making annual pledges for the schools. They even went so far as to propose to replace the old building "formerly used as a public school" with a modern structure.[23]

Such enthusiasm and support for a separate parochial school system came forth before the state's final decision had been made public. That came two days later when the *Evening Record* published in full the attorney general's response. In a September 9, 1913, letter to L. A. Colee, the chairman of the county school board, West requested that the county no longer use any county school funds to support school nos. 12 and 13, explaining that the practice of paying the Sisters of St. Joseph as public-school teachers was, indeed, a violation of Article XII, Section 13 of the state constitution and added that Sections 5 and 6 of its declaration of rights must also be considered. Section 5 stated, "The free exercise and enjoyment of religious profession and worship shall forever be allowed in this State, etc., and Section 6 stated, "No preference shall be given by law to any

22. At the Third Plenary Council held in 1884, the American Catholic Church officially required the establishment of parochial schools; Kinzer, *An Episode in Anti-Catholicism*, 13.

23. "Catholics Make Plans for Parochial Schools," *SAER*, September 23, 1913, 1.

church, sect or mode of worship, and no money shall ever be taken from the public treasury directly or indirectly in aid of any church, sect or religious denominations, or in aid of any sectarian institution." West then stated that the provisions of the constitution were "self-executing"—that is, not requiring acts of the legislature to be in force—and limiting the powers and actions of all public officials. He declared, "The appropriation or use of any portion of the school funds of St. Johns county to support a school conducted in this way, in my opinion, violates the constitutional inhibition referred to, and is therefore unauthorized."[24]

Thus ended the thirty-five-year arrangement whereby the Sisters of St. Joseph taught in the public-school system.[25] It was not a quiet decision by the sisters to simply withdraw from the public schools. It was the result of great public discussion and a constitutional interpretation of the practice by the state's attorney general. Both the Catholic community and the public-school adherents seemed to embrace the separation with great anticipation of brighter futures for both systems.

Meanwhile, the Catholic Church began to look at another one of the bills that was signed into law after the 1913 legislative session. Although it was not obviously anti-Catholic, it had a profound effect on the Catholic schools for blacks run by the Sisters of St. Joseph. On April 23, 1913, Representative E. D. Prevatt of Clay County introduced House Bill 415, "An Act Prohibiting White Persons from Teaching Negroes in Negro Schools, and Prohibiting Negro Teachers from Teaching White Children in White Schools in the State of Florida, and Providing for the

24. "Final Decision in School Matter," *SAER*, September 25, 1913, 3.

25. The arrangement that Verot achieved in Savannah in 1870 and hoped to emulate in St. Augustine was ended in December 1916 after a lawyer fought against it on the grounds that the Georgia constitution prohibited the use of public funds for sectarian purposes. Although the Sisters of St. Joseph withdrew from the public schools, the Sisters of St. Benedict in San Antonio, Pasco County, and the Sisters of the Holy Names of Jesus and Mary in Key West and Tampa continued to teach in public schools for several more years; Gannon *Rebel Bishop*, 190–91, 116, and 91.

Penalty Therefor." The act provided that violators could be fined up to five hundred dollars or imprisoned in the county jail up to six months.[26] It was read for the first time by its title and referred to the Committee on the Judiciary A.

The next day, the committee reviewed the bill, recommended its passage, and placed it on the Calendar of Bills for its second reading. It was taken up again on May 17, and though some amendments to exempt reform schools were considered, the bill passed on unchanged to its third reading, where it received a unanimous vote in support of passage. The measure was engrossed that same day and sent over to the Senate for consideration. On June 3, Senator John P. Wall from Putnam County, just south of the Clay County line, moved that the rule requiring the readings of a bill to occur on separate days be waived and that House Bill 415 be taken up and considered. His motion was approved, and the bill immediately moved on through its second and third readings and was approved unanimously. On June 4 the bill was referred to the Committee on Enrolled Bills. The next day, the committee found it to be correctly enrolled, and it was referred to the Joint Committee on Enrolled Bills, which also found it to be correctly enrolled. On June 6 it was again found to be correctly enrolled and sent to the governor, who signed it into law on June 7, 1913.[27]

Thus, the bill was quickly shepherded through the legislative process and passed without eliciting any great debate or any notice by the senators who had quashed several of the other anti-Catholic bills. Unlike the Anti-Garb Bill, there was no discussion of this bill in the newspapers, only its inclusion in the lists of bills the legislators had considered on a given day and

26. *General Acts and Resolutions Adopted by the Legislature of Florida at Its Regular Session 1913 under the Constitution of A.D. 1885* (Tallahassee: T. J. Appleyard, 1913), 1:311.

27. *Journal of the State House of Representatives of Florida* (Tallahassee: T. J. Appleyard, 1913), 670, 823, 1540, 2509, 2559, 2561, and 2636; *Journal of the State Senate of Florida* (Tallahassee: T. J. Appleyard, 1913), 2279–2280.

its passage and signing into law by the governor. Perhaps it was seen primarily as a restriction on blacks and was, therefore, not controversial.

By the fall of 1913, however, with the school year about to commence, William J. Kenny, bishop of the Catholic Diocese of St. Augustine, asked the diocese's attorney to examine the law and its potential impact on the black schools run by the Sisters of St. Joseph. Actually, the law could affect every Catholic school for African Americans in Florida at that time. In the Diocese of Mobile, which included all of Florida west of the Apalachicola River, Catholic sisters taught black student in Pensacola, at St. Joseph's School, which had four teachers and 190 students, and in Warrington, at St. John the Evangelist School, which had one teacher and thirty-four students. In the Diocese of St. Augustine, two Sisters of the Holy Names of Jesus and Mary taught 125 students at St. Peter Claver School in Tampa, and two of the same order taught ninety-five students at St. Francis Xavier School in Key West. The Sisters of St. Joseph had charge of St. Benedict the Moor School in Ybor City, where three sisters taught 125 students; Peter Claver School in Fernandina, where two sisters taught twenty-nine students; and St. Benedict the Moor School in St. Augustine, where three sisters taught sixty-five students.[28]

On September 3, 1913, Alston (A. W.) Cockrell of Cockrell and Cockrell in Jacksonville wrote Kenny that he thought the law was unconstitutional because it did not apply equally to all races. Looking at Section 1 of the printed as well as the original enrolled act on file with the Florida secretary of state, he noted that the wording differed from the title of the actual law.

28. Thomas Jesse Jones, ed., *Negro Education: A Study of the Private and Higher Schools for Colored People in the United States* (New York: Arno Press and the *New York Times*, 1969), 180; reprint of U.S. Office of Education Bulletin, 1916, no. 38, Government Printing Office, 1917. *The Sisters of Saint Joseph of Saint Augustine, Florida: Our First One Hundred Years, 1866–1966*.

Section 1 read, "From and after the passage of this Act it shall be unlawful in this State, for white teachers to teach negroes in negro schools, and for negro teachers to teach in white schools." Cockrell elaborated:

There is a distinction made between white teachers and negro teachers. The white teachers are only inhibited from teaching negro children in negro schools, being not prohibited from teaching any one other than negroes in the negro schools, whereas negro teachers are prohibited from teaching at all in white schools. At first blush, the distinction may seem to be a distinction without difference but I think that this is not so.... This discrimination, in my opinion, makes the act void.

In advising the bishop, he said,

Theoretically, since the act is void, the proper course would be to pay no attention to it.... Practically, however, this might result in the Sisters being subjected to embarrassment by prosecutions or threatened prosecutions or possibly by imprisonment. Then too, ... the courts might ... hold it constitutional. So it may be ... best ... to interview the prosecuting officer in each county where the Sisters teach negro children, explaining to him wherein the act is violative of the constitution and secure some arrangement not to prosecute; or if this be impossible, to secure some arrangement by which a test case can be made with the agreement that no action be taken, except in the test case, until after the test case is concluded.[29]

Some of Cockrell's reasoning in the letter is obscure, but it appears that Bishop Kenny took his attorney's advice and paid no attention to the law.

The next month Bishop Kenny, who had just turned sixty,

29. Alston (A. W.) Cockrell of Cockrell and Cockrell, Jacksonville, to Rt. Rev. W. J. Kenny, St. Augustine, September 3, 1913, Diocese of St. Augustine records, reel 3, box 3-W-22; microfilm on file at P. K. Yonge Library, University of Florida, Gainesville. The mistake in the enrolled version may have come about because of the rush to get the bill passed and signed into law before the end of the legislative session. For whatever reason, it was on the basis of its unequal application to white and black teachers that Cockrell deemed the law unconstitutional and advised Bishop Kenny to ignore it. Cockrell did not raise any question of whether the law applied to private as well as public schools.

died. He had been in failing health, but his death from pneumonia on October 23, 1913, while on a trip to Baltimore, was quite unexpected. It is not known if Kenny had any intention to force the issue about the sisters' black schools, but Cockrell's counsel to ignore the law seems to have been wise, for the sisters continued to open their black schools in the fall as usual with no outcry from any corner.

Bishop Kenny was succeeded by Irishman Michael J. Curley, the mission priest in De Land, Florida, who had been stationed in St. Augustine briefly nine years before. Michael J. Curley was born October 12, 1879, in Athlone, County Westmeath, Ireland. His early schooling was under the Marist Brothers. When he was sixteen, he entered Mungret College in Limerick and earned a B.A. from Royal University of Ireland in 1900. Following a visit from Bishop John Moore, the prelate of the Diocese of St. Augustine, Curley volunteered to one day serve in the United States. He attended the Urban College of the Propaganda in Rome, received his Licentiate of Sacred Theology in 1903, and was ordained to the priesthood on March 19, 1904. The following autumn, as promised, he arrived in Florida to become the pastor of St. Peter's Church in De Land. In 1905, he served as chancellor of the Diocese of St. Augustine and as secretary to the bishop William John Kenny. After the death of Bishop Kenny, Pope Pius X appointed Curley the fourth bishop of St. Augustine on April 3, 1914. He was consecrated on June 30, 1914, at the age of thirty-four, the youngest Catholic bishop in the United States at that time.[30]

Curley's return to St. Augustine as the new bishop was highly anticipated, as he had "won the highest esteem and the warm regard of the people of [St. Augustine] regardless of denomination." He was further described in the St. Augustine paper as "a scholar of rare attainment, a preacher of exceptional

30. Page, "Curley," 106.

ability and a man of very pleasing personality. He is a young, energetic and zealous worker and as a bishop will be a force that will exert a great influence for the good of the entire State."[31]

The address Curley gave at a reception held for him by St. Augustine's Knights of Columbus and the Daughters of Isabella on July 3, 1914, showed that he was not one to shy away from confrontation. Citing St. Augustine's long history as a Catholic city, he said, "Here then no apologies are needed for our existence, and I owe no man any explanation of my return to this dear old city as Catholic bishop of this diocese.... We are of the present, with our vision focused cheerfully and courageously on the years to be."[32]

Because Florida's legislature met biannually in the odd-numbered years during the early 1900s, 1914 was an off year. During that time there was little anti-Catholic activity. In 1915, the legislature did meet, and the *Tallahassee Democrat* proudly reported in its May 6, 1915, issue that Representative William Henry "Bill" Mapoles from Walton County had been noticed by *The Menace*, identified by the *Democrat's* editors as "the great Anti-Catholic paper," for his introduction of a bill providing for a state investigation of Catholic convents. *The Menace's* article actually decried the *Tampa Tribune's* denunciation of Mapoles's bill and its praise of the work carried on in the convents. Regarding the representative, the Tampa paper said, "Mapoles has probably been reading The Menace, a publication which makes war on the Catholic church, without much regard to whether it deals in facts or falsehoods in such warfare. The State of Florida ought to pray for early deliverance from this brand of intolerance and from legislation of the Maypole type." The *Tallahassee Democrat*, however, accused the *Tribune's* editors of "hunger[ing] for the bum blessings of Rome more than they

31. "Father Curley Made Bishop, Appointed by Pope on April 2," *SAER*, April 2, 1914, 1.
32. "Public Reception Tendered Bishop Michael J. Curley," *Jacksonville Florida Times-Union*, July 3, 1914, 3, 8.

thirst for righteousness of human freedom."[33] This exchange shows the clear divide between the urban community of Tampa and the rural community of Tallahassee.

The main focus during the legislative session, however, was the upcoming elections in 1916. Of particular note was the entry of Sidney J. Catts into Florida's political arena. Catts, a Baptist preacher originally from Alabama, briefly served a church in DeFuniak Springs in Florida's rural panhandle before deciding to run for governor in 1916. He was considered a joke by the long-established Democrats in Tallahassee, but they underestimated the strong influence his anti-Catholic rhetoric would have in the rural areas of the state. Catts appealed to the prevailing patriotism and anti-Catholicism that was sweeping the South. His supporters put forth his platform, which clearly demonstrated his strategy to take advantage of anti-Catholic sentiments:

Nothing in Florida above the Nation's flag. As Roman Catholicism puts her allegiance to the Pope above the flag, Mr. Catts stands against her invasion of the State of Florida in her politics. As Roman Catholicism opposes our public school system, Mr. Catts opposes Roman Catholicism in the State of Florida in the realm of education. As Roman Catholicism believes in the celibacy of the priesthood and the confessional, Mr. Catts stands squarely against them, and is ready to fight from the State of Florida this great menace to the peace of home, the maintenance of our public schools, and the enjoyment of quiet religion at all hazards.[34]

His strategy worked. Fueled by the diatribes of Tom Watson and the other anti-Catholic writers of the day, Catts was a powerful opponent to the well-known Democratic veteran W. V. Knott. Governor Park Trammell was nearing the end of

33. "Rep. Mapoles Gets Space in *The Menace*," *Tallahassee Daily Democrat*, May 6, 1915, 1.

34. Catts campaign flyer reproduced in Michael Newton, *The Invisible Empire: The Ku Klux Klan in Florida* (Gainesville: University Press of Florida, 2001), 37, photo 9.

his single term—all that was allowed under Florida law at that time—and cast his eye about for which political seat he would next seek. He settled upon a run for the United States Senate, opposing the incumbent, Nathan Bryan.

The newspapers of 1916 were filled with news of the various political campaigns. In mid-April, however, papers across the state, out of state, and even in Europe reported the arrest of three Sisters of St. Joseph on Monday, April 24, the day after Easter, and in the midst of a celebration of the fiftieth anniversary of the sisters' arrival in Florida, when they came to teach the newly freed slaves. Sister Mary Thomasine Hehir was the principal of St. Benedict the Moor School, the black parochial school located in Lincolnville. She, along with two other sisters who taught there, was ordered to appear before the county judge, accused of violating the 1913 law that made it illegal for white teachers to instruct blacks in black schools. Based on interviews with Sisters of St. Joseph who were there on the scene, Jane Quinn wrote,

Between nine and ten o'clock on Easter Monday morning the prisoner, Thomasine, was led to court. She went out the back gate of Hospital [Aviles] Street toward the courthouse, accompanied by the priest and the superior general, while the other Sisters watched apprehensively from the second floor porch [of the convent]. Old-timers in the convent thought the reason they chose the back street was "to avoid a tumult on St. George Street," although local sentiment was not really at such a fever pitch.[35]

The two teachers accepted the offer of bonding out and were released under their own recognizance, but Sister Thomasine refused it.[36] The judge allowed her to be held at the con-

---

35. Quinn, *Story of a Nun*, 206.
36. In his 1993 dissertation, Dennis states that according to Sr. Mary Albert Lussier, then archivist for the Sisters of St. Joseph, it was widely believed that Bishop Curley advised Sister Thomasine to refuse to pay the bond in order to call greater attention to the case; McCarron, "Catholic Schools in Florida," 100.

St. Benedict the Moor School, St. Augustine, 1916.
Sister Thomasine Hehir, SSJ, the principal, is the sister in the middle of the top row.

Courtesy of the Archives of the Sisters of St. Joseph of St. Augustine, St. Augustine, Florida.

vent in the custody of Father O'Brien, rather than being sent to the county jail. The papers reported that the St. Johns County sheriff had been instructed by Governor Trammell to make the arrest after he received a petition advising him that the law was being violated. The petition came from an unnamed black man identified only as possibly being an employee of the Surprise Store, a St. Augustine department store. Some papers reported the complaint had been made by three black men employed at the Surprise Store.[37] From the start the arrest was seen as a preliminary step in testing the law, and it was expected that the case would go to the state or even the United States Supreme Court.[38]

37. St. Augustine city directories for 1914 and 1915 show that the Surprise Store employed three black porters.
38. "Sisters of St. Joseph Have Been Arrested," *SAER*, April 24, 1916, 1; "Recent State Law Is to Be Tested in St. Augustine," *Jacksonville Florida Times-Union*, April 25, 1916, 4;

Because the case involved a state law, the trial was held in the Circuit Court before Judge George Cooper Gibbs. The first hearing was held May 4. Sister Mary Thomasine, represented in court by Alston Cockrell, the attorney who advised Bishop Kenny, pleaded not guilty. While the case was still pending, teaching at the Catholic black schools across the state was suspended. As the outcome would also affect Baptist black schools, there was much interest even among non-Catholics. The papers in St. Augustine and Tampa, where Catholic sisters taught blacks, were sympathetic and outraged by the arrests. A report from St. Augustine said,

The incident has naturally created a great deal of talk here, much indignation has been expressed, and it seems deplorable that any law should be countenanced which has for its object the prevention of gratuitous education of the colored boys and girls of the state by white teachers. It seems a pity that the Sisters of St. Joseph should not only be hampered in their free educational work, but also be embarrassed by arrest for their noble efforts in behalf of the uneducated children.

The result of this case will be awaited with keen interest by the people of this city and county especially. In fact, it is of statewide interest, so long as it will test the constitutionality of a legislative act which precludes the proper education of the negroes of Florida.[39]

In rural parts of the state, however, there was support for the arrest. The *Lake City Index*, for example, praised Governor Trammell and the sheriff for doing their duty to enforce the law and said it was "glad that negroes brought this case."[40]

On May 21, the judgment came. Judge Gibbs ordered Sister Thomasine to be released, for he found that she had not violated

<hr />

"Test State Law on Teaching Negroes," *Tampa Morning Tribune*, April 25, 1916, 1; and "Three Nuns Arrested for Teaching Negroes," *Atlanta Constitution*, April 25, 1916, 1.

39. "Recent State Law to Be Tested in St. Augustine," *Florida Times-Union*, April 25, 1916, 4.

40. "Trammell Is Right on This," *Lake City Index*, quoted in the *Tallahassee Daily Democrat*, May 18, 1916, 4.

the 1913 act.[41] He explained that the state clearly had the authority to rule that whites could not teach blacks in public black schools and that blacks could not teach whites in public schools, but it had no authority to apply the law to private schools. He further ruled that the law was unconstitutional because it violated the Florida state constitution, specifically Section 1, which states that all men are equal before the law and have the inalienable right of possessing and protecting property and pursuing happiness, and Section 12, which says private property cannot be taken without just compensation. He ruled the law also violated Article XIV of the United States Constitution, which says no state shall make or enforce any law that shall abridge the privileges or immunization of citizens of the United States. Life, liberty, and property cannot be taken without due process. He ruled that the 1913 law violated these constitutional principles because it deprived teachers of privileges that were not denied to any other class of citizens.[42]

On the surface the 1916 arrest of the three Sisters of St. Joseph appears to be just another example of the anti-Catholic spirit of the times. Author Jane Quinn believed that to be so, for she wrote:

It is difficult to explain why the petition to arrest Thomasine was made by a black, unless one may assume that the politicians who wanted to create the incident as a test and perhaps out of anti-Catholic sentiment being whipped up by Sidney Catts in his gubernatorial campaign, thought it would bear more weight with public opinion for a black to call for the arrest.... It is a good guess that the political climate of the day suggested to the instigation of the action that it would be seemly for them to have a black object to the Sisters teaching at St. Benedict's.[43]

41. "Judge Gibbs Orders Release of Sisters," *SAER*, May 22, 1916, 1.
42. Copy of court file in the suit "Ex Parte Sister Mary Thomasine," law no. 778, docket no. 3, page 97; on file ASSJSA. Gibbs did not afford the same rights to black teachers.
43. Quinn, *The Story of a Nun*, 205.

Several curious factors, however, lend support to the idea that the arrest was arranged by the Catholic Church itself, rather than its enemies, to force a test case of the 1913 law. First, there had been little discussion of the bill in the press, not even in the Catholic-friendly *Tampa Morning Tribune*, when it was proposed during the 1913 legislative session. More attention was paid to the Anti-Garb Bill that was proposed and passed in the House in May but failed in the Senate. This bill prohibited the use of sectarian clothing or religious insignias by public-school teachers. It would have affected not only the Catholic sisters, who wore habits and crosses, but also Protestants, such as some Methodists who wore Epworth League pins. Perhaps, as suggested before, the bill that prohibited whites from teaching "negroes" was seen as anti-black, rather than anti-Catholic, and was, therefore, not considered very newsworthy. Second, the law that prohibited white persons from teaching blacks was signed into law on June 7, 1913, yet it was not enforced until the sudden arrest of the sisters two-and-a-half years later. Third, if the petition was a legitimate complaint, why was it brought forward in St. Augustine, a historically Catholic community, rather than a place such as Lake City, where anti-Catholicism was a strong influence? If planned as a test case, St. Augustine would have been a much friendlier venue. Fourth, why was the petitioner against the sisters left without any clear identification? This was in great contrast with the highly publicized petition filed by some leading citizens of St. Augustine in the summer of 1913, which demanded that the use of public funds to support the Catholic free schools cease and led to the withdrawal of sisters from employment in the public-school system. Fifth, was it merely a coincidence that the day of the arrest, the day after Easter, coincided with the day of celebration to commemorate the arrival of the Sisters of St. Joseph from France fifty years before, specifically to teach blacks? Why were they celebrating the anniversary that day in April, when it was in September that the sisters had arrived?

It seems reasonable to propose that the Catholic Church did, indeed, arrange the petition to Governor Trammell that led to the arrest of the sisters. Bishop Curley, a strong, young, and zealous leader, was not one to let the law go unchallenged. With the official separation of the Sisters of St. Joseph from the St. Johns County public-school system in September of 1913 and with a strong parochial school association then in place, there would be no doubt that St. Benedict the Moor and the other black schools run by Catholic sisters were private schools. Perhaps, with confidence that the sisters would win, Bishop Curley chose to pursue a test case as suggested by the diocese's lawyer. The prospect that Catts, an openly anti-Catholic candidate, might win the gubernatorial election the next year perhaps further persuaded him that it was time to pursue the matter.[44]

The Sisters of St. Joseph were at the center of two legal cases, one of which ended the practice of Catholic sisters teaching as part of the public-school system and dealt with questions that continue to arise in addressing what the separation of church and state means. The second case clarified the distinction between the legislature's authority over public and private institutions. It spoke more to the rights of whites than to those of blacks and upheld the right of the state to enforce the segregation of schoolteachers as well as students.

The cases may have played a role in the political success of Sidney Catts in his race for the governor's office, as he often made references to the Catholic threat to the public schools. For Governor Trammell, it provided a safe way for him to maintain the support of anti-Catholics without obviously attacking the church. True, he signed into law the prohibition of

44. Robert Rackleff states that the test case was "set up by the church," but provides no documentation to substantiate the assertion; see Rackleff, 358–59fn20.

whites teaching blacks in black schools, but when the case arose two-and-a-half years later, he merely told the sheriff to enforce the law. Trammell ran well in Florida's rural counties and took the Senate seat from Nathan Bryan, who was seen as being sympathetic to Catholics.

Bishop Curley, the new, forceful bishop, openly fought Governor Catts's Convent Inspection Law, a measure that became law in 1917 but was never enforced, and as suggested, may have engineered the test case in 1916. When Curley was asked by the civil authorities to simply "withdraw the Sisters from the colored schools," he replied that "he was the spiritual shepherd of white and colored alike and he would not desert one of his spiritual children."[45] His leadership was noticed by his superiors, and in 1921 he was made the archbishop of Baltimore, the most prestigious bishopric in the United States. He held the position until his death in 1947.

For the Sisters of St. Joseph of St. Augustine, once they had the firm support of a strong parochial school system, they were probably glad to be freed from the public-school system that limited their ability to teach Catholic values. It is not known if Sister Thomasine, the heroine of the Catholic community, was party to the generation of the test case, if indeed, the church was behind it. Because the sisters did not speak out in public, we do not know what she thought of the incident. It was probably good to have the ambiguity of the law settled, and she, very likely, was simply pleased to serve to that end. For blacks, seemingly the last ones to be considered throughout the ordeal, there was really no change; the racism of the times continued. Now, at least, they were ensured the continuation of the availability of a Catholic education, the very reason the Sisters of Joseph came from France fifty years before.

45. *Florida Catholic*, May 23, 1947, 3.

Chapter 8

The Sisters of St. Joseph Expand into Georgia

⟜

Although Savannah, Georgia, is located only about 176 miles north of St. Augustine, it is very different from the Ancient City in nearly every respect, except for its proximity to the Atlantic Ocean. Like St. Augustine, Savannah has a colonial history, but one that is linked to Protestant England rather than Catholic Spain.

Although Savannah has English roots, as in Florida, its first European inhabitants were Spanish missionaries. Beginning in 1566, within a year of the founding of St. Augustine, missionary efforts were in full force, especially among the Guale people near what became Savannah. Early Jesuit missionary efforts failed, but they were succeeded by Franciscans, who established Mission Santa Catalina de Guale on St. Catherines Island. The friars established a string of missions along the coast between there and Florida, but in 1597, the Guale at St. Catherines Island revolted, and three Franciscans lost their lives at Sapalo Island.

Stresses on the Spanish continued, especially when the English established Charles Town, South Carolina, in 1670, and then attacked the mission at Santa Catalina in 1680. Although successful in repelling the English, the Spanish and

Guale people abandoned the mission soon thereafter. Pressure from England continued, and increasingly larger areas of the northern part of La Florida gave way to the expansion of England's Caroline colony into what became the English colony of Georgia in 1733, starting with the establishment of Savannah. The Spanish mission came to an end in 1742, when the English defeated a Spanish attempt to take Charles Town at the Battle of Bloody Marsh near present-day Brunswick, Georgia. Georgia was thereby firmly established as an English colony, and Roman Catholicism was outlawed there.

With the establishment of the United States in 1789, religious freedom came to Georgia, and within the year, a small number of Catholics left Maryland and settled in Georgia, where they sought economic opportunity. They established Locust Grove, the first Catholic settlement in Georgia, very near the site that later became the town of Washington, Georgia.

Archbishop John Carroll, a leading Patriot during the American Revolution, was the first American Catholic bishop. His see was Baltimore, Maryland, but he had responsibility for all the United States. Georgia's Catholics came under Bishop John England when, in 1820, a diocese based in Charleston, South Carolina, was established. Under his leadership, the Church of St. John the Baptist was completed in Savannah in the 1830s. Bishop England died in 1842, leaving a much stronger Catholic presence in the South.

A Georgia-based Catholic diocese was established in 1850; Savannah, with a growing number of Irish immigrants, was the see for its bishop. The Diocese of Savannah was huge, encompassing all of Georgia and the eastern part of Florida. The first bishop of the diocese, Francis Xavier Gartland, was consecrated in November 1850. Georgia covered 59,000 square miles in area and had a population of about one million people. Even so, Gartland oversaw only about 5,500 Catholics in Georgia and Florida combined. Five years later, under his leadership, in Georgia alone, there were 4,000 Catholics scattered throughout the state. Bishop Gartland died after tending to the ill during a yellow fever epidemic in 1854.

John Barry became the second bishop of the diocese in 1857. While pastor of the Catholic parish in Augusta, he had ministered to yellow fever victims in 1832 and 1839. After the 1839 epidemic, he turned his home into an orphanage. When he became the bishop of Savannah, he moved the orphanage to Savannah, where it became known as the Barry Male Orphan Asylum. Barry died in 1859 while on a fundraising trip in France.

These were the men who laid the groundwork for Bishop Verot, who assumed oversight of the Diocese of Savannah soon after the Civil War began. As related earlier, Verot had first come to Florida from Maryland with the honorary title of bishop of Danaba to serve as vicar apostolic over the Florida portion of the Diocese of Savannah. St. Augustine was his base of operations in Florida. On July 14, 1861, Pope Pius IX appointed him the third bishop of the Diocese of Savannah, with authority over Georgia as well as Florida. As bishop, in 1863 he established St. Patrick's, a second Catholic church in Savannah. It was in a remodeled cotton warehouse on the corner of West Broad and Liberty Street. Before and during the Civil War, Verot strongly defended the Southern cause, earning him the moniker, "Rebel Bishop." To the surprise and consternation of many white citizens of Savannah and St. Augustine, after the Civil War Verot became one of the strongest champions for the newly freed slaves.

In 1870, Florida was separated from the Diocese of Savannah to create a new diocese based in St. Augustine. Given the choice of the two jurisdictions, Verot chose Florida, and became the first bishop of the Diocese of St. Augustine, which encompassed all the state east of the Apalachicola River. The Diocese of Savannah came under the new leadership of Bishop Ignatius Persico. The story of the work of the Sisters of St. Joseph in Savannah and other parts of Georgia is the subject of this chapter. The sisters in Georgia took a somewhat different path from the one taken by the Sisters of St. Joseph in Florida.

In February 1867, five months after the first Sisters of St. Joseph from Le Puy, France, arrived in St. Augustine to begin teaching the freed slaves, Mother Sidonie Rascle sent five sisters from their house to begin working with the black people of Savannah. French sisters Julie Roussel, Joséphine Deleage, and Marie Joseph Cortial, as well as postulants Catherine Kennedy (an American soon to take her religious name of Sister St. John) and Ellen Ronin (soon to be known as Sister St. Paul) took up residence in a house at the corner of Perry and Floyd streets in downtown Savannah. Sister Julie, who had founded the house in Mandarin, Florida, near Jacksonville, reluctantly acted as the superior of the Savannah colony until Mother Hélène Gidon arrived from France in October to assume the post. The day after their arrival in Savannah, they started teaching basic academic subjects as well as Catholic catechism to fifty "colored" children, using a building behind St. John the Baptist Cathedral.

The sisters regularly reported to the Sisters of St. Joseph motherhouse in Le Puy, France, describing their work, but also giving their impressions of Savannah. In addition to St. Augustine's and Savannah's different historical roots, the physical and economic differences of the two cities could not have been greater. Sister Joséphine, writing from Savannah to the motherhouse in Le Puy, described Savannah as being a "very beautiful city where all that is wanted can be found, whereas St. Augustine is quite poor, nonetheless, I miss it now and then." Sister Julie gave more details about Savannah's physical appearance, commenting particularly about its wide streets and open squares, with trees that formed canopies over the walkways. Her one negative comment was about the many Protestant "temples" and how different they were from the Catholic cathedral. Such were some of the advantages and disadvantages of being in Savannah rather than in St. Augustine.[1]

By July 1867, the sisters had around 110 black children as students, whom they taught without charge. It was not long until they also taught 120 tuition-paying adults at night. The children's classes usually had anywhere from twenty to seventy students. Sister Joséphine taught small boys, while Sister Marie Joseph taught the little girls. The sisters dearly loved their pupils and became highly indignant when anyone criticized any of them, though they were frustrated over the lack of consistent class attendance. Although the sisters taught basic academic subjects, most of their letters back to Le Puy spoke enthusiastically of their work in religious instruction, especially when any of their many Protestant students showed real interest in Catholic practices. They were ever hopeful of making converts, but never forced the issue.

The letters of the sisters reveal their attitudes toward their charges after they had been teaching them for nearly a year and a half. Sister Joséphine wrote of her work with about sixty small black boys, "I have the boys' class. I like the work very much and I believe I am like a mother who thinks her children are handsome, even when they are rather ugly; mine, it is true, are not very pretty; however, I cannot get used to hearing them reviled and despised; I am angered by those who do so." After Sister Marie Joseph became very ill in 1867, she returned to the St. Augustine motherhouse, and Sister St. Pierre was sent to replace her in teaching the little black girls in Savannah. Sister St. Pierre wrote, "I am in charge of the little girls; they are 70 in number, but usually I have only 50 or 60. A few among them are very

1. Letter no. 48, Sister Joséphine Deleage, Savannah, to Mother Agathe, Le Puy, May 12, 1867, ASSJSA; Letter no. 53, Sister Julie Roussel, Savannah, to Mother Agathe, Le Puy, July 10, 1867, in McGoldrick, *Beyond the Call*, 144.

devilish, but very obedient for two or three minutes when I have scolded them well. Sister St. John comes sometimes to help me for half an hour in the morning."[2]

Earlier, when Verot announced to his parish in Savannah that the sisters would be arriving from St. Augustine to teach the blacks in Savannah, many in the congregation were horrified. By October 1868, however, the local paper expressed strong support for their work:

Bishop Verot procured several members of the society of the Sisters of St. Joseph, and the school has been conducted by them in the rear of the Cathedral of St. John the Baptist. It now numbers several hundred scholars, who improve rapidly under the admirable teaching of the Sisters. We are glad to see a movement of this kind in our midst, and would recommend that it be generally followed up by all church organizations, so that strangers [that is, Northerners] may not come here and gain an influence over our black population which will be neither for their good nor ours.[3]

A similar reversal of attitude was seen in St. Augustine.

During this early period, as in St. Augustine, the sisters were confronted with competition from Protestant missionaries from the American Missionary Association. Mother Hélèn Gidon commented in one of her letters, "There are white persons, who, through interest, also dedicate themselves to instructing the colored; they are, of course, Protestants, paid by the state, who do not withdraw from any sacrifice to assist them for their purpose." Speaking of the Protestant school in Savannah, she said,

The establishment is magnificent; I don't understand how we happen to have any Protestant children; what attracts them to us? Mother

---

2. Letter no. 12, Sr. M. Joséphine Deleage, Savannah, to Mother Agathe, Le Puy, June 13, 1868, ASSJSA; Letter no. 14, Sister St. Peter Borie, Savannah, to Sister Marie de Sales, Le Puy, June 20, 1868, ASSJSA.

3. *Savannah Morning News*, "Catholic Schools for the Blacks," October 13, 1868.

Sidonie will have described for you this type of school; just imagine, they [the Protestants] count up to 1100 children, while among our three schools we have only 150. There are in the city several private schools. Judge, then, the number of colored people there are in Savannah and the small number of Catholics![4]

Her sentiments were correct. The competition between the Protestants and the Catholics in Savannah at that time, indeed, was so lopsidedly in favor of the Protestants that correspondence from the missionaries to their American Missionary Association administrators in New York does not even mention the work of the Sisters of St. Joseph.

The following article seems to explain why the sisters had so few black students. The *Savannah Morning News* of February 16, 1870, included a report on private schools in Savannah, written by J. W. Alvord, general superintendent of education, and submitted to Maj. Gen. O. O. Howard, commissioner of the Freedman's Bureau, on January 14, 1870:

The Catholics have a school of about sixty pupils managed by the Bishop [Verot] and taught by the *St. Joseph Sisters, an order in France trained* expressly for African missions. By especial dispensation by the Pope a band of them have been sent here, and others to St. Augustine and Jacksonville, Fla.... After looking in at one of these schools, with very polite reception by the teacher, I called upon the acting bishop [Father J. Hamilton, who was the administrator during Bishop Verot's absence when he was at the Vatican Council in Rome]. The call was a pleasant one. He complained, however, that your officers had refused to their church the aid given under the law to the other parties.

I promised, on his invitation, to examine the school more thoroughly, and if found to be teaching the *elements* of an *English education* would report in favor of receiving such assistance. But knocking for admission the next morning, the teacher held the door partly open and positively forbade my entrance—said "the father (after my call)

4. Letter no. 3, Mother Hélèn Gidon, Savannah to Mother Agathe D., Le Puy, May 13, 1869, ASSJSA.

had ordered her not so to do." I was of course surprised, but parleyed pleasantly; told her that "the father" had invited me to "visit the school whenever I wished!" but in vain. She "presumed the permission had been reconsidered" and said that "the teachers were a priesthood," "took no proof," "were mainly teaching religion" &c., and reiterated her positive refusal to admit me. I could only express my regrets, and on leaving sent my official card to "Father Hamilton" with the message that I was very sorry not to be able to see the school; that our Government made no distinction in religious denominations, and that if the school could be *reported on our blanks*, it would have most cheerfully granted the usual bureau aid. On the back of the card I noted that I should be happy to see him at the Beach Institute [a large private school supported with Freedman's Bureau funds] at any time during the day, but he did not call. This bishop should not complain of you hereafter.[5]

The sisters were, indeed, giving religious instruction, but it is unclear as to whether the teaching of Catholic piety and theology took precedence over their teaching of standard academic subjects. It is likely that such was the case, given their lack of proficiency in speaking English during those early years in Savannah.

The awkwardness of this situation did not prevent the successful implementation five months later of Bishop Verot's plan to incorporate the Catholic schools into the Savannah public-school system, something he had been working toward for eight years. The plan's details were finally worked out by Father Hamilton while Verot was still in Europe. The "Savannah Plan," as it came to be known, was adopted by the Chatham County Board of Education on May 17, 1870. It essentially provided that the Catholic schools in Savannah would operate under the authority of the superintendent of the school system. The Catholic schools would operate just like any other public school, except for the following provisions: if possible, qualified teachers assigned to the Catholic schools would be Catholics; they would employ standard textbooks, except for history texts,

5. *Savannah Morning News*, February 16, 1870.

which would be those commonly used in Catholic schools; each day would begin with the reading of scripture, taken from a Bible chosen by the teacher (that is, not the Protestant King James version); the trustees of any Catholic building could withdraw it from the use of the board of education, provided they gave three months' notice; holidays would be those that were usually given in Catholic schools (e.g., Catholic feast days); and religion could be taught, but only separately from the regular curriculum and outside of regular school hours.[6]

In the midst of these transactions, on March 11, 1870, Pope Pius IX created the Diocese of St. Augustine, and shortly thereafter, Verot became the first bishop of St. Augustine. Under the circumstances, it is quite understandable that he left the details of the school plan to Father Hamilton. In October, Verot took up residency in St. Augustine as the new bishop and turned Savannah's Catholics and their schools over to the care of their new bishop, Ignatius Persico.

Savannah's Catholic public schools fared well under Verot's school plan, and by April 23, 1872, the *Savannah Morning News* reported on the school examinations for all the schools in town, including the private Massie School, the Cathedral School (Catholic), St. Patrick's School (Catholic), and a Colored School. As part of the school agreement, the Sisters of St. Joseph taught at the Cathedral School under their given names, rather than their religious names. At the close of the public examination ceremonies, officials congratulated the students and teachers for their successes, but most especially the public/Catholic alliance for providing education for all students. At the next year's closing examinations, one of the guests, a public educator, also praised the Savannah Plan, saying that the "system was proper, right and just," and noted how the number of students in the Savannah school system had grown from 400 scholars in 1866 to

6. Gannon, *Rebel Bishop*, 184–85.

2,500 in 1873, two to three years after the Catholics became part of the system.[7] The schools now uniformly taught subjects customary for an "English curriculum": arithmetic, recitation, calisthenics, dialogue, geography, spelling, and reading, as suited for each age group. The detailed report described the activities and examinations of each of the schools, reporting the number of scholars in each age group. The Cathedral School, located at the corner of Perry and Abercorn streets, included grammar, intermediate, and primary departments, and had a total of 338 pupils.

When Verot had recruited the Sisters of St. Joseph from Le Puy, he had emphasized the need for the freed slaves to receive ministry, but he had hoped that the Sisters of St. Joseph would also take care of Savannah's many orphans, black and white. In July 1867, as the sisters' schools in Savannah began growing in enrollment, Bishop Verot finally broached the idea of the sisters' expanding their work to include taking care of white boys, ages twelve and under, who had been orphaned during the Civil War. He asked Sister Julie Roussel if she thought the motherhouse in France would respond positively to such a proposal. Sister Julie told him no but said that they might think differently when it came to America. Verot acknowledged that large boys had been a problem for the Sisters of Charity in Savannah, and that they had had to abandon that ministry. Preadolescent boys, however, were a different matter.[8] Verot's request was not really out of the question, for the Sisters of St. Joseph from the days of their founding in the mid-seventeenth century had taken care of orphans in France. To his delight, the motherhouse in Le Puy supported the proposed work, and by the next year, the Sisters of St. Joseph in Savannah, besides

7. *Savannah Morning News*, "School Examinations—Massie and Cathedral Schools Examined by the Board of Examiners," April 23, 1872; and "Closing School Examinations—Persico Saying Farewell—Great Praise of the Public/Catholic School Arrangement," *Savannah Morning News*, April 25, 1873.

8. Letter no. 55, Sister Marie Julie Roussel, Savannah, to Our Rev. Mother [Le Puy], July 15, 1867, ASSJSA.

teaching, had taken on the administration of the Orphan Male Asylum. Verot purchased the Scarborough House, located on W. Broad Street, to serve as a convent and an orphanage. In 1869, the city council was so pleased with the sisters' work that it gave them a one-lot parcel of land to carry on that ministry.

In September 1867, the sisters were still waiting to begin their work with the orphans. Sister St. Pierre finally arrived at the end of the year from St. Augustine to take the place of Sister Marie Joseph, who was gravely ill and had returned to St. Augustine. On December 23, 1867, Sister Clémence also arrived in Savannah. Five days later, the two postulants received their habits as novices; Catherine Kennedy became Sister St. John [or St. Jean], and Helen Rouin became Sister St. Paul. With a full complement of sisters now in place, Bishop Verot announced that the Sisters of St. Joseph would be "entrusted with the care of the [white] orphan boys." The public response was good, and a collection of $600 was received to support the sisters' work. Their new assignment was something the local residents supported wholeheartedly, as compared to the prejudices they faced against their education work with the blacks. As explained by Mother Hélèn,

His Lordship [Verot] has had a fortuitous thought to place us in charge of the white orphan boys; it is the means of establishing good relations between us and many families who can do good for the Community [the Sisters of St. Joseph]. The inhabitants of the South in the United States have such a pronounced aversion for the colored people since the war [Civil War] that it seems, excepting persons of great Christianity, they cannot like people in charge of educating them [the blacks].[9]

The Sisters of St. Joseph in Savannah proceeded to assume the care of the thirty-eight young white boys. Their duties

9. Letter no. 1, Mother Hélèn Gidon, Savannah, to Rev. Mother, Le Puy, January 9, 1868, ASSJSA.

included taking care of the boys' clothing, grooming them, bathing the youngest, teaching them good manners and decorum, caring for the dormitories, and teaching classes. Sisters Clémence and St. Pierre carried out these tasks. Until they obtained a larger facility, the orphans went to the free Catholic School that was open to other children as well. The schoolmaster supervised them after class, seeing that the orphans studied for an hour. Sister Clémence oversaw their spiritual growth, making sure they said their morning and evening prayers.

Commenting in the same letter on the good effects of the sisters' efforts, Mother Hélèn proudly related to the motherhouse in France, "If you could just see how contented these poor children are to have the sisters to watch over them instead of the young careless man who amused himself with them and who slapped them roughly when he was in bad humor." Satisfaction with their efforts was widespread, including among the women patrons of the orphanage, who helped raise funds and made clothes for the boys.[10] Another letter written by Mother Hélèn on March 26, 1868, commented on the ever-growing reputation of the sisters' work: "The children are very well behaved, very respectful toward Sister [Clémence], who is a true mother for them. She is very busy with 40 children.... It is already noticed with pleasure that Sisters are in charge of their children. They are always clean and more polite. Here everyone is interested in an orphan and loves the persons who take care of them." She reported that "many persons who were quite opposed to our work [with the blacks] put aside their prejudices, and indifferent (persons) now show us some affection. Sister St. Pierre also reported on the success of the orphanage under Sister Clémence's leadership: "She is very contented with the boys. She loves them very much; she takes them to walk twice a week and on Sunday after Vespers almost

10. Letter no. 6, Mother Hélèn Gidon, Savannah, to Community in Yssingeaux, France, February 23, 1868, ASSJSA.

always. We go across town; everyone looks at us as though we were some curiosity; they [the boys] assemble as in Le Puy on Procession days.... Monseigneur wanted us to make the rounds of all the streets for the edification of the residents; we have never been able to achieve such a fine promenade as that."[11]

The work of the sisters with orphans by all accounts was a huge success, for the orphans and for the sisters, who as a result gained great esteem among Savannah's citizens. Mother Hélèn, however, enjoyed that success only briefly, dying from chest congestion, perhaps a heart attack, on December 3, 1869. Protestants as well as Catholics attended the High Mass that was held at St. Patrick's Church, and Sister Joséphine, who had been her assistant, took on the responsibilities of mother superior in Savannah.[12] Her assistant was Sister St. Pierre, and Sisters Clémence and St. John became her councilors.

The 1870 census shows that the St. Joseph's Orphan Asylum, as it was listed, was under the direction of Mother Joséphine, age forty; Sister St. Pierre, age thirty-two; Sister Clémence, age twenty-eight; Sister St. John, age twenty-five; Sister St. Paul, age twenty-two; and Sister St. Patrick, age twenty-five. Mother Joséphine and Sisters St. Pierre and Clémence were from France; Sister St. John, who had been among the first novices in St. Augustine, was from New York; and Sisters St. Paul and St. Patrick were from Ireland. The number of orphans had dropped from a range of thirty-eight to forty to only twenty-six. The boys ranged in age from four years to thirteen years, most of them born in Georgia.

The sisters had successfully undertaken their new work, but a much more profound change came the next year, when on March 1, 1870, Bishop Verot became the pontiff for the newly

11. Letter no. 9, Mother Gidon, Savannah, to Mother Agathe, March 26, 1868; Letter no. 14, Sr. St. Pierre Borie to Sr. Marie de Sales, Le Puy, June 20, 1868, ASSJSA.
12. Letter no. 28, Mother Joséphine, Savannah, to Rev. Mother, Le Puy, December 14, 1869, ASSJSA.

created Diocese of St. Augustine, with oversight of most of the state of Florida. The Diocese of Savannah then came under a new leader, an Italian cleric named Ignatius Persico. Verot, upon becoming the bishop of St. Augustine, no longer had any authority in the Diocese of Savannah. Writing from Rome, where he was when his new appointment was announced, Verot tried to comfort the Sisters of St. Joseph's superior in Le Puy: "The Sisters in Savannah will always be at least virtually under my jurisdiction. The bishop I have had named for Savannah [Persico] is a good man who will always be in agreement with me, and will always do whatever I ask him.[13] Mother Joséphine reported to Le Puy that although Persico did not visit them often, "he is all heart," and had told them, "My dear daughters, I am your bishop, your father, your friend, have confidence."[14] They retained their ties with Le Puy, but Bishop Persico acted swiftly in March 1871, administratively separating the Sisters of St. Joseph, who were now under his charge, from their former motherhouse in St. Augustine. He changed their official name to the Sisters of St. Joseph of Georgia. Although Sister Joséphine and the other sisters were under his authority, they still maintained close relationships with their beloved sisters in Florida.

By October of 1871, the Savannah sisters opened their own novitiate to take in new members. The work of the sisters in Georgia expanded, and in the spring of 1872, Bishop Persico bought a much-needed larger facility, the abandoned medical college building, for the sisters and orphans. The previously used Scarborough House had proved to be "unpleasantly located" and "very damp and unhealthy." Mother Joséphine described the new building: "I have just learned that there is going to be a very large building, only recently constructed for a 'Medical College,' put up for sale. The façade is 62 feet and the length, 66 feet. It

13. Verot to Madame le Supérieure, writing from Rome, May 2, 1870, ASSJLP.
14. Letter no. 11, Mother Joséphine to Rev. Mother Leocadie Broc, Le Puy, January 14, 1871, ASSJSA.

is four stories high. I went to see it immediately with good Father Lewis and Sister St. Peter. It will do for us perfectly. It will be put up for auction in three or four weeks and Monseigneur [Persico] intends to conclude the deal for us." Despite her high hopes, it was clear that the Sisters of St. Joseph in Savannah were struggling. Mother Joséphine reported that their community in Savannah had only five professed sisters, one of whom was a lay sister, and three novices. They "lived from day to day," and Bishop Persico was concerned about their financial situation. The situation was precarious.[15]

At this juncture, Bishop Persico, who was elderly and in poor health, stepped down and was replaced by a new prelate, William H. Gross, on April 27, 1873. The change added even more uncertainty to the sisters' future. Bishop Gross was a much younger and energetic man, one who was capable of ministering to the needs of the 20,000 Catholics in the Diocese of Savannah. He was also a decisive man, used to being in charge and being obeyed.

William Hickley Gross was born in Baltimore, Maryland, in 1837, and entered the Redemptorist Order in 1857. He completed his seminary training in Annapolis, Maryland, in March 1863, and served the wounded from both the North and the South during the Civil War. Gross was introduced to the Deep South after the war, when he participated in a series of missions in Georgia and Florida in 1868 at the request of Bishop Verot. Between January and April 13, 1868, he preached missions in Savannah, Augusta, Macon, Columbus, Atlanta, St. Augustine, and Jacksonville.[16]

15. Sisters of St. Joseph of Georgia Annals, hereafter cited as SSJGA Annals, October 1872, typescripts, no. 501.7, housed at the Archives of the Sisters of St. Joseph—Augusta Province, St. Louis, Mo., hereafter cited as CSJA; McGoldrick, *Beyond the Call*, 246–47; Letter no. 26, Mother Joséphine Deleage, Savannah, Georgia, to Father Superior, Le Puy, April 24, 1872, in McGoldrick, *Beyond the Call*, 246–47.

16. Gross's vivid letters telling of the missions are published in the *Redemptorist North American Historical Bulletin*, no. 20 (December 2003).

THE SISTERS OF ST. JOSEPH EXPAND INTO GEORGIA

These experiences as a missionary in Georgia prepared Gross to assume the prelacy of Savannah. The Catholics of Savannah welcomed him warmly, remembering his highly successful missions held in the city five years before. At the age of thirty-six, Gross was the youngest bishop in the United States at that time. Young and seemingly tireless, he created the *Southern Cross*, a newspaper to keep Catholics throughout his diocese informed about Catholic matters; he used funds raised by Bishop Persico to build a new Cathedral of St. John the Baptist in Savannah, to replace the one destroyed during the Civil War. He also founded Pio Nono College in Macon, a short-lived higher education institution that later became a secondary school.[17]

Gross made his first canonical visit to the sisters on August 17, 1873. He reappointed Sister Joséphine as the general superior and, according to the Annals, "expressed satisfaction at the state of affairs ... and assured the Sisters of his paternal affection and great desire to promote the interest and welfare of their Institution." Mother Joséphine wrote to their father superior in Le Puy to advise him of their transition to another new and dynamic bishop in Georgia: "Our personnel grows little by little. Soon, I hope it is at any rate the intention of [Bishop Gross] to found another house in Georgia. His Grace [gives] us the [honor?] of a visit to see us from time to time; but very briefly. His occupations are so multiple, [they] do not permit him to converse with us as long as we would like. Mgr. Gross justifies his name. He is equal to 144 Bishops." Perhaps Mother Joséphine meant "lives up to his name," for the word "gross" in French means big, large, great, or considerable. Although small in stature and youthful in appearance, Bishop Gross was, indeed, larger than life, for as Mother Joséphine continued, "He is all powerful, he obtains

17. *Savannah Republican*, May 3, 1873, quoted in *Freeman's Journal*, May 17, 1873; Rev. Andrew Skeabeck, CSSR, "Most Rev. William Gross: Missionary Bishop of the South; Georgia and Its Fifth Bishop, 1873–1875," *Records of the American Catholic Historical Society of Philadelphia* 66 (1956): 78–94.

all he wants. He has undertaken the construction of a new Cathedral [finishing the new St. John the Baptist]. One hopes to be able to say mass in a little [while?]. He also is getting ready to build a college [Pio Nono, in Macon, Georgia]; already the materials are gathered." Gross also began replacing some of the other religious personnel in Georgia. Sister Joséphine's final comment was, "Our bishop today is very popular, he pleases everyone. [He] is above all a distinguished preacher; he gives a great number of missions that produce a grand good." During this time, the sisters taught about forty colored girls, charging $2.00 a month for tuition, and started a small school for white boys under the age of twelve in the autumn of 1874, thus enabling the sisters to contribute to their own support and not to be a burden on the orphanage.[18]

As Mother Joséphine noted, Bishop Gross took control of his diocese, but little did she know what was in store for the Sisters of St. Joseph of Georgia. He made his second canonical visit in May 1875, and as the Annals succinctly record it, "made some changes." Gross demanded that the Sisters of St. Joseph sever their ties with the motherhouse in Le Puy, France, and that they be changed from being under pontifical right—that is, directly under the pope—to diocesan right under Gross's direct control as the bishop of the diocese. He gave the sisters twenty-four hours to accept these conditions or to leave his diocese. Such a demand was monumental and may have taken even Bishop Verot by surprise, but Gross had acted within his prerogative as the local ordinary and in accordance with the constitution of the Sisters of St. Joseph. Because Verot was no longer the bishop over the sisters, he could do nothing to prevent the change. He wrote the Congregation of the Propaganda about the turn of events:

18. SSJGA Annals, August 17, 1873, CSJA; no. 55, Mother Joséphine, Savannah, to Father Superior, Le Puy, April 5, 1874, ASSJSA; SSJGA Annals, Aug 1875, 10, CSJA.

When the diocese of St. Augustine was separated from the diocese of Savannah in 1870, there were Sisters of the Congregation of St. Joseph in both Savannah and St. Augustine whom I had brought over from France with the at least virtually expressed condition that they would retain their ties to the Superior General of the order in Le Puy. Bishop Gross does not understand this, and desires to have absolute jurisdiction over them. The Superior of the community in Savannah [Sister Joséphine Deleage] received an order last month from Bishop Gross to leave Savannah within 24 hours.[19]

Faced with Gross's ultimatum, Mother Joséphine Deleage resigned as the superior of the Sisters of St. Joseph of Georgia. She left Savannah and briefly returned to the Sisters of Joseph in St. Augustine, later becoming the superior of a new foundation in Palatka, Florida. Gross appointed Sister St. Pierre Borie to serve as superior pro-temp in Georgia until the remaining sisters in Savannah could officially elect a new mother superior. Sister Clémence Freycenon was chosen in an election in July 1875.[20] The Sisters of St. Joseph in Savannah at that point included six professed sisters, two lay sisters, and seven novices.

In 1875, Bishop Gross arranged for the Sisters of St. Joseph and the boys' orphanage to move from Savannah to Washington, Georgia, a small community west of Savannah, near Augusta. He felt that the rural atmosphere would be better for the boys than the city of Savannah had been. Meanwhile, he recruited other religious orders to take over the teaching duties in Savannah. Bishop Gross's plan was totally unexpected and traumatic for the Sisters of St. Joseph of Georgia. According to the Annals,

19. Verot to Secretary of the Congregation of Propaganda; letter draft written in Latin in the Archives of the Diocese of St. Augustine, n.d., as quoted in Gannon, *Rebel Bishop*, 135fn63. Verot misstated Bishop Gross's demand; Gross ordered the sisters to either accept the change to become a diocesan community or to leave the diocese within twenty-four hours. Bishop Verot died in June 1876. John Moore succeeded him in May 1877.

20. SSJGA Annals, May 1875, CSJA. No mention was made of the severing of ties with the Le Puy motherhouse.

The Convent was in a flourishing condition, and prosperity seemed to bless all undertakings. Like a thunderbolt came the summons to give up the comfortable abode and to begin the struggle and removal to another part of Georgia [from Savannah to Washington].... With sad hearts, but resigned to God's holy will the Sisters prepared to leave Savannah. Mother Clémence quietly made arrangements for the departure, there was no murmuring but with prayers for God's protection in their new home the Sisters left their dear convent.[21]

Washington, located in Wilkes County, Georgia, was founded in 1780 and bears the distinction of being the first town ever named after George Washington. This fact would cause confusion for the Sisters of St. Joseph nearly two hundred years later. Many of the current buildings in the downtown area of the town date from the 1870s, the same period in which the sisters arrived. One of the primary industries in Washington at that time was the processing, selling, and shipping of cotton. The town's residential buildings still reflect the wealth and prominence the community had prior to the Civil War; the path of Sherman's March to the Sea had bypassed it. The sisters arrived in 1876, at the end of the Reconstruction period. The downtown had grown from twenty-four to forty-eight businesses between 1860 and 1870, but a huge economic resurgence was still to come in the 1890s and early 1900s. Even so, Washington remains a small town. Its highest population to date was 4,662 in 1980; in 2020, the population had fallen to 4,134.

As in many prosperous antebellum communities, large plantation houses were located on the outskirts of Washington, especially on the east side of the downtown area. Former slaves settled primarily in three areas, one of which was along Whitehall Road, on land owned by Nicholas Wylie. He had bought the land from Jesse Mercer (1769–1841), one of the most prominent Baptist leaders in Georgia and the South in the nineteenth century.

21. SSJGA Annals, August 1910, 114, CSJA.

He was a pastor, philanthropist, publisher of Baptist newspapers, and one of the founders of Mercer University in Macon, Georgia. He also was a delegate at the Georgia constitutional convention in 1798 and wrote the section of the Georgia constitution that guaranteed religious liberty in the state. During Reconstruction, Wylie was an entrepreneur and sold land or rented houses to the freed blacks on land that had once been part of his extensive land holdings; 3,200 acres were in Wilkes County and 300 acres were in or adjacent to Washington. The area where the blacks settled became known as Wylieville, later as Freedmanville, Freedman, and most recently, Whitehall.[22] It was Nicholas Wylie's personal residence with outbuildings and some acreage that the Catholic diocese, under Bishop Gross's direction, purchased from the Wylie estate to establish the boys' orphanage in Washington.

The January 14, 1876, edition of the *Washington Gazette* reported to the residents of Washington, Georgia, what was happening in their community: "On last Wednesday four sisters of the order of St. Joseph arrived in our town." The presence of the sisters was big news for the community of approximately 2,000 residents, for more sisters and the young boys from the Orphan Male Asylum in Savannah were soon to follow.

Such an undertaking was somewhat of a gamble. Washington, like nearly all of Georgia's other communities, was decidedly Protestant, even though nearby Locust Grove had been established by early Catholic settlers and is considered the cradle of Georgia Catholicism. The initial step toward the relocation of the Savannah orphanage was taken when in 1873 Bishop Gross visited Washington as the guest at the home of General Robert Toombs. A former U.S. representative and senator and then the first secretary of state for the Confederacy and a brigadier general in the Confederate army, Toombs was widely revered by

22. National Register of Historic Places, Washington Historic District, Washington, Wilkes County, Ga., Reference no. 04001319, 20, 22, 29–35.

the citizens of Washington. They were "aghast" when "the grandest Georgian of them all" was "indifferent to criticism" about his hosting of such a visitor.[23] Because of Toombs's endorsement, however, Bishop Gross was accepted and then widely admired because of his charm and rhetoric in defense of Catholicism. Many of Washington's Protestants even started to visit services at the local Catholic church.

The second step was to employ the negotiating skills of Father James M. O'Brien, the Catholic priest who resided in Washington. He was ordained on January 6, 1874, the first priest ordained by Bishop Gross. Gross sent him to Washington, Georgia, where O'Brien was the priest for St. Patrick's Church and oversaw missions in fifteen counties. He was very popular and highly regarded by many Catholics as well as Protestants in Washington. Maguire described the situation: despite Gross's successful visit in 1873,

the prejudice [against Catholics], was still alive for when in 1876 Bishop Gross removed the Male Orphanage, under the charge of the Sisters of St. Joseph, from Savannah to Washington the purchase of a home had to be conducted with greatest diplomacy, else they could not have procured an inch of ground.... In taking charge of the orphans and the sisters, Fr. O'Brien had a duty at once difficult and delicate. For their coming was anything but agreeable to the non-Catholics of Washington, and great was the consternation when it was learned that they were to occupy the former residence of Jesse Mercer, the Father of the Baptist Church in Georgia and whose home had been used as a Baptist Seminary. Mercer University in the City of Macon is named for him.[24]

Newspaper records, however, show that land developer Nicholas Wylie had purchased the Mercer property in 1848 and

23. Nellie T. Maguire, "Catholicity in Washington, Ga.: The Beginning and Progress of Catholicity in Washington, Wilkes Co., Georgia," *American Catholic Historical Researches* 11, no. 1 (January 1894): 24.
24. "Father O'Brien Has Passed Away," *Atlanta Constitution*, May 12, 1900, 7; Maguire, "Catholicity in Washington, Georgia," 25–26.

tore down or removed the Mercer House to build his own mansion there. The Catholic purchase was, indeed, of the former Mercer property, but the house on it was that of Nicholas Wylie. This was confirmed by comparing a photograph of the Wylie House with a photograph of the sisters' orphanage. Both photos show the same entrance with colossal columns. Sanborn maps further confirm the presence of the columns and the transformation of the building as the sisters expanded it with additions over the years.[25]

The diocese's purchase included fifty acres and a two-story house with eight rooms, another two-story building, and two one-and-a-half-story buildings. Besides the orphanage proper, there would be a school for the orphans, as well as another separate school for other children of the community. The education of the orphans would include standard academic subjects as well as vocational training in basic trades, including farming on the extensive acreage. Seventeen Sisters of St. Joseph would support the asylum under Fr. O'Brien's direction.[26]

Bishop Gross was very pleased to see his plans for the move of the orphanage from Savannah to Washington falling into place. Most accounts mention his belief that the fresh country air and additional space would be good for the boys, but one account gives an underlying reason for the move. Gross needed the old medical college building where the orphans were cared for, to give it to the Sisters of Mercy "in payment for some ground adjoining the Cathedral." The new cathedral was one of his

25. Eliza A. Bowen, *The Story of Wilkes Co., Georgia: Collection of Articles by Miss Eliza A. Bowen of Wilkes County Who Wrote Stories of Wilkes County People and Published Her Articles in the Washington (Georgia) Gazette and Chronicle from 1886–1897* (Marietta, Ga.: Continental Book, 1950), 115; Robert Marion Willingham, *Washington, Georgia* (Charleston, S.C.: Arcadia, 2000); "Two Model Schools: The Catholic Girls' Academy in Washington; The Orphanage and Its School—A Stroll over the Grounds and Building—A Remarkable Business Success," *Atlanta Constitution*, June 30, 1889, 12; Sanborn Maps, Washington, Ga., 1890, 1896, 1903, 1909, and 1917.

26. *Dedication of Saint Joseph's Home, May 30, 1932, and Brief Sketch of St. Joseph's Male Orphanage, Washington, Wilkes County, Georgia* (n.p., n.p.), 2.

major projects.[27] Father O'Brien purchased the Wylie property in time for the sisters' and boys' arrival in January 1876. Their arrival in Washington from Savannah was reminiscent of the situation faced by the first Sisters of St. Joseph who arrived in St. Augustine from Le Puy in 1866; they, too, were not expected at that time.

When Mother Clémence and Sisters St. John, Aloysius, and Scholastica arrived in Washington, they located the old Wylie House and found it to be cold and empty except for two wooden benches, and there was no sign of anyone to meet them. There was no food except for the leftovers of their previous day's lunch. They found out later that the sisters' letter notifying the local Catholics of their intended arrival had been misdirected to Washington, D.C. The situation was quickly remedied, though, once Washington's Catholic community learned they were there. A young girl who was among the parishioners from St. Patrick's Church who came to help recalled, "When we reached the old Wiley House, which had been purchased for them [the sisters], we found the four black-robed figures seated on an upturned box, gazing in dismay at the bare walls and empty rooms."[28] Their despair was soon lifted, as under Father O'Brien's direction, the buildings were made livable within two weeks, ready for the arrival of fifty to sixty boys and thirteen other sisters. The convent part of the buildings was also to serve as a mother-house for the Sisters of St. Joseph of Georgia.

Bishop Gross did not make his first canonical visit to the Sisters of St. Joseph of Georgia in Washington until June 1877, about a year-and-a-half after their arrival there. Letters he wrote

27. "The Work of the Sisters of St. Joseph in Washington, Georgia," in Sisters of St. Joseph of Georgia typescript V [p. 1], CSJA; see mention of Gross's plans for the cathedral, in Letter no. 55, Mother Joséphine, Savannah, to Father Superior, Le Puy, April 5, 1874, ASSJSA. The move to Washington was in January 1876, so the Savannah yellow fever epidemic in July–August of that year was not an immediate impetus for their move, as some have suggested.

28. *Souvenir of the Silver Jubilee, 1876–1901* (Washington, Ga.: St. Joseph's Academy, 1901), 4, 9; held in the Mary Willis Library, Washington, Ga.

to Reverend Mother Mary Louise at the Carmelite Convent in Baltimore, his confidant, reveal much about his attitudes toward his work. Writing from Washington, he described the long hours he had spent ministering to Protestant and Catholic alike, in various parts of Georgia, only to be hit with a barrage of requests when he arrived in Washington for a respite. He wrote:

Pretty well worn out by this long and heavy work, I came to this beautiful little town, fully determined to enjoy a rest—and to endear [endure] or to answer the huge pile of letters which had accumulated. I have here the orphanage under charge of the Sisters of St. Joseph. Their house is beautifully situated. No sooner had I arrived, than the priest informed me of the large number expecting confirmation—and of course his Lordship would on the occasion make a few remarks—a sermon three quarters of an hour long! Then the people begged to have a word or so from their beloved Bishop—which meant a sermon nearly every evening. Then the Sisters had not seen their dear Bishop for a year and each one wanted to have a little talk with the beloved Bishop for only five minutes—and you know how long are ladies' five minutes! Besides all that, each wished also to go to confession to Monseigneur—And then how could the Bishop leave them without giving at least one or two conferences: accordingly I am booked for a conference to-day—and, to-morrow—Last night I gave a lecture for the benefit of the orphans! This is rather a peculiar way of taking a rest! But these religieuses are very pious and good, and I don't like to refuse a favor when I can do it.[29]

In Washington, the orphanage's daily routines continued as they had in Savannah, and continued for decades. Father O'Brien's annual reports, including full financial records, were published in the Atlanta newspapers. One example, "Feeding the Orphan," comes from the *Atlanta Constitution* of March 12, 1888. The report provides a good overview of life at the institution.

29. William H. Gross, bishop of Savannah, Washington, Wilkes Co., Ga., to Rev. Mother, Carmelite Convent, Baltimore, Md., June 27, 1877, Bishop Gross Letters, Record Group X (ten) Biddle Street, series 2, box 2, folders 1–8, film M 9571, SCM 9571, on file in the Maryland State Archives.

Examinations of students were a common public event at this time, and the orphan scholars showed their academic prowess along with their counterparts in the sisters' private schools. O'Brien observed that the quality of learning institutions can be judged by their examinations and declared, "Taking the examinations as a criterion they will necessarily conclude that the schools provided for the orphan boys are equal, if not superior to many provided for more favored children." He also commented, "A sense of duty compels me to state in behalf of the self-sacrificing Sisters of St. Joseph, who have the management of domestic affairs, that they spare no pains or labor to make the orphanage a home in the true sense of the word for the poor boys committed to their care, and if they do not grow up to be good Christian men and useful citizens it will not be the fault of the devoted sisters." The 1880 census record lists Sr. St. Pierre as the director of the orphanage, which housed thirteen boys at that time; the 1910 census lists Mother Clémence as the director, when there were forty-six boys housed at the orphanage.

In addition to their daily care for the boys, the sisters also obtained support for the orphanage through various fundraisers, such as a cotton raffle, and received private donations, even from non-Catholics. A group of women that O'Brien referred to as the "lady collectors" also gathered donations that augmented the support received from the diocese. With the move to Washington, another source of support was the production of the boys' sixty-four-acre farm, which yielded cotton, milk, butter, eggs, and vegetables.

In 1888, ninety-four boys lived in the orphanage in Washington. Boys came from all over Georgia, but mostly from Savannah, Atlanta, and Augusta. Twenty-four boys were able to return to their families or were placed with adoptive parents, leaving seventy at the orphanage. Over the next several decades, the orphan population averaged about fifty boys.

Once the orphanage was firmly established, the sisters sought to start a boarding–day school for girls, and on October 15, 1876, enough funds were raised by the sisters from friends in the North to purchase a nearby two-story house, "the Old Randolph Place," to open the doors of St. Joseph's Academy for Young Ladies. The school for girls ages ten to eighteen at first had only one boarder, Lizzie Briody of Savannah; three more came within the first year. This was the first institution started by the Sisters of St. Joseph as their own property, not of their diocese.[30] The academy continued to grow rapidly, despite competition from the already existing secular Washington Female Seminary.

An advertisement for the academy appeared in many regional newspapers. The ad in the September 27, 1877, issue of the *Washington Gazette* described the school as being in the suburbs of Washington and devoted to the moral and intellectual improvement of young ladies. A school year had two five-month sessions, a fall term from the first Monday in September and a spring term beginning on the first Monday in February. The curriculum was quite broad, typical of a nineteenth-century finishing school. It included orthography, reading, writing, grammar, rhetoric, composition, history, natural philosophy, geography, botany, arithmetic, algebra, geometry, French and Latin, piano and organ, drawing, and watercolor painting. Skills expected of well-bred women of the time were also taught; fancy work, embroidery, wax flowers, lacemaking, and plain and fancy needlework were taught to the boarders at no extra charge. By 1878, the sisters had to add wings to the building, and the State of Georgia granted the academy a charter; it was Georgia's first Catholic female institution. Mother St. John Kennedy (the former novice Catherine Kennedy) was the superior, and Sisters Clémence, Aloysius, and Mary Rose taught at the school, supported by tuition fees.

30. SSJGA Annals, October 1876, CSJA.

As St. Joseph's Academy progressed, Fr. O'Brien saw the need for strong religious education for the children of the parish in Sharon, Georgia, a small community about thirteen miles south-southwest from Washington. With Bishop Gross's permission, Fr. O'Brien asked Sister Clémence, who was then the general superior of the Sisters of St. Joseph of Georgia, to send sisters to open a school to teach the children of the parish for the approximately two hundred Catholics in Sharon. On January 29, 1878, Sister François (Francis) Burke and three other sisters arrived in Sharon and settled into a sparsely furnished, four-room house that had been found for them by a Mr. O'Keefe and Father O'Brien. The sisters started teaching at the local parish school almost immediately.

In November of that year, Bishop Gross gave the sisters permission to build a convent and a boarding school for the boys in Sharon; girls were to be taught as day students. The sisters started two sodalities for girls, one for the older girls and another for the younger ones. Before the end of 1878, a Sharon resident, Edward Croke, donated five acres for the construction of a boarding school. Sister Francis, the superior, and Sisters Scholastica Scott and William Anna Hogan began the school. Mother Clémence was the superior of the school when the building was completed in 1880. Sacred Heart Seminary for Young Boys opened with fifteen students, but from 1900 to 1910 it averaged a student body of sixty to seventy boys. In 1919, there were seventy-five boarders, including boys from other Georgia communities and states in the Southeast. The superior in 1909 had renovated the second-floor convent area, adding steam heat and providing individual rooms for the sisters. One of the favorite annual events for the entire St. Joseph community in Georgia was a baseball game between the boys of the orphanage and the boys of Sacred Heart Seminary. The event usually took place in Sharon, with plenty of cheering by the girls from the academy in

Sisters of St. Joseph of Georgia, St. Joseph's Academy for Young Ladies, Washington, Georgia, late 1890s. Mother St. John Kennedy is number 1 and Sister St. Peter Borie is number 5.

Courtesy of the Archives of the Sisters of St. Joseph of Carondelet, St. Louis Province, St. Louis, Missouri.

Washington and by the sisters as they pulled for "their" respective boys from either the orphanage or the seminary. The St. Joseph's Academy for Young Ladies continued to prosper in the following years. The young women students assisted the sisters in their work with the orphans and among Washington's black and poor white citizens.[31]

Despite the traumatic changes that Bishop Gross initiated among the Sisters of St. Joseph when he became their bishop in 1873, his plans worked out well, and he was liked by the sisters during his tenure over them. The Annals expressed how much Gross would be missed when he was appointed to another post. In January 1885, the sisters in Washington received a telegram from him "announcing his appointment to the archbishopric of Oregon City. This of course threw a gloom over the whole

31. "The Work of the Sisters in Sharon, Georgia," first typescript [pages 1–3]; and "Sacred Heart Seminary, Sharon, Georgia, 1878–1946, Second Account" [pages 1–3], in Georgia Sisters of St. Joseph VII, typescripts, CSJA; *Souvenir of the Silver Jubilee*, 7.

Community for their bishop had grown very near and dear to all the inmates of the Orphanage, Academy, and Convent in Sharon." He stopped in Washington for a visit with the sisters in December 1889 on his return from a trip to Rome. He was warmly received, and festivities were held in his honor. As Gross left to return to Oregon, the sisters were "bidding adieu to a true and valued friend."[32] As the prelate of the Diocese of Savannah, he had been very concerned about the broad scope of concerns in his diocese and saw difficult relocations of sisters and institutions as a necessary part of accomplishing his goals in Georgia as a whole. Bishop Gross died in Baltimore, Maryland, on November 14, 1898, at age sixty-one.

Bishop Thomas A. Becker, the prelate of the Diocese of Wilmington, Delaware, succeeded Gross; he was consecrated the sixth bishop of Savannah on March 26, 1886. Becker was born in Pittsburgh, Pennsylvania, the son of strict Presbyterian parents, but converted to Catholicism while a student at the University of Virginia. He studied at the College of Propaganda Fide in Rome and was ordained there on July 18, 1859. After serving in several positions, he was appointed secretary to Archbishop Martin J. Spalding of Baltimore. As he was serving as a parish priest in Richmond and conducting a boys' school there, Pope Pius IX appointed him the first bishop of the Diocese of Wilmington, Delaware, on March 3, 1868, at the age of thirty-six, and on August 16 he was consecrated. He was a scholar: he wrote articles in the *American Catholic Quarterly Review* in support of the establishment of a Catholic university in the United States and was one of the founders of the Catholic University of America, which opened in Washington, D.C., in 1889. Bishop Becker died at the orphanage in Washington, Georgia, on July 28, 1899.[33]

St. Joseph Academy for Young Ladies had gained an excel-

32. SSJGA Annals, 34, 43, CSJA.
33. BeVard, *One Faith, One Family*, 93–95.

lent reputation in the Southeast. Perhaps one of its most prominent students was Agnes Watson, a girl from Thomson, Georgia, who attended St. Joseph's briefly in 1899 and 1900. She was notable not for herself but for her father, who was none other than Tom Watson, who spread anti-Catholicism across the South through his publications, *Watson's Magazine* and the *Jeffersonian Magazine*. In 1920, the sisters received a letter inquiring if it was true that Tom Watson sent his daughter to a Roman Catholic school. Sister Sacred Heart replied:

Mother Aloysius wishes me to answer your letter as I was in Washington, Georgia, when Agnes Watson attended our school. She entered the fall term of 1899, and I think to March or April, 1900, then she withdrew on account of illness.

When Agnes married Mr. Lee, a widower with two small boys, she sent the children to our boarding school in Sharon, Ga. Last year two of Mr. Tom Watson's nephews were at the same school, Sacred Heart Seminary.

Agnes was ever devoted to the Sisters, sending loving messages to the year of her death; we in turn had remembrances of her.

Our relations with Mr. Watson were limited to business letters and nothing unpleasant resulted from the correspondence.

We sincerely regret the stand he has taken and do not believe he expresses his true views as regards our Church and clergy.

We pray for him daily and know if we were in need he would not be found wanting. His affection for his daughter would weigh much in considering her teachers.[34]

Tom Watson would not have considered his behavior in sending his daughter to a convent school to be contradictory. The anti-Catholic section of each issue of *Watson's Magazine* included this header on the editorial page:

34. Letter from Sister Sacred Heart, Mount Saint Joseph, Augusta, Ga., to Mr. James Farrell, September 1920, printed in the *Tablet*, April 21, 1928. The *Tablet* was a Catholic weekly newspaper published by the Tablet Publishing Co. of the Diocese of Brooklyn, beginning in 1908; clipping on file at CSJA.

For the individual Roman Catholic who finds happiness in his faith, I have no word of unkindness. Some of my best friends are devout believers in their "Holy Father." If anything contained in these chapters dealing with the hierarchy causes them pain, and alienates their good will, I will deplore it.

The Roman Catholic ORGANIZATION is the object of my profoundest detestation—NOT the belief of THE INDIVIDUAL.[35]

The Sisters of St. Joseph, no matter where they were based, were eager to pursue a new ministry as soon as their current one began to bear fruit. In 1886, Bishop Becker gave the sisters permission to open a mission in Atlanta, a city where there were relatively few Catholics. They rented a house on Capitol Avenue for the establishment of a school for boys in 1894 to complement the work of the Sisters of Mercy, who had already established a girls' school in the growing city. Fifty boys began classes on October 1 in the rented building in the first year, with the help of Father Benjamin J. Keiley, the pastor of the Immaculate Conception Parish in Atlanta. Sister de Sales was principal and the superior of the convent, Sister Patricia was the housekeeper, and Sisters Regis, Clare, and Ignatius were the teachers. The next year Mother Clémence, who was provincial superior of the Sisters of St. Joseph of Georgia at the time, bought property on Pryor Street, and the sisters built a new school known as Loretto Academy, an elementary school. It opened on September 8, 1895.[36]

The sisters' institutions were thriving, but as the decades passed, so did the sisters who had been part of the original contingent sent from St. Augustine to serve in Savannah in 1867. Sister St. Pierre Borie, called Sister St. Peter by the students, died at age fifty-nine on May 26, 1896. She served thirty years as a religious, suffering from poor health much of the time. According to her lengthy obituary in the Annals of the Sisters of

35. *Watson's Magazine*, July–December 1910; Google digitized version online, original at University of Virginia.
36. [Nellie Maguire], typescript, "Sisters of St. Joseph of Georgia," 22, CSJA.

St. Joseph of Georgia, she "devoted herself to the care of the poor and sick, especially to the needs of the poor colored people." This was in keeping with her call when, as a novice, she had come to serve the newly freed slaves in St. Augustine in 1866. After working among the blacks in the Ancient City, she was among the initial group sent by Mother Sidonie Rascle to help the mission in Savannah. She worked in the boys' orphanage in Savannah and moved to Washington, Georgia, when Bishop Gross relocated the orphanage there.

Because of her health problems, Sister St. Pierre transferred to St. Joseph's Academy, where she was on the faculty. A former student during the Silver Jubilee celebration for the academy in 1901 fondly reminisced, "I remember how we used to tease dear old Sister St. Peter to take us to the woods—which looked so cool tempting away in the distance, but her invariable answer [in her strong French accent] was, 'No, no de snake will bit you, and den I will have de remorse on conscience,'" and "Dear old Sister St. Peter, how many souls there were awaiting her in Heaven— souls that she had snatched from death by her unwearied charity." According to the Annals, she also began

visitations to the poor and the sick, making her name a household word. To the needy colored people she was an Angel of Mercy, being untiring in her efforts to aid them in every way.... In her charity she was solicitous for the welfare of the soul as well as the body. A memoranda found after her death showed she had baptized over one hundred fifty persons [primarily newborn babies]. She possessed a charming child-like manner that endeared her to the poor and won their confidence, and in the death of St. Peter all felt that a true friend had departed.

Father O'Brien performed her funeral services, "a touching tribute to her memory being the throng of colored people who sadly sought to show their affections, by going to her last resting place."[37]

37. SSJGA Annals, 56–57, CSJA.

Less than three years later, Mother St. John Kennedy died on March 11, 1899, after a painful five months of suffering. As described in the convent's annals, she had a "slight stroke of paralysis then a complication of diseases set and life became a weary martyrdom." She was not one of the initial group of sisters who came from France in 1866 but was closely tied to them. In secular life she was known as Katherine "Kate" Kennedy. She was born in Oswego, New York, on September 24, 1844, and at age twenty-two became one of the first postulants with the Sisters of St. Joseph in St. Augustine. Mother Sidonie sent her, as a novice named Sister St. John, to assist with the mission in Savannah in 1867. She taught in the school for little black boys and visited the sick and the needy. Bishop Gross appointed her the mistress of novices because, as an American, she could communicate easily in English.

In January 1877, Mother Clémence Freycenon, due to health concerns, resigned as the general superior of the Sisters of St. Joseph of Georgia, and Sister St. John was elected to the position on January 21. She was reelected every three years by the sisters and served as the general superior until 1894. The federal census records of 1880 show that Mother St. John was also the superior of St. Joseph's Academy for Young Ladies, assisted by seven teaching sisters. There were eighteen boarders as well as day students. Over the next decade, the students in the census record numbered thirty-three students, taught by seventeen sisters, one of whom was Mother Clémence.[38] Mother St. John was beloved by the students of St. Joseph's Academy, known for being caring, kind, and gentle. In 1895, she became the superior at Sacred Heart Seminary in Sharon and remained at that post until her death.

Father James M. O'Brien played an essential role in the

38. U.S. Federal Census Population Schedules for Georgia, 1880 and 1900. The 1900 census taker misidentified the Sisters as being Sisters of Charity.

successes of the Sisters of St. Joseph of Georgia. He enjoyed the absolute confidence of Bishop Gross and was entrusted with the administration of the orphanage in Washington; he was also a strong support for the sisters' other institutions in various places in Georgia. He was devoted to the orphans, earning him the moniker, "the friend of the orphan in Georgia." O'Brien was assigned to whatever tasks in the diocese that called for Bishop Gross's confidence, but he always returned to Washington. Suffering from an abscess on his kidney, he was sent to Johns Hopkins Hospital in Baltimore, where he died on May 11, 1900. He lay in state at the Church of the Immaculate Conception in Atlanta. His body was returned then to Washington, Georgia, for his desire was to be "buried with his people." Both Catholics and non-Catholics mourned his loss.[39]

Mother Clémence Freceynon died from a heart attack at the age of sixty-nine, on August 5, 1910, while serving as the superior of St. Joseph's Orphanage in Washington. Like Sister St. Pierre, Clémence had come to America as a novice from Le Puy, France, to establish the original Sisters of St. Joseph of St. Augustine community. Mother Sidonie included her in the group that she sent to Savannah. When Mother Joséphine resigned as the general superior of the Sisters of St. Joseph of Georgia and returned to St. Augustine, Bishop Gross appointed Sister St. Pierre to be the general superior until one could be elected by the community. The election occurred in 1875, and Sister Clémence was chosen and served for about a year-and-a-half of the three-year term, stepping down because of ill health. Sister St. John took her place in May 1877. Within three years, Clémence began serving in administrative roles again. She was appointed to be the superior of Sacred Heart Seminary in Sharon from 1880 to 1894, and again was elected to be the general superior

39. SSJGA Annals, May 1900; "Father O'Brien Has Passed Away," *Atlanta Constitution*, May 12, 1900, 7.

in Washington from 1894 to 1897, and then again in 1903. At the end of that term, in 1906, she became the superior of the Orphanage in Washington, the post she was holding when she died.

Sister Clémence came to America to minister to the "dear blacks," but most of her ministrations were to young white boys, either orphans or students. The last focus of her work in Georgia had been at the orphanage. According to her obituary in the *Washington Reporter*, under her care, the boys' home had "grown from an eight room house and a few orphan boys to a large and splendidly equipped Orphanage that is caring for a hundred unfortunate boys. Mother Clémence had planned for an even longer future for this institution and at the time she was called away, the contractor was erecting a $20,000 addition which has prospered and widened in its scope under her administration."[40] Mother Clémence had been sick only two days before she died, but those writing the Annals said that she seemed to know death was coming and was well prepared. Further commenting, they said, "She had seen the Community grow from a mere colony of four or five … to a sisterhood of over fifty. All looked upon her as a Mother in her 70th year, 45th in religion." By another account, "Mother Clémence had always prayed that her final confession would be uttered in her native French. Her prayer was answered. A French Jesuit, giving a mission near Washington, was present when the great woman died." The death of Mother Clémence, the last of the original French sisters from Le Puy in Georgia to die, seems to have been a harbinger of the decades to come, the beginning of the end for the Sisters of St. Joseph of Georgia.

Disaster struck St. Joseph's Academy in Washington when a fire was discovered in the middle of the night on November 20,

40. "Mother Clemence Dies Suddenly," *Washington Reporter*, August 12, 1910, n.p.; microfilm at the Mary Willis Library, Washington, Ga.; SSJGA Annals, 116–17, CSJA; Msgr. Noel C. Burtenshaw, ed., *Georgia Bulletin*, Atlanta, "History of the Sisters of St. Joseph of Georgia," in *Southern Cross*, December 6, 1984, 7.

1912. At 3:30 in the morning, a sixteen-year-old student awoke to the smell of smoke and roused the sisters. They rang the fire alarm and went down the corridors, groping through smoke to get the girls out of the building and into the cold night air. Unlike the older girls and sisters on the second floor, the younger students on the third floor had time to take some of their personal items. The sisters' quarters on the second floor were destroyed. Mother Aloysius, the superior of the academy, was not there at the time, as she was on her way from Sharon, Georgia, to Atlanta. The people of Washington rushed to help. Most of the fifty-four boarders who were from Georgia went to their own homes, and out-of-state girls stayed in Washington with citizens who opened their homes to them. One bright spot was that the orphanage was not damaged. No mention was made about accommodations for the five displaced sisters, but it is likely that they moved into the orphanage.

The main building of the academy and a recently built stone chapel and auditorium were damaged. The library books, some furniture, and all school records were saved, but less than half of the loss was covered by insurance. The sisters sent out an appeal:

To the alumnae, patrons and many friends of St. Joseph's Academy, Washington, Ga. Early Tuesday morning, November 20, our school was entirely destroyed by fire. The labor of 36 years at an investment of $200,000, with an insurance of $30,000 represents our work. The clothing etc. of the sisters is a total loss. In our great need we call upon our friends for assistance. Any a mount however small, gratefully received and acknowledged.[41]

After the death of Bishop Becker in 1899, Father Benjamin J. Keiley, a protégé of Bishop Becker, became the seventh bishop of Savannah on June 3, 1900. At Becker's request, Rome had allowed Keiley to follow Bishop Becker to Georgia, where he

---

41. *Augusta Herald*, November 25, 1912, 2.

appointed Keiley the pastor of Immaculate Conception Church in Atlanta, vicar general of the diocese in 1886, and rector of the Cathedral of St. John the Baptist in 1896.

Bishop Keiley evaluated the sisters' situation after the fire, hoping they would be able to replace the destroyed buildings with support from the people of Washington. The townspeople fervently hoped to keep the academy in Washington because it was an important aspect of the town's economy, but officials in Atlanta and Augusta both made strong pitches for its relocation to their communities. Augusta's offer was too much to compete with, and on December 5, 1912, the *Washington Gazette*'s headlines read, "Washington Loses St. Joseph Academy / Augusta Wins in Spirited Three-Cornered Contest. Orphanage to Remain, May be Enlarged." By mid-December, businessmen in Augusta had already begun collecting funds toward the $15,000 needed to close the deal. The *Augusta Herald* reported, "The bishop of Savannah and the Sisters of St. Joseph, under whose direction the college [academy?] is run will be to Augusta Wednesday to settle the details of the establishment of the school here. One of the important matters is selecting a temporary home for the school, which is to open in Augusta after the holidays." By December, the sisters and eighteen high school girls were living with the sisters in Dickey Cottage on Monte Sano Avenue. Some of the girls were members of the graduating class of 1913.

Work progressed on the construction of a new building for the academy at 2426 Wrightsboro Road, but "On December 13, 1913, the news came of the failure of the Irish American Bank in which were part of our borrowed fund. This was the greatest blow coming as it did through trusted friends." Because great progress had already been made on the construction, there was no alternative but to borrow more money to complete the building; the St. Louis Mercantile Co. lent them another $37,000. According to the Annals, "The Sisters were crushed under the immensity of the debt, but hoped Our Lord would come to our relief." After nearly thirty-seven years in Washington, on June 1, the sisters took possession of the academy under its new name, Mount Saint Joseph. The new convent established in Augusta became the motherhouse of the Sisters of St. Joseph of Georgia. The orphanage (now called St. Joseph's Home), its boys, and its sisters remained in Washington. Mount Saint Joseph Girls' Academy in Augusta opened in the new building with thirty-five boarders and fifty day pupils on September 9, 1915.[42]

The sisters' financial situation remained dire, and two years later, a letter from Festus Wade, the president of the mortgage company that held title to the property, related to Mother Agnes Gonzaga, CSJ, that Mother Alphonse and Sister of the Sacred Heart of the Sisters of St. Joseph in Augusta had visited him that morning in St. Louis. They owed his company between $175,000 and $180,000. The sisters continued to run the Sacred Heart parish school in Savannah (to which they returned in 1916) and the St. Anthony parish school established in 1918 in Atlanta. Their plan had been to mortgage the other properties they owned, their flagship institutions of Sacred Heart Seminary for boys in Sharon and the Loretto School for boys in Atlanta, to obtain a loan from the Mercantile Trust to pay for the new convent/school. Wade told Rev. Mother Agnes, "We are about to take over the Properties; in fact, it has all been agreed between us that we will take possession and rent to them [the sisters] temporarily until some plan can be worked out to sell it [the property] or otherwise dispose of it. I have suggested to them that they talk to you with the idea of amalgamating with your community [Carondelet Sisters of St. Joseph]."[43]

On September 30, 1915, Mother Alphonse at Mount St.

---

42. SSJGA Annals, 129–30, CSJA; Sr. Laura Ann Grady, CSJ, "A History of Mount St. Joseph," *Marianite* 12, no. 10 (October 2013): 5.

43. Festus J. Wade, president, Mercantile Trust Company, St. Louis, to Rev. Mother Agnes Gonzaga, CSJ, St. Louis, September 11, 1915, CSJA.

Joseph wrote to Mother Agnes in St. Louis, saying that their bishop supported their becoming part of the Carondelet Sisters of St. Joseph. The problem was their terrible financial condition. She wrote, "We are ready to resign all rights to our present convent to the St. Louis Mercantile Co. They will lose nothing and we will be free of debt," adding, "The St. Louis Mercantile Co. seems loath to dispossess us."[44] Indeed, correspondence with the company shows that the creditors diligently tried to suggest financial solutions to keep the sisters solvent. Mother Agnes wrote to Mother Alphonse about a week later, expressing her sympathy for the Georgia sisters' situation:

[The Lord] has pressed the cross heavily upon the shoulders of your community. Do not lose heart. I can say nothing definite to you now but will soon—I know this that your good community is one of the fervent, well organized ones which it would be a pleasure for Carondelet to fold in its motherly arms and I hope that may come.... Meanwhile, we'll all pray and pray, and pray.... No words can tell how sorry we are but Courage!—the darkest hour precedes the dawn—"[45]

That same day, Mother Agnes also wrote Wade a message that revealed her concerns: "I have no objection whatever to the amalgamation but it may be quite out the question for us to assume the debt."[46] The sisters in St. Louis had debts of their own resulting from rain damages to their property.

Archbishop John Glennon, the archbishop of the Diocese of St. Louis from 1903 to 1946, advised Mother Agnes Gonzaga to at least go look at the Sisters of St. Joseph's property in Augusta, saying there was no rush, given that the Mercantile Company was allowing them to rent quarters from them. He

44. Sister Mary Alphonse, Mt. St. Joseph, Augusta, Ga., to Mother Agnes Gonzaga, September 30, 1915, CSJA.
45. Sr. Agnes Gonzaga [CSJ], St. Joseph's Academy, St. Louis, Mo., to Mother Alphonse, SSJGA [Augusta, Ga.], October 5, 1915, CSJA.
46. Sr. Agnes Gonzaga, CSJ, St. Louis, Mo., to Mr. Wade, St. Louis St. Mercantile Company, October 5, 1915, CSJA.

acknowledged, however, that there were no other religious communities showing much enthusiasm for taking over the property. He also advised Mother Agnes to get not only the explicit approval, but also the cordial sympathy of the bishop of Savannah, as well as the sympathy and support of the local clergy and the unanimous support of the sisters themselves. Less than a month later, he informed Mother Agnes that the Sisters of St. Joseph in Augusta, "having definitely declared themselves as unwilling, under present circumstances, to affiliate with you; and furthermore, seeing no hope of such affiliation in the future, makes it impossible for you to take any further step, even if you are willing to assume the obligation incident to the affiliation." Her reply the next day was probably a reflection of her regret over the situation, but also of some relief, for she said that she would like to help the sisters of Georgia, but their debt was beyond their ability to help them, and besides that, giving them funds would be "like putting money down a hole."[47]

In March of 1916, Wade devised another solution for the Georgia Sisters of St. Joseph's problems. He proposed to Mother Agnes that the Carondelet Sisters of St. Joseph could buy the convent/school in Augusta, which had just been completed in 1914, for a mere $150,000. It was worth $250,410, but the company needed to dispose of it quickly. He offered terms of $25,000 down and $1,000 a month at 5 percent interest per annum. This, too, was turned down, and Wade wrote back,

We have made every possible effort to help the Sisters at Augusta, but unfortunately, neither they nor the bishop will accept the only kind of help we could give them.

As we are going to take a substantial loss on the building, and

47. Archbishop John J. Glennon, archbishop's house, St. Louis, to Rev. Mother Agnes Gonzaga, St. Joseph Academy, St. Louis, Mo., October 11, 1915; Archbishop John J. Glennon, St. Louis, to Rev. Mother Agnes Gonzaga, SSJ, Academy, St. Louis, November 15, 1915; Mother Agnes Gonzaga to Archbishop, Most Rev. J. J. Gilmore, D.D., St. Louis, Mo., November 16, 1915, CSJA.

as the poor Sisters are going to lose their all, I did not see why they should be otherwise embarrassed. I know their intentions are alright but they are badly advised, and their judgement is very poor.

There is a wonderful opportunity there for the establishment of a new school. I presume you are not aware that we have finally taken title of the property ourselves.[48]

In April 1916, the sisters in Augusta received notice from the Mercantile Company that their school and convent in Augusta had sixty days to pay their debt or they would have to move out, and gave them until May 30, 1916, to relocate.[49] The sisters had no idea what they were going to do.

Then, on April 29, 1916, the sisters' hope that "Our Lord would come to our relief," as recorded in their Annals after the failure of the Irish American Bank in 1913, was realized. Mrs. R. T. Semmes (also known as Katie Flannery Semmes), a former student of the sisters, came to their rescue when she "purchased and presented" to them a nearby estate, Chateau Le Vert, on Bellevue Avenue in Augusta for Mount St. Joseph Academy. She also bought and gave them the Sacred Heart Academy property in Sharon, thereby enabling the sisters to continue their tuition-funded schools. The practically new convent/school they had to give up was sold to a syndicate and converted into the Linwood Hotel. It was later bought by the federal government and became a hospital for World War I soldiers; the structure remains on its original site of the Charlie Norwood Uptown Veterans Hospital.[50]

The Sisters of St. Joseph of Georgia, who fought so hard to survive as an independent foundation of the Order of the Sisters of St. Joseph, finally resigned themselves to defeat. Sister

48. Festus Wade, St. Louis Mercantile Company, St. Louis, to Sister Agnes Gonzaga, St. Louis, March 16, 1916, CSJA.

49. SSJGA Annals, 4–5, CSJA.

50. "Chateau Le Vert Given to Sisters of St. Joseph," *Atlanta Constitution*, April 30, 1916, 5; SSJGA Annals, 4–5; Sr. Laura Ann Grady, CSJ, "A History of Mount St. Joseph," 5.

Aloysius at Mount St. Joseph, Augusta, wrote to the mother superior of the Carondelet sisters in St. Louis on May 30, 1919. By that time, though their financial matters were probably stabilized, they were in desperate need for more subjects [postulants] to carry on their ministries. She resurrected the question of possible affiliation with the Carondelet Sisters of St. Joseph.

A lack of subjects was nothing new to the sisters. The South was a difficult "field to plow" because it was so overwhelmingly Protestant, unlike the urban areas of the North. The sisters of Georgia had actually raised the question of affiliating with the Carondelet Sisters of St. Joseph themselves as early as May 21, 1912, exactly six months before the devastating fire in Washington. Sister Aloysius requested a copy of the Carondelet rule, as the one they had in Washington was the old French rule; she also asked for a copy of the book of customs. Sister Aloysius said they considered the Carondelet sisters to be "the fountain head" in America, and that, although the Lord was blessing them, they were poor and needed more subjects. The rule and book were sent. In her thank-you letter to the mother of the Carondelet house, Sister Aloysius said that the question of affiliation "has been spoken of in a general way many times and not in a serious manner." There would be pros and cons. She was fine with the idea, Bishop Keiley was asking about it, and even the pope was in favor or the idea.

Nothing came of the proposal, however, until the hope of the Sisters of St. Joseph of Georgia as a distinct foundation literally went up in blazes in November 21, 1912. The "fire" continued, sometimes raging and sometimes smoldering, until 1922, when the fifty-five remaining Georgia sisters voted nearly unanimously to affiliate. With the approval of Rome, on February 13, 1922, the Sisters of St. Joseph of Georgia ceased to exist and became the Sisters of St. Joseph of Carondelet, Augusta Province. The change that occurred that day was more than just a change in name. The Southern culture of the Georgia community was obliterated. As described by Msgr. Noel Burtenshaw, as the leadership transferred to the Northern sisters of Carondelet, "many of those superiors made it clear that the southern style religious life that had been developed over a 55-year period was now over. Many radical changes were ushered in and quickly adopted by the Georgia sisters, but their old community that had developed in Washington was missed for many years afterward.[51]

However, the Sisters of St. Joseph of Georgia did not just disappear. As the Carondelet Sisters of St. Joseph in the Augusta Province, the fifty-five women and their successors continued the remaining ministries begun before the 1922 affiliation with the Carondelet Sisters of St. Joseph based in Carondelet, Missouri:

> St. Joseph's Home (Orphanage), Washington, Ga. 1876–1967
> Sacred Heart Seminary (School for Boys), Sharon, Georgia, 1878–1946
> St. Joseph's Convent, Brunswick, 1900–1960
> Sacred Heart Convent, Atlanta, 1909–55
> Mount St. Joseph Academy (School for Girls), Augusta, Georgia, 1912–66
> Sacred Heart Parish School, Savannah, 1916–54
> St. Anthony's Parish School, Atlanta, 1918–57

Sister Eulalia Murray, who entered the Sisters of St. Joseph of Georgia in June 1913, was the last woman to enter religious life as a member of the order before it amalgamated with the Sisters of St. Joseph of Carondelet. She died on March 2, 1987.

51. Msgr. Noel C. Burtenshaw, "History SSJ of Georgia," 8.

Conclusion

⟿

The story of the Catholic sisters of St. Augustine, Florida, from the mid-nineteenth century through the first decades of the twentieth century is one of "firsts"—the first officially recognized convent school in Florida, the first Roman Catholic white order to minister to freedmen after the Civil War, and the first Catholic orphanage in Florida. Within the first six decades of their arrival in Florida, these pioneering women of the veil, Sisters of Mercy followed by Sisters of St. Joseph, laid the foundations for the ongoing presence of the Catholic Church in Florida and Georgia. This book tells their stories as they carried on their ministries to both blacks and whites and other "dear neighbors" who needed their help during a time of rapid change in the South.

The story of the Catholic women religious in Florida begins with the arrival of the Sisters of Mercy from Providence, Rhode Island, to St. Augustine in 1859. Coming from New England, they were accustomed to strong anti-Catholic sentiments. What they found, however, was an old town with Catholic roots and a people who accepted them. Their St. Mary's Academy for white girls was a highly regarded institution and instilled the ideals of domesticity that were common to both Catholics and Protestants. Rather than drawing young women away to convent life, as Protestants feared, they instilled in their students a sense of submissiveness and piety and taught them the drawing room skills expected of a lady in America. Yet, as Sister Elizabeth Kolmer, ASC, has pointed out, "These women were apparently oblivious to concepts of 'the Victorian lady' and 'the cult of domesticity.'"[1] The example of their own submissiveness sprang from the vow of obedience that they took when becoming women religious. The vow of obedience, along with the vows of chastity and poverty, were what defined women religious' lives for them and set them apart from all others. This vow was sometimes tested with the Sisters of Mercy and the Sisters of St. Joseph in Florida and in Georgia when dealing with their bishops, demonstrating the power that bishops held.

The Sisters of Mercy returned to the Ancient City after the Civil War and reopened St. Mary's Academy. They were there when the eight Sisters of St. Joseph arrived from Le Puy, France, in 1866 to teach newly freed slaves. The Sisters of Mercy provided much needed support for these French sisters, who could not speak English, were unaccustomed to the South, and were impoverished. Unlike the Sisters of Mercy, the St. Joseph Sisters' black students did not pay tuition. The support provided by the Sisters of Mercy and by other congregations to the French Sisters of St. Joseph throughout their journey to St. Augustine demonstrated the international network available to Catholic women religious around world. The Sisters of Mercy stayed in St. Augustine for only ten years, but their groundbreaking work in the Ancient City and the help they provided to the Sisters of St. Joseph was indispensable.

The Sisters of St. Joseph of St. Augustine quickly began the work of their mission and opened a school for black boys shortly after their arrival in the Ancient City. Unlike most women religious who went to Northern, urban parts of the United States to serve fellow immigrants from their native land, the first

1. Sr. Elizabeth Kolmer, ASC, "Catholic Women Religious and Women's History: A Survey of the Literature," in *The American Catholic Religious Life: Selected Historical Essays* (New York: Garland, 1988), 13.

Sisters of St. Joseph who came to St. Augustine came to the predominantly rural American South, where there were few Catholics. Their mission field was in a place entirely different from France, environmentally and culturally. Never before had they seen black people, the very ones they came to serve. The biggest obstacle, however, was not their initial lack of English-speaking skills or cultural differences, but the competition they faced from the Protestant missionaries of the American Missionary Association (AMA), who were already well established in St. Augustine and other Florida communities.

The letters that both the sisters and the AMA missionaries sent back to their respective superiors show that the rivals were really similar in their sincere desires to save black souls. In addition to that desire, however, many of the AMA missionaries were motivated by a sense of needing to atone for the United States' sin of supporting slavery and by the desire to instill good Yankee values, such as hard work and thrift, to turn the former slaves into good citizens. The Sisters of St. Joseph, on the other hand, were motivated by an understanding that their own salvation depended upon obedience to the call to convert others to the Roman Catholic faith. This explains why their emphasis was on Roman Catholic doctrine and piety rather than Bible study and why they felt so passionate in opposing the Protestant "heretics." They were motivated by religious beliefs rather than political or social concerns about blacks or the future of the United States. Their desires were not entirely self-serving, however, for their unvarnished letters reveal a passion for the "dear blacks." The ministry of the pioneer Sisters of St. Joseph of St. Augustine, the first Catholic order dedicated to ministering to the needs of the freedmen after the Civil War, was no token effort, but a heartfelt mission.[2]

2. Efforts among blacks by religious orders were sometimes very limited; see Margaret Susan Thompson, "Philemon's Dilemma: Nuns and the Black Community in Nineteenth-Century America; Some Findings," *Records of the American Catholic Historical*

The letters from both the sisters and the American Missionary Association allow a much fuller understanding of the competition between Catholics and Protestants as they vied for black souls after the Civil War. Heretofore, the Sisters of St. Joseph were the prime storytellers for their predecessors and only mentioned that the early sisters were resisted in their efforts. So, too, the many studies of the American Missionary Association only note that there was Catholic opposition, but do not provide any detail. Through the letters that the French Sisters of St. Joseph sent back to their motherhouse in Le Puy, France, and the letters and the reports that the AMA missionaries submitted to their head office in New York, we gain a more complete picture. The story of the missionaries, both Catholic and Protestant, shows the struggles and joys both sides encountered, only to see the freedmen elude them and establish their own denominations as many blacks rose to the challenge and opportunities of their newfound freedom to reject the paternalistic spiritual offerings of white churches.

In the late nineteenth and early twentieth centuries, the sisters' work among blacks, poor whites, and elite whites spread to other communities in Florida. By 1905, the sisters had ten foundations and schools, spreading from Fernandina to Ybor City to Miami, but most were in the northeast part of the state. The rivalry between the Protestants and Catholics was particularly intense during the Reconstruction Era. Reconstruction officially ended in 1876, but distrust between Catholics and Protestants remained. Florida's 1877 and 1888 yellow fever epidemics, though tragic, provided opportunities for the Sisters of St. Joseph of

---

Society of Philadelphia 96, no. 1–4 (March–December, 1986), 5. The work of the Ursulines in French colonial and antebellum New Orleans, as recounted by author Emily Clark, in *Masterless Mistresses*, strongly contrasts that of the Sisters of St. Joseph of St. Augustine. The Ursulines unabashedly embraced slavery, whereas the "peculiar institution" horrified the Sisters of St. Joseph. Like the Ursulines, however, they made no attempt to change American society other than to seek to enable blacks to be good American citizens and, hopefully, Catholic.

St. Augustine to minister to non-Catholics and gain good will, respect, and gratitude. Several sisters lost their own lives from the yellow jack. Under a government contract, the sisters also had the opportunity to instruct the Apaches who were held at Fort Marion in St. Augustine in 1887.

During this period, the Sisters of St. Joseph of Georgia was founded in Savannah; Bishop Gross moved the boys' orphanage to Washington, Georgia, in 1876. They built a girls' academy next door to the orphanage the next year, and a school for young boys soon followed in Sharon, Georgia. These institutions afforded the sisters in Florida and Georgia not only great opportunity to influence young Catholics, but also to impart Catholic ideals to other youth, for many of their students were Protestants. Through their students, the Sisters of St. Joseph were sometimes able to voice their views in ways they could not themselves. As historians Carol Coburn and Martha Smith point out, "Unlike white, Protestant women who honed their political skills and established a 'public voice' on social issues involving women and children, nuns did not. Limited ... by 'convent manners' that emphasized humility, obedience, selflessness, and public silence, nuns demonstrated their influence but rarely gave voice to it."[3] What the sisters could not do, alumnae from St. Joseph's Academy in St. Augustine, such as May Mann Jennings, perhaps the most politically powerful woman in nineteenth-century Florida, could do. Had May been Catholic, rather than Baptist, the way to the governor's mansion, by way of marriage to the governor, would have been closed to her. The Christian social values and skills that she learned at the academy, however, remained a part of her life and were channeled toward her statewide endeavors, thus enabling the sisters to have an indirect impact on the state. The extensive work of Sister Mary Ann among the poor and needy of Jacksonville also spoke loudly and won her the

3. Coburn and Smith, *Spirited Lives*, 222.

devotion of the residents and officials of the city of Jacksonville, who affectionately called her "Jacksonville's Angel of Mercy."

The last decade of the nineteenth century was a time of comfortable progress for the Sisters of St. Joseph in St. Augustine. Their schools and academies were well established and highly regarded, including the fine facility for the African Americans in St. Augustine: St. Cecelia's School, later known as St. Benedict the Moor. At an unexpected moment, a crushing blow came, not from Protestants, but from their own bishop. Formerly warm and supportive of the sisters' work, Bishop John Moore abruptly removed Mother Lazarus L'hostal, an act that stunned her, the sisters, and their superiors in France. Moore deposed her on the pretext that she had disobeyed a papal decree—ironically, one that was intended to protect sisters from superiors who abused their power. The episode coincided with the bishop's separation of the Sisters of St. Joseph from the motherhouse in Le Puy. This was even more devastating to the community and brought an end to the French mission; Irish sisters, instead of French ones, filled the places of leadership for decades to come.

As the new century progressed into its second decade, anti-Catholicism, heretofore so lacking in the antebellum South, suddenly struck the sisters. In response to complaints by some leading citizens, Florida's attorney general ruled that the sisters' employment as part of the public-school system, something that had been a part of several counties' education programs since 1878, was unconstitutional. As a result, the sisters withdrew from the public schools and the diocese began building a statewide parochial school system. Then, a rash of anti-Catholic legislation came out of the Florida legislature. A 1913 law making it illegal for whites to teach blacks in black schools was directed primarily at the Sisters of St. Joseph of St. Augustine. The work they had come to Florida to do and had carried on for fifty years was suddenly illegal. This book proposes that the 1916 arrest of the sisters who taught at St. Benedict the Moor School in St. Augustine was engineered by Bishop Michael J. Curley as a way to settle the constitutional questions attached to the 1913 law. The sisters were vindicated when, as Curley must have expected and hoped, the court ruled the law unconstitutional and inapplicable to private schools. It is tempting to consider the sisters' teaching of their black students contrary to the 1913 law as an act of civil disobedience on their part. This view, however, disregards the roles of bishops Kenny and Curley in directing the sisters' actions. The sisters' arrest is more rightly interpreted to be a result of their faithfulness to their vow of obedience to their superiors than an act of civil disobedience against their government.

The arrest of the three Sisters of St. Joseph was a major turning point for the sisters and the Catholic Church in Florida. The court's ruling cleared the way for the sisters to continue their ministry. The sisters' nearly simultaneous withdrawal from teaching in the public-school system alleviated the ambiguities of women religious teaching in a secular environment. There was, however, another consequence; it also removed them from regular contact with non-Catholics, thereby limiting their spheres of influence.

This change was in keeping with a new Code of Canon Law adopted by the Catholic Church in 1917–18. Earlier decrees in 1900 and 1901 had elevated the status of sisters who had ministries outside convents, placing them on a par with cloistered sisters. On the one hand, the change was a welcomed recognition of the sisters' work, but it brought with it serious consequences. The Vatican now imposed restrictive regulations and required detailed reports every five years. The result was that "innovation, risk taking, and responding to the contemporary needs of people, which were the trademarks of the sisterhoods prior to 1920, were discouraged in favor of rigidity, uniformity, regulation, and following 'the letter of the law.' The vow of obedience became the overriding concern."[4] As Amy Koehlinger clearly explains, because of their new status, the sisters' ministries were "restricted largely to established Catholic spheres—congregational schools and hospitals and diocesan parishes." The wide-ranging spheres of influence that they had enjoyed in the nineteenth century were now limited by the imposition of a "cloistered mentality" that distanced them from the world. The "convent culture" that resulted "dominated religious life for women from the 1920s through the 1950s."[5]

In Michael J. Curley, the Sisters of St. Joseph of St. Augustine had a bishop who was progressive in his thinking, and the new canon law's impact on them may have been less harsh than it was for other congregations. He promoted higher education for the sisters beyond the Teacher Training Institute they had established in 1890 and allowed some to attend the University of Florida or the Catholic University of America to earn advanced degrees. Such training enabled the sisters to maintain excellence in their schools, and the standards for education in general were elevated. Curley also urged stronger recruitment of new sisters from the United States, rather than depending so much on France and Ireland, and abandoned the European class distinction of lay and choir sisters. Sisters voted in their first presidential election in 1928, when Catholic Al Smith was a candidate, a sign of the Catholic Church's new place in mainstream American society.

The Florida Sisters of St. Joseph's teaching and other ministries continued and, indeed, expanded after 1920, with the addition of four hospitals, four homes (for the aged, unwed mothers, and two children's homes), and five special education centers. They established eighty-seven new foundations between 1911 and 1962. Even so, the impact of the new canon laws was

4. Coburn and Smith, *Spirited Lives*, 224.
5. Amy L. Koehlinger, *The New Nuns: Racial Justice and Religious Reform in the 1960s* (Cambridge, Mass.: Harvard University Press, 2007), 25.

evident. The new foundations, mostly new schools, were well within the sisters' normal sphere. Noticeably lacking were new schools for African Americans, represented only by St. Pius V School, which opened in Jacksonville in 1921, and Saint Augustine School, which opened in Miami in 1956–59, during the segregation era. The days of pioneering, risky ministries were over. The twentieth-century Sisters of St. Joseph of St. Augustine continued to build on the foundation laid by the eight French sisters from Le Puy, but now in much less controversial ways.

As women religious, the Sisters of St. Joseph, in Florida and in Georgia, assumed a life that was counter to the prevailing ideas concerning a woman's domestic responsibilities to marry and raise her own children, duties that were considered essential to maintain stability in society. It was their commitment to their vows and the rules of their orders and their devotion to a life of service that empowered them to become beloved and respected members of Florida's and Georgia's Catholic communities as they mentored rising generations of Southern black and white youth and helped the "dear neighbor." The effectiveness of their ministries was even recognized by Protestant women who "envied, resented, admired, and competed with nuns."[6] Catharine Beecher, who largely defined American ideas of domesticity, explained that her image of unified society "was a Protestant parallel to the Catholic pattern of close interaction between social and religious forms. Protestant women should have the same social support for their religious and moral activities as Catholic nuns received from their society" rather than being relegated to quiet lives at home.[7]

Mary J. Oates clearly shows how the Catholic sisters' freedom from the constraints of American domesticity allowed them to carry on wider works of mercy that other women,

6. Coburn and Smith, *Spirited Lives*, 222.

7. Kathryn Kish Sklar, *Catharine Beecher: A Study in American Domesticity* (New Haven, Conn.: Yale University Press, 1973), 171.

Protestant or Catholic, were unable to pursue. The sisters' ability to devote their entire lives to such service set them apart from their Protestant counterparts; few AMA teachers spent their lives serving the freedmen. In the American Catholic Church, most social welfare missions were performed by sisters, not the laity, for in the nineteenth century most Catholics were poor and unable to support institutions or ongoing ministries. The lay ministries that did exist, most notably the St. Vincent de Paul Society established in 1845, were nearly all run by men. Catholic laywomen, such as the "Ladies of the Roman Catholic Church" and "Daughters of Isabella," would, however, hold fundraisers, such as fairs, to support the sisters' work. The sisters were able to fulfill the Catholic principle that "the gift of personal service [not just the contribution of money] was an essential component of the definition of charity."[8] Reliance on the sisters' work with the poor and needy meant that lay Catholic women did not form the same kinds of social service groups that became the hallmark of Protestant benevolent efforts in the nineteenth century.

By the early twentieth century, the influence of Catholic women worldwide began to expand beyond the realm of church and home, even as women religious experienced tighter church control of their activities beginning in 1917. The 1910s saw the creation of numerous charitable lay groups, such as the National Conference of Catholic Charities, founded at the Catholic University of America in 1910; the League of Catholic Women, founded in 1911; the Catholic Women's Union, founded in 1916; and the National Council of Catholic Women, founded in 1920. Ironically, many of these women's groups were patterned after similar Protestant groups.

The story of the nuns in Florida and Georgia in the nineteenth and early twentieth centuries shows that the strong

8. Oates, *Catholic Philanthropic Tradition in America*, 10, 13, and 39. See also Deirdre M. Moloney, *American Catholic Lay Groups and Transatlantic Social Reform in the Progressive Era* (Chapel Hill: University of North Carolina, 2002).

anti-Catholicism associated with the North in the 1850s did not hold sway in the South during that period, though it flared up briefly in the 1910s. It also demonstrates the irony that these women, whose lives were restricted by their religious vows, particularly the vow of obedience, were at the same time, because of those restrictions, free to go to strange lands in ways that were "out of bounds" for most other women, as demonstrated by their successful establishment of black schools. Their teachings for white girls, however, were consistent with the prevailing values and prescribed behaviors for American women, as evidenced by the stories of the alumnae from St. Joseph's Academy in St. Augustine and at least one alumna of St. Joseph's Academy in Washington, Georgia. Writing for the booklet published for the fiftieth anniversary of the academy in 1901, Nellie T. Maguire,[9] who later became a local historian, hearkened back to the expectations for young women of the previous century: "The past days, whether of weal or woe, heartfelt thanksgiving is prayerfully given to God; that He bless the coming years and enable the sisters to so educate their girls to be models of true womanhood, this is their aim and prayer. They wish for their children lives of devoted Christians, that they be the stay and consolation of their parents, ever showing by word and example that they are convent girls, embodiments of noble, virtuous lives."[10] Women religious, supposedly rebellious and dangerous women, were actually part of the establishment, fulfilling the expectations of a white, male-dominated society.

Father Pierre Medaille, the Jesuit priest who assisted the first Sisters of St. Joseph in establishing their new congregation in 1650, defined their mission as "to practice all the holy spiritual and corporal works of mercy of which women are capable."[11]

9. Father Pablo Migone, "A Journey of Dedication through Education: Sisters of St. Joseph," *Labyrinthine Mind*, February 3, 2011, http://www.patheos.com/blogs/labmind/2011/02/a-journey-of-dedication-through-education-sisters-of-saint-joseph.html.
10. *Souvenir*, 7.
11. Vacher, Des *"régulières,"* 8, 788.

The early Sisters of St. Joseph of St. Augustine and of Georgia accomplished their mission admirably. They came from France to serve the newly freed slaves, but their ministries reached across the spectrum of humanity that they encountered: Catholic and Protestant, rich and poor, old and young, and yes, black and white. Placed against the background of the experiences of blacks, women, and Catholics in the South, the Sisters of St. Joseph enrich our understanding of life in Florida and Georgia from 1866 to the 1920s, during the eras of Reconstruction and Progressivism, and demonstrate that Catholics, though a minority in the South, played no small role in shaping aspects of Florida's and Georgia's history.

Appendix A

FOUNDATIONS OF THE SISTERS OF ST. JOSEPH OF ST. AUGUSTINE, 1866–1905

All schools and institutions were legally racially segregated during this period.

First Foundation, St. Augustine, 1866

1867	Free schools for blacks and for white boys
1869	Free school for white girls
1877	St. Joseph's Academy for white girls
1887	Teaching Apaches at Fort Marion
1889	St. Agnes School, North City, for whites
1898	St. Cecelia's School/St. Benedict the Moor for blacks
1916	Cathedral Parish School for whites

Second Foundation, Savannah, Georgia, 1867

1870	Transferred to the Diocese of Savannah

Third Foundation, Mandarin, 1874

1874	Free schools for blacks and for white boys and girls
1881	St. Joseph's Academy for young white boys
1916	St. Joseph's Parochial School for whites

Fourth Foundation, Jacksonville, 1868

1868	Free schools for blacks and for whites
1886	St. Mary's Home, orphanage for white girls

Locations of the Foundations and Institutes of the Sisters of
St. Joseph of St. Augustine and of Georgia.

1900   St. Joseph's Academy for white girls
1891   Immaculate Conception School for whites
1921   St. Pius School for blacks

Fifth Foundation, Fernandina, 1872

1872   Free schools for blacks and for whites
1874   St. Peter Claver School for blacks
1879   St. Joseph's Academy for white girls

Sixth Foundation, Palatka, 1876

1876   Day schools for blacks and for whites
1881   Academy of the Sacred Heart for white girls

Seventh Foundation, Elkton, 1882

1882   St. Ambrose School for white girls

Eighth Foundation, Orlando, 1889

1891   St. Joseph's Academy for white girls

Ninth Foundation, Ybor City, 1891

1892   St. Joseph's Academy for white girls
1903   St. Benedict the Moor School for blacks

Tenth Foundation, Miami, 1905

1905   St. Catherine Academy for white girls

Appendix B

WPA CHURCH RECORDS, STATE LIBRARY OF FLORIDA

Black churches established in Florida up to 1900. Some white churches are included as indicated.

Fernandina

1864   First Colored Baptist Church

1870   Macedonia African Methodist Episcopal (AME)

1870   New Zion Baptist Church

1885   Mt. Pleasant Baptist Church

1886   Mt. Calvary Baptist Church

1890   Ebenezer Baptist Church (First Colored Baptist Church)

Note: No black Roman Catholic Church, predominantly Baptist

Palatka

1858   St. Monica's Roman Catholic Church (white and black)

1866   Bethel AME

1869   Mt. Tabor First Baptist Church

1882   Payne's Chapel AME

1882   St. Mary's Episcopal (originally St. Philip's; changed name in 1907)

1886   Mt. Nebo Baptist Church

1889   Mt. Zion Primitive Baptist Church

1890   Mt. Vernon Presbyterian Church

Note: No black Roman Catholic Church

St. Augustine

1565 The Cathedral, Roman Catholic (white and black)

1763 Trinity Episcopal Church (white)

1824 Memorial Presbyterian Church (white)

1833 Bethel Methodist Episcopal Church. White and black members, but mostly "colored."

1845 First Methodist Episcopal Church, South, King and Riberia Streets (white)

1870 Trinity AME Church, on Bridge Street

1873 New St. Paul AME Church, 85 Central Avenue

1874 First Baptist Church, 81 St. Francis Street

1875 St. Mary's Baptist Church, 69 Washington Street

1876 Mather Perit Presbyterian Church

1881 Zion Baptist Church, 96 Evergreen Avenue

1886 North City Baptist Church, next to 15 Bernard Street

1888 St. Luke's AME Church, Evergreen Avenue

1891 St. Cyprian's Protestant Episcopal Church, corner of Lovit and Central Streets

1898 St. James Baptist Church, corner of W. King and Whitney Streets

1911 St. Benedict the Moor Catholic Church, first black Catholic church in Florida

Jacksonville (five in or near Mandarin, as noted)

1834 St. John's Episcopal Church (white)

1838 Bethel Baptist Church at corner of Pine (Main) and Union Streets. Name changed to Bethel Baptist Institutional Church when it was incorporated on November 16, 1894

1838 First Baptist Church (white)

1840 First Presbyterian Church (white, no mention of black members)

1847 Immaculate Conception Roman Catholic Church (white and black)

1858 First Baptist Church of Mandarin (black?)

1859 Mandarin Methodist Church (white?), Rt. 6, 2¼ mi. SE of Mandarin

1860 St. Joseph's Catholic Church, Loretto (Mandarin) (white and black)

1865 Midway AME Church, 1654 Van Buren (First AME in Florida)

1866 Mt. Zion AME Church, 201 E. Beaver Street

1868 Mt. Olive AME Church, Pippin and Franklin Streets

1868 St. Luke's Missionary Baptist Church, E. Church Street (from Bethel Baptist)

1870 Church of the Good Shepherd Episcopal (white)

1870 St. Paul AME Church, 201 Johnson Street

1871 Spring-Hill Baptist Church, Buckman Street (from Bethel Baptist)

1872 First Baptist Church of Oakland, 1137 Jessie Street

1872 St. Andrews Episcopal Church (white)

1873 Mt. Zion AME Church, on Route 6, U.S. Hwy 47 to Mandarin Street

1875 St. Stephen's Episcopal Church (white)

1875 Union Congregational Church, 236 W. Church Street

1877 St. John's Lutheran Evangelical Church, Laura and Ashley Streets (white)

1878 New Hope AME Church, Tyler Street

1878 Shiloh Metropolitan Missionary Baptist Church, Logan Street (from Bethel Baptist)

1878 St. John's Missionary Baptist Church, Albert Street (from Bethel Baptist)

1878 St. Paul Missionary Baptist Church, Stonewall Street

1879 Mt. Lilla Missionary Baptist Church, 638 W. 2nd Street

1880 Bethel Methodist Episcopal Church, 6 miles North of Mandarin Street

1880 Church of Our Savior Episcopal, in Mandarin Street (white)

1881 Church of Our Savior Episcopal (white)

1881 Harmony Missionary Baptist Church, Julia and State Streets

1882 Mt. Olive Primitive Baptist Church, Cleveland Street

1882 St. Philip's Protestant Episcopal Church (colored)

1883 First Christian Church, Church Street

1883 St. Philip's Episcopal (white)

1884 Day Spring Baptist Church, 1105 Jefferson Street

1884 Union Church, Lawton Street

1885 All Saints Episcopal Church (white)

1886 New Mt. Olive Missionary Baptist Church, Hart Avenue and Barnett Street

1886 Phillips Congregational Church, South Jacksonville

1887   Mt. Pleasant Missionary Baptist Church, Ashley and
        Van Buren Streets, renamed Pleasant Grove Primitive Baptist
        after 1902.
1888   St. Matthew Baptist Church, 28th Street
1888   White-Springs Baptist Church, Louisiana Street
1889   Asbury AME Church, 3208 Phyllis Street
1889   Central Baptist Church, 115 W. State Street
1889   Seventh Day Adventist Church, Jessie Street
1889   St. Joseph Methodist Episcopal (from Ebenezer Methodist
        Episcopal)
1889   St. Paul's Church, Jacksonville Beach
1890   Emmanuel Episcopal Church (white)
1891   Jacksonville Church of New Jerusalem
1891   Jacksonville Citadel (Salvation Army)
1892   Beulah Missionary Baptist Church, Ionia Street
1892   Mt. Calvary Baptist Church, Dora and Spruce Streets
1892   St. Stephens AME Church, 5th and Davis Streets
        (sponsored by New Hope AME)
1893   St. Mary's Chapel Episcopal (white)
1896   Springfield Advent Christian Church, 16th Street
1898   St. James AME Church, 2196 Forest Street
1899   Fellowship Missionary Baptist Church, Barnett Street
1899   Mt. Moriah AME Church, 101 Oak Street
1900   Mt. Moriah Baptist Church, Louisiana Street
1915   Holy Rosary Catholic Church, Laura Street and Cottage
        Avenue (sponsored by Immaculate Conception). Closed 1922?
1921   St. Paul's Roman Catholic, Park and Acosta Streets. Possibly
        should be St. Pius V.

BIBLIOGRAPHY

Primary Sources

Manuscript and Archival Collections

American Missionary Association Papers. Amistad Research Center, New Orleans, La.

Annals of the Sisters of St. Joseph of Georgia, 1867–1921. Archives of the Sisters of St. Joseph of Carondelet. St. Louis, Mo.

Bishop William H. Gross to Rev. Mother Louise Peckocheck, 1873–95. Maryland State Archives, Annapolis, Md.

Diocese of St. Augustine Papers. On microfilm. P. K. Yonge Library, University of Florida, Gainesville.

Drexel, M. M. Katharine, Convent, to Bishop William Kenny, Dioceses of St. Augustine. P. K. Yonge Library, Gainesville: University of Florida.

Drexel, Rev. Mother Katharine, to Bishop John Moore, Diocese of St. Augustine [1894–1903]. Archives of the Sisters of the Blessed Sacrament, Bensalem, Pa.

Florida State Board of Health. Yellow Fever Epidemic Incoming Correspondence. RG 894, Series 868. Florida State Archives, Tallahassee.

"Information on the Sisters of Mercy Who Were in St. Augustine Florida, (1859–1869)." Copy of this manuscript (301.2) pasted in the back of the Record Book, on file at the Archives of the Sisters of St. Joseph of St. Augustine, St. Augustine.

May Mann Jennings Papers. P. K. Yonge Library, University of Florida, Gainesville.

McEervey, Sister M. Aquin. "History of the 'Macon' Novitiate, Mount De Sales Academy." Typescript from the Archives of the Mother House, Bethesda, Maryland. On file at the Archives of the Sisters of St. Joseph of St. Augustine, St. Augustine, Fla.

"Mother McAuley Sisters of Mercy." Typescript. Sisters of Mercy Archives, Macon, Ga.

Notices Nécrologiques des Soeurs de St. Joseph de 1912 á 1942. Report from

Maison-Mère de la Congrégation de St-Joseph, Du Puy. Archives of the Sisters of St. Joseph, Le Puy, France.

Pascua Florida, 1889–1908. Archives of the Sisters of St. Augustine, St. Augustine.

Sisters of St. Joseph of St. Augustine. Correspondence [1865–1916]. Copies of original transcripts of letters at Sisters of St. Joseph Archives, Le Puy, France; some typed copies of letters at Archives of the Sisters of St. Joseph of St. Augustine, St. Augustine.

Sisters of St. Joseph of St. Augustine. Letterbooks [1865–1916]. Archives of the Sisters of St. Joseph, Le Puy, France.

Sisters of St. Joseph of St. Augustine. Records Srs. of St. Joseph, St. Augustine, 1866–1937. Archives of the Sisters of St. Joseph of St. Augustine, St. Augustine.

[Sister St. Andrew McLaughlin, SSJ, ed.]. "Jacksonville's Angel of Mercy: Sister Mary Ann and an Abridged Account of St. Mary's Home, Jacksonville, Florida. Unpublished manuscript, ca. 1940), unpaginated [5–9]. Photocopy of the original manuscript, which is housed in SSJSA, St. Augustine.

Typed Notes from the Archives of the Sisters of Mercy, Providence, R.I., no. 301.2, on file at the Archives of the Sisters of St. Joseph of St. Augustine, St. Augustine.

Typescripts of Historical Accounts of the Institutions of the Sisters of St. Joseph of Georgia, no. 501.9. Archives of the Sisters of St. Joseph of Carondelet, St. Louis, Mo.

Works Progress Administration. Survey of Church Records Manuscripts. 1935. State Library of Florida, Tallahassee.

Newspapers

American Missionary 50, no. 3 (March 1896).

Atlanta Constitution, April–May 1916.

Augusta Herald, 1912.

Freeman's Journal, May 17, 1873.

Jacksonville Florida Times-Union, July–December 1888; July 1914; March–May 1916.

Jacksonville Weekly Florida Union, September–December 1877.

St. Augustine Evening Record, 1913–17.

St. Augustine Examiner, 1859–69.

Savannah Morning News, 1868, 1870, 1872–73.

Tallahassee Daily Democrat, April–May 1915; May 18, 1916.

Tallahassee Semi-Weekly True Democrat, 1913.

Tampa Morning Tribune, May 31, 1913, April 1916.

Washington [Ga.] Gazette, 1877, 1912.

Washington [Ga.] Reporter, 1910.

Government Documents

Bush, George Gary. *History of Education in Florida.* Bureau of Education Circular of Information no. 7, 1888. Washington, D.C.: Government Printing Office, 1889.

Carroll, Henry K. *Report on the Statistics of Churches in the United States at the Eleventh Census: 1890.* Washington, D.C.: Government Printing Office, 1894.

General Acts and Resolutions Adopted by the Legislature of Florida at Its Regular Session 1913 under the Constitution of A.D. 1885. Tallahassee: T. J. Appleyard, 1913.

Jones, Thomas Jesse, ed. *Negro Education: A Study of the Private and Higher Schools for Colored People in the United States.* New York: Arno Press and the *New York Times*, 1969. Reprint of U.S. Office of Education Bulletin, 1916, no. 38, Government Printing Office, 1917.

Journal of the State House of Representatives of Florida. Tallahassee: T. J. Appleyard, 1913.

Journal of the State Senate of Florida. Tallahassee: T. J. Appleyard, 1913.

Kennedy, Joseph C. G. *Population of the United States in 1860: Compiled from the Original Returns of the Eighth Census.* Washington, D.C.: Government Printing Office, 1864.

Murray, R. D. "Treatment of Yellow Fever." In *Yellow Fever: Its Nature, Diagnosis, Treatment, and Prophylaxis, and Quarantine Regulations Relating Thereto, by Officers of the U.S. Marine Hospital Service.* Washington, D.C.: Government Printing Office, 1898. Reproduced in Yellow Fever Studies. New York: Arno Press, 1977.

Sheats, W. N. *Biennial Report of the Superintendent of Public Instruction.* 1895.

Sisters of St. Joseph. *Constitutions of the Congregations of the Sisters of St. Joseph.* New York: O'Shea, 1884.

U.S. Census. Miscellaneous Statistics, 1860.

U.S. Census. Population Schedules for St. Johns County, Florida, 1860.

U.S. Census. Population Schedule for Georgia, 1880 and 1900.

U.S. Census. Population Schedules for Providence County, Rhode Island, 1860.

Books and Reports

1911–1936 Silver Jubilee of the Church of St. Benedict the Moor, February 2nd, 1936. St. Augustine, 1936.

Adams, Charles S., ed. *Report of the Jacksonville Auxiliary Sanitary Association of Jacksonville, Florida, Covering the Work of the Association during the Yellow Fever Epidemic of 1888.* Jacksonville, 1889.

Barton, Clara. *The Red Cross in Peace and War.* Meriden, Conn.: American Historical Press, 1899.

Burritt, Elihu. *Jacksonville, Florida: Experiences in a Stricken City.* Jacksonville: Riverside, 1888.

Carroll, Sister Mary Theresa Austin, RSM. *Leaves from the Annals of the Sisters of Mercy in Four Volumes. Vol. 4, Containing Sketches of the Order in South America, Central America, and the United States: By a Member of the Order of Mercy.* New York: P. O'Shea, 1895.

Congrégation de Saint-Joseph Du Puy. *Religieuses Décédées, Depuis le mois de Janvier jusqu'au mois de Juillet 1889.* 1877 and 1888.

de Tocqueville, Alexis. *Democracy in America: The Complete and Unabridged Volumes I and II.* First published in 1835. Translated by Henry Reeve. New York: Bantam Dell, 2004.

Horsey, C. W., M.D. "Report of the Epidemic of Yellow Fever at Fernandina, Florida, August, September and October, 1877." *Proceedings of the Florida Medical Association, Session of 1878.* Jacksonville: Union Book and Job Rooms, 1878.

Ketcham, William. "Bureau of Catholic Indian Missions." In *The Catholic Encyclopedia.* Vol. 7. New York: Robert Appleton, 1910. Accessed Sept 11, 2021. http://www.newadvent.org/cathen/07745a.htm.

Kirsch, Johann Peter. "Council of Trent." In *The Catholic Encyclopedia.* Vol 15. New York: Robert Appleton, 1912. Accessed Sept 11, 2021. http://www.newadvent.org/cathen/15030c.htm.

Lanslots, D. I., OSB. *Handbook of Canon Law for Congregations of Women under Simple Vows.* 8th ed. New York and Cincinnati: Frederick, 1919.

Papi, Hector, SJ. *Religious Profession: A Commentary on a Chapter of the New Code of Canon Law.* New York: P. J. Kenedy and Sons, 1918.

Rypert, C. J. "Notes in the Saddle." *American Missionary* 41, no. 4 (1887). http://cdl.library.cornell.edu/cgi-bin/moa/moa-cgi?notisid=ABK5794-0041-69.

Saint-Jure, J.-B. *The Religious: A Treatise on the Vows and Virtues of the Religious State.* New York: P. O'Shea, 1882.

Sternburg, George M. *Report on the Etiology and Prevention of Yellow Fever.* Washington, D.C.: Government Printing Office, 1890. http://books.google.com/books?id=qZ-Od89oQyoC&printsec=titlepage&dq=Yellow+fever+suscep.

Veale, James. "Florida." In *The Catholic Encyclopedia.* Vol. 6. New York: Robert

Appleton, 1909. Accessed September 11, 2021. http://www.newadvent
.org/cathen/06115b.htm.

Vermeersch, Arthur. "Religious Profession." In *The Catholic Encyclopedia*.
Vol. 12. New York: Robert Appleton, 1911. Accessed September 9, 2021.
http://www.newadvent.org/cathen/12451b.htm.

Verot, A. The Right Rev. *A Tract for the Times: Slavery and Abolitionism,
Being the Substance of a Sermon Preached in the Church of St. Augustine,
Florida, on the 4th Day of January 1861, Day of Public Humiliation Fasting
and Prayer*. New ed. New Orleans: Printed at the "Catholic Propagator"
Office, 1861.

Watson's Magazine. Vol. 5 (1910).

Welsh, Herbert. *The Apache Prisoners in Fort Marion, St. Augustine, Florida*.
Philadelphia: Office of the Indian Rights Association, 1887.

Ye Heroes of Ye Epidemic by One of Ye Heroes T.O.B. Jacksonville: DaCosta,
1888.

"Yellow Fever: Description of the Plague at Fernandina: How the Priests and
Sisters Devoted Themselves to the Noble Work of Ministering to the
Stricken." Undated clipping from *Catholic Mirror* [1877].

Secondary Sources

Aleil, Pierre-Francois et al. *Haute-Loire*. Paris: Christine Bonneton, 2001.

Austin, Rachel A. "Negro Churches: Supplement to (W. W. Rice's article)."
Typescript of 11 leaves for the Federal Writers' Project. Bound with "Negro Churches," compiled by Alfred Farrell, field worker; John A. Simms,
editor [s.l.: s.n., 1936].

Bloom, Khaled J. *The Mississippi Valley's Great Yellow Fever Epidemic of 1878*.
Baton Rouge: Louisiana State University Press, 1993.

Boles, John B., ed. *Masters and Slaves in the House of the Lord: Race and
Religion in the American South, 1740–1870*. Lexington: University Press
of Kentucky, 1988.

Bowen, Eliza A. *The Story of Wilkes Co., Georgia: Collection of Articles by
Miss Eliza A. Bowen of Wilkes County Who Wrote Stories of Wilkes
County People and Published Her Articles in the Washington (Georgia)
Gazette and Chronicle from 1886–1897*. Marietta, Ga.: Continental,
1950.

Brewer, Eileen Mary. *Nuns and the Education of American Catholic Women,
1860–1920*. Chicago: Loyola University Press, 1987.

Brief History of the Churches of the Diocese of St. Augustine, Florida. Parts 2 and
6. Saint Leo, Fla.: Abbey Press, 1923.

BeVard, Mary Jane, ed. *One Faith, One Family: The Diocese of Savannah, 1850–2000*. Syracuse, N.Y.: Signature, 2000.

Buker, George E. "The Americanization of St. Augustine, 1821–1865." In *The Oldest City: St. Augustine, Saga of Survival*, edited by Jean Parker Waterbury, 151–79. St. Augustine: St. Augustine Historical Society, 1983.

Burtenshaw, Noel C. "History of the Sisters of St. Joseph of Georgia." *Southern Cross*, December 6, 1984, 6–8.

Burton, David H. *Clara Barton: In the Service of Humanity*. Westport, Conn.: Greenwood, 1995.

Byrne, Patricia, CSJ. "French Roots of a Women's Movement: The Sisters of St. Joseph, 1650–1836." Ph.D. diss., Boston College, 1985.

Clark, Emily. *Masterless Mistresses: The New Orleans Ursulines and the Development of a New World Society, 1727–1834*. Chapel Hill: University of North Carolina Press, 2007.

Coburn, Carol K., and Martha Smith. *Spirited Lives: How Nuns Shaped Catholic Culture and American Life, 1836–1920*. Chapel Hill: University of North Carolina Press, 1999.

Cochran, Thomas Everette. *Public School Education in Florida*. Lancaster, Pa.: New Era, 1921.

Colburn, David R. *Racial Change and Community Crisis: St. Augustine, Florida, 1877–1980*. New York: Columbia University Press, 1985.

Coleman, Very Reverend William V. *The Church in South Georgia*. Savannah: Catholic School System, Diocese of Savannah, 1967.

Cott, Nancy. *The Bonds of Womanhood: "Woman's Sphere" in New England, 1780–1835*. New Haven, Conn.: Yale University Press, 1977.

Curran, Robert Emmett. *Papist Devils: Catholics in British America, 1574–1783*. Washington, D.C.: The Catholic University of America Press, 2014.

Curry, J. L. M. *A Brief Sketch of George Peabody, and a History of The Peabody Education Fund Through Thirty Years* (1898). New York: Negro Universities Press, 1969.

Curtis, Sarah A. *Educating the Faithful: Religion, Schooling, and Society in Nineteenth Century France*. DeKalb: Northern Illinois University Press, 2000.

Cushman, Joseph D. *A Goodly Heritage: The Episcopal Church in Florida, 1821–1892*. Gainesville: University Press of Florida, 1965.

Davis, Cyprian, OSB. *The History of Black Catholics in the United States*. New York: Crossroad, 1991.

Davis, T. Frederick. *History of Jacksonville, Florida and Vicinity, 1513 to 1924*. A facsimile reproduction of the 1925 edition with Introduction by Richard A. Martin. Gainesville: University Press of Florida, 1964.

Deagan, Kathleen, and Darcie MacMahon. *Fort Mose: Colonial America's Black Fortress of Freedom*. Gainesville: University Press of Florida, 1995.

Dedication of Saint Joseph's Home, May 30, 1932, and Brief Sketch of St. Joseph's Male Orphanage, Washington, Wilkes County, Georgia. 1932.

De Sales, Francis. *Introduction to the Devout Life*. Translated and edited by John K. Ryan. New York: Image Doubleday, 1989.

Dolan, Jay P. *The American Catholic Experience*. New York: Doubleday, 1985.

Dolan, Josephine A. *Nursing in Society: A Historical Perspective*. Philadelphia: W. B. Saunders, 1978.

Dyer, Frederick N. *The Physicians' Crusade against Abortion*. Sagamore Beach, Mass.: Science History Publications, 2005.

Ellis, John H. *Yellow Fever and Public Health in the New South*. Lexington: University Press of Kentucky, 1992.

Jones-Wilson, Faustine C., et al. *Encyclopedia of African-American Education*. Westport, Conn.: Greenwood, 1996.

Ewens, Mary, OP. *The Role of the Nun in Nineteenth-Century America: Variations on the International Theme*. Thiensville, Wisc.: Caritas, 2014.

Fairlie, Margaret C. "The Yellow Fever Epidemic of 1888 in Jacksonville." *Florida Historical Quarterly* 19, no. 2 (October 1940): 95–108.

Farrelly, Maura Jane. *Papist Patriots: The Making of an American Catholic Identity*. Oxford: Oxford University Press, 2012.

Fialka, John J. *Sisters: Catholic Nuns and the Making of America*. New York: St. Martin's, 2003.

Flynt, Wayne. *Cracker Messiah: Governor Sidney J. Catts of Florida*. Baton Rouge: Louisiana State University Press, 1977.

Fox-Genovese, Elizabeth. *Within the Plantation Household: Black and White Women of the Old South*. Chapel Hill: University of North Carolina Press, 1988.

Francis, Mark R., CSV. "Liturgy and Popular Piety in a Historical Perspective." In *Directory on Popular Piety and the Liturgy: Principles and Guidelines, A Commentary*, edited by Peter C Phan, 39–43. Collegeville, Minn.: Liturgical Press, 2005.

Friedman, Jean. *The Enclosed Garden: Women and Community in the Evangelical South, 1830–1900*. Chapel Hill: The University of North Carolina Press, 1985.

Gallagher, Charles, Ph.D. *Cross and Crozier: The History of the Diocese of St. Augustine*. n.p.: Editions du Signe, 1999.

Gannon, Michael V. *Rebel Bishop: Augustin Verot, Florida's Civil War Prelate*. Milwaukee: Bruce, 1964.

———. *The Cross in the Sand: The Early Catholic Church in Florida, 1513–1870*. Gainesville: University Press of Florida, 1965.

Gillard, John T., SSJ. *The Catholic Church and the American Negro*. Baltimore: St. Joseph's Society Press, 1929.

Gillis, Chester. *Roman Catholicism in America*. New York: Columbia University Press, 1999.

Goldenburg, Gary. *Nurses of a Different Stripe: A History of the Columbia University School of Nursing, 1892–1992*. New York: Columbia University School of Nursing, 1992.

Grady, Sr. Laura Ann, CSJ. "A History of Mount St. Joseph." *Marianite* 12, no. 10 (October 2013): 4–6.

Graham, Thomas. *The Awakening of St. Augustine—The Anderson Family and the Oldest City: 1821–1924*. St. Augustine: St. Augustine Historical Society, 1978.

———. "The Flagler Era." In *The Oldest City: St. Augustine: Saga of Survival*, edited by Jean Parker Waterbury, 181–209. St. Augustine: St. Augustine Historical Society, 1983.

Grant, Mary A., and Thomas C. Hunt. *Catholic School Education in the United States: Development and Current Concerns*. New York: Garland, 1992.

Graveline, Noël. *Le Puy-en-Velay: Excitement, Colours and Fun*. Beaumont, France: Editions Debaisieux, 2003.

Greenberg, Mark I., William Warren Rogers, and Canter Brown Jr., eds. *Florida's Heritage of Diversity: Essays in Honor of Samuel Proctor*. Tallahassee: Sentry, 1997.

Harris, Harry L., and John T. Hilton, eds. *A History of the Second Regiment, N.G.N.J., Second N.J. Volunteers (Spanish War), Fifth New Jersey Infantry, Together with a Short Review Covering Early Military Life in the State of New Jersey*. Patterson, N.J.: Call Printing and Publishing, 1908.

Harvey, Karen. *St. Augustine and St. Johns County: A Pictorial History*. Virginia Beach, Va.: Donning, 1980.

Healy, Kathleen, RSM, ed. *Sisters of Mercy: Spirituality in America 1843–1900*. New York and Mahwah, N.J.: Paulist Press, 1992.

Higham, John. *Strangers in the Land: Patterns in American Nativism, 1860–1925*. Westport, Conn.: Greenwood, 1981. Originally published by Trustees of Rutgers College in New Jersey, 1955.

Hill, Samuel S., ed. *Encyclopedia of Religion in the South*. Paperback ed. Macon, Ga.: Mercer University Press, 1997.

Hine, Darlene Clark. *Black Women in White: Racial Conflict and Cooperation in the Nursing Profession, 1890–1950*. Bloomington and Indianapolis: Indiana University Press, 1989.

Huggins, Nathan Irvin. *Protestants against Poverty: Boston's Charities 1870–1900*. Westport, Conn.: Greenwood, 1971.

Humphreys, Margaret. *Yellow Fever and the South*. New Brunswick, N.J.: Rutgers University Press, 1992.

Jedin, Hubert. "Council of Trent." In *New Catholic Encyclopedia*. Vol. XIV. New York: McGraw-Hill, 1967.

Jenkins, Sally. *The Real All Americans: The Team That Changed a Game, a People, a Nation*. New York: Doubleday, 2007.

Johnston, Sidney P. "Florida's Historic Black Public Schools": Multiple Property Submission prepared for the Florida Division of Historical Resources, 2003.

Jones, Jacqueline. *Soldiers of Light and Love: Northern Teachers and Georgia Blacks, 1865–1873*. Chapel Hill: University of North Carolina Press, 1980.

Joseph, Brother Paul. "Institute of the Brothers of the Christian Schools." *Catholic Encyclopedia*. Vol. 8. New York: Robert Appleton, 1910. Accessed April 23, 2022. http://www.newadvent.org/cathen/08056a.htm.

Kauffman, Christopher J. *Ministry and Meaning: A Religious History of Catholic Health Care in the United States*. New York: Crossroad, 1995.

Keuchel, Edward F. "Sister Mary Ann: 'Jacksonville's Angel of Mercy.'" In *Florida's Heritage of Diversity: Essays in Honor of Samuel Proctor*, edited by Mark I. Greenberg, William Warren Rogers, and Canter Brown Jr., 99–111. Tallahassee: Sentry, 1997.

Kinzer, Donald L. *An Episode in Anti-Catholicism: The American Protective Association*. Seattle: University of Washington Press, 1964.

Koehlinger, Amy L. *The New Nuns: Racial Justice and Religious Reform in the 1960s*. Cambridge, Mass.: Harvard University Press, 2007.

Kolmer, Sr. Elizabeth, ASC. "Catholic Women Religious and Women's History: A Survey of the Literature." In *The American Catholic Religious Life: Selected Historical Essays*, edited by Joseph M. White, 1–13. New York: Garland, 1988.

Kuhns, Elizabeth. *The Habit: A History of the Clothing of Catholic Nuns*. New York: Doubleday, 2003.

A Little Sketch of the Work of the Sisters of Mercy in Providence, Rhode Island, from 1851 to 1893. Providence: J. A. and R. A. Reid, Printers, 1893.

"Letters from St. Augustine." *The Ancient City Genealogist*. St. Augustine Genealogical Society, St. Johns County, Florida, 4, no. 1 (April 1993): 11.

Libster, Martha M. *Herbal Diplomats: The Contribution of Early American Nurses (1830–1860) to Nineteenth-Century Health Care Reform and the*

Botanical Medical Movement. Wauwatosa, Wisc.: Golden Apple Healing Arts, 2004.

Lucian, Justin, FSC, compiler of notes. "The Brothers of the Christian Schools in St. Augustine, Florida, 1859–1863." Memphis, Tenn.: Christian Brothers University. For Private Circulation, 2003. Held by the Florida Collection, State Library of Florida, Tallahassee.

Maguire, Nellie T. "Catholicity in Washington, Georgia: The Beginning and Progress of Catholicity in Washington, Wilkes Co., Georgia." *American Catholic Historic Researches* 11, no. 1 (January 1894): 17–28.

Maher, Sister Mary Denis, CSA. *To Bind Up the Wounds: Catholic Sister Nurses in the U.S. Civil War*. Baton Rouge: Louisiana State University Press, 1989.

Mannard, Joseph G. "Maternity ... of the Spirit: Nuns and Domesticity in Antebellum America." In *The American Catholic Religious Life: Selected Historical Essays*, edited by Joseph M. White, 129–48. New York: Garland, 1988.

Martin, Richard A. *The City Makers*. Jacksonville: Convention Press, 1972.

Mary Alberta, Sister, SSJ. "A Study of the Schools Conducted by the Sisters of St. Joseph of the Diocese of St. Augustine, Florida, 1866–1940." Master's thesis, University of Florida, 1940.

Mattick, Barbara E. "Ministries in Black and White: The Catholic Nuns of St. Augustine, 1859–1869." In *"Lives Full of Struggle and Triumph": Southern Women, Their Institutions, and Their Communities*, edited by Bruce L. Clayton and John A. Salmond, 109–25. Gainesville: University Press of Florida, 2003.

Mazzonis, Querciolo. *Spirituality, Gender, and the Self in Renaissance Italy: Angela Merici and the Company of St. Ursula (1474–1540)*. Washington, D.C.: The Catholic University of America Press, 2007.

McCarron, Dennis Michael. "Catholic Schools in Florida, 1866–1992." Ph.D. diss., Florida State University, 1993.

McCarthy, Thomas P., CVS. *Guide to the Catholic Sisterhoods in the United States*. Washington, D.C.: The Catholic University of America Press, 1952.

McDannell, Colleen. *The Christian Home in Victorian American, 1840–1900*. Bloomington: Indiana University Press, 1986.

McGoldrick, Sister Thomas Joseph, SSJ. "The Contributions of the Sisters of St. Joseph of St. Augustine to Education, 1866–1960." Master's thesis, University of Florida, 1961.

———. *Beyond the Call: The Legacy of the Sisters of St. Joseph of St. Augustine, Florida*. n.p.: Xlibris, copyright held by the author, 2008.

McLaughlin, Sister St. Andrew, SSJ, ed. "Jacksonville's Angel of Mercy: Sister Mary Ann and an Abridged Account of St. Mary's Home, Jacksonville, Florida." Unpublished manuscript, c. 1940, unpaginated [5–9], photocopy of original manuscript housed in the Archives of the Sisters of St. Joseph of St. Augustine.

McNally, Michael J. *Catholic Parish Life on Florida's West Coast, 1860–1968*. St. Petersburg: Catholic Media Ministries, 1996.

Merritt, Webster. *A Century of Medicine in Jacksonville and Duval County*. Gainesville: University Press of Florida, 1949.

Mickler, Sister Julia, SSJ. *Sheaves Gathered from the Missionary Fields of the Sisters of St. Joseph in Florida, 1866–1936*. St. Augustine: Diocese of St. Augustine, 1936.

Migone, Father Pablo. "A Journey of Dedication through Education: Sisters of St. Joseph." *Labyrinthine Mind*, February 3, 2011. http://www.patheos .com/blogs/labmind/2011/02/a-journey-of-dedication-through-education-sisters-of-saint-joseph.html.

Miller, Barbara Elizabeth. "Tallahassee and the 1841 Yellow Fever Epidemic." Unpublished master's thesis, Florida State University, 1976.

Miller, Randall M. "A Church in Cultural Captivity: Some Speculations on Catholic Identity in the Old South." In *Catholics in the Old South: Essays on Church and Culture*, edited by Randall M. Miller and Jon L. Wakelyn, 11–52. Macon, Ga.: Mercer University Press, 1983.

Miller, Randall M., and Jon L. Wakelyn, eds. *Catholics in the Old South: Essays on Church and Culture*. Macon, Ga.: Mercer University Press, 1983.

Moloney, Deirdre M. *American Catholic Lay Groups and Transatlantic Social Reform in the Progressive Era*. Chapel Hill: University of North Carolina Press, 2002.

Mormino, Gary R., and George E. Pozzetta. *The Immigrant World of Ybor City: Italians and Their Latin Neighbors in Tampa, 1885–1985*. Urbana: University of Illinois Press, 1987.

Morrow, Diane Batts. *Persons of Color and Religious at the Same Time: The Oblate Sisters of Providence, 1828–1860*. Chapel Hill: University of North Carolina Press, 2002.

Muldrey, Sister Mary Hermenia, RSM. *Abounding in Mercy: Mother Austin Carroll*. New Orleans: Habersham, 1988.

Murphy, Miriam T. "Catholic Missionary Work among the Colored People of the United States, 1776–1866." *Records of the American Catholic Historical Society* 35, no. 2 (June 1924): 101–36.

National Register of Historic Places. Washington Historic District, Washington, Wilkes County, Ga., Reference no. 04001319.

Newton, Michael. *The Invisible Empire: The Ku Klux Klan in Florida*. Gainesville: University Press of Florida, 2001.

Nordstrom, Justin. *Danger on the Doorstep: Anti-Catholicism and American Print Culture in the Progressive Era*. Notre Dame, Ind.: University of Notre Dame Press, 2006.

Oates, Mary J. *The Catholic Philanthropic Tradition in America*. Bloomington: Indiana University Press, 1995.

O'Brien, David. *Public Catholicism*. New York: Macmillan, 1989.

Ochs, Stephen J. *Desegregating the Altar: Josephites and the Struggle for Black Priests, 1871–1960*. Baton Rouge: Louisiana State University Press, 1990.

O'Connor, Sister Mary Loretto, RSM, AM. *Merry Marks the Century*. Providence: Sisters of Mercy, 1951.

Page, David P. "Bishop Michael J. Curley and Anti-Catholic Nativism in Florida." *Florida Historical Quarterly* 45, no. 2 (October 1966): 100–117.

Paul, Brother Joseph. "Institute of the Brothers of the Christian Schools. In *The Catholic Encyclopedia*, vol. 8. New York: Robert Appleton, 1910. Accessed April 23, 2022. http://www.newadvent.org/cathen/08056a.htm.

Phan, Peter C., ed. *Directory of Popular Piety and the Liturgy, Principles and Guidelines: A Commentary*. Collegeville, Minn.: Liturgical Press, 2005.

Pond, William L. "This Is Yellow Fever." *Journal of the Florida Medical Association* 8 (August 1971): 48–50.

Pryor, Elizabeth Brown. *Clara Barton: Professional Angel*. Philadelphia: University of Pennsylvania Press, 1987.

Quinn, Jane. *The Story of a Nun: Jeanie Gordon Brown*. St. Augustine: Villa Flora Press, Sisters of St. Joseph, 1978.

———. "Nuns in Ybor City: The Sisters of St. Joseph and the Immigrant Community." *Tampa Bay History* 5, no. 1 (Spring/Summer 1983): 24–41.

Rackleff, Robert B. "Anti-Catholicism and the Florida Legislature, 1911–1919." *Florida Historical Quarterly* 50, no. 4 (1971): 352–65.

Rapley, Elizabeth. *The Dévotes: Women and Church in Seventeenth-Century France*. Montreal and Kingston: McGill-Queen's University Press, 1993.

Richardson, Joe M. *The Negro in the Reconstruction of Florida, 1865–1877*. Florida State University Studies 46. Tallahassee: Florida State University, 1965.

———. "'We Are Truly Doing Missionary Work': Letters from American Missionary Association Teachers in Florida, 1864–1874." *Florida Historical Quarterly* 54, no. 2 (October 1975): 178–95.

———. *Christian Reconstruction: The American Missionary Association and Southern Black, 1861–1890*. Athens: University of Georgia Press, 1986.

Rivers, Larry Eugene, and Canter Brown Jr. *Laborers in the Vineyard of the Lord: The Beginnings of the AME Church in Florida, 1865–1895.* Gainesville: University Press of Florida Press, 2001.

Schroeder, H. J., OP. "Canons Concerning Justification." In *Canons and Decrees of the Council of Trent,* 42–46. Rockford, Ill.: TAN, 1978.

Seventy-Five Years in the Passing with the Sisters of Mercy, Providence, Rhode Island, 1851–1926. Providence: Providence Visitor Press, 1926.

Shofner, Jerrell. *Nor Is It Over Yet: Florida in the Era of Reconstruction.* Gainesville: University Press of Florida, 1974.

The Sisters of Saint Joseph of Saint Augustine, Florida: Our First One Hundred Years, 1866–1966. St. Augustine: Sisters of St. Joseph, 2000.

"Sisters of Mercy in Macon." *The Bulletin of the Catholic Laymen's Association of Georgia,* December 12, 1925, 5.

Skeabeck, Rev. Andrew, CSSR. "Most Rev. William Gross: Missionary Bishop of the South; Georgia and Its Fifth Bishop, 1873–1875." *Records of the American Catholic Historical Society of Philadelphia* 66 (1956): 78–94.

Sklar, Kathryn Kish. *Catharine Beecher: A Study in American Domesticity.* New Haven, Conn.: Yale University Press, 1973.

Souvenir of the Silver Jubilee, 1876–1901. Washington, Ga.: St. Joseph's Academy, 1901. Held at the Mary Willis Library, Washington, Ga., 1901.

Straight, William M. "The Yellow Jack." *Journal of the Florida Medical Association* 8 (August 1971): 31–47.

Taves, Ann. *The Household of Faith: Roman Catholic Devotions in Mid-Nineteenth-Century America.* Notre Dame, Ind.: University of Notre Dame Press, 1986.

Thompson, Margaret Susan. "Philemon's Dilemma: Nuns and the Black Community in Nineteenth-Century America; Some Findings." *Records of the American Catholic Historical Society of Philadelphia* 96, no. 1–4 (March–December 1986): 3–18.

Vacher, Marguerite. *Des "régulières" dans le siècle: Les soeurs de Saint-Joseph du Père Médaille aux XVII et XVIII siècles.* Clermont-Ferrand, France: Soeurs de Saint-Joseph de Clermont-Ferrand et Éditions Adosa, 1991.

Van Balen Holt, Mary. *Meet Katharine Drexel: Heiress and God's Servant of the Oppressed.* Ann Arbor, Mich.: Charis, Servant Publications, 2002.

Vance, Linda D. *May Mann Jennings: Florida's Genteel Activist.* Gainesville: University Press of Florida, 1985.

Vicchio, Stephen J., and Sister Virginia Geiger, eds. *Perspectives on the American Catholic Church, 1789–1989.* Westminster, Md.: Christian Classics, 1989.

Welsh, Herbert. *Apache Prisoners in Fort Marion, St. Augustine, Florida*. Philadelphia: Office of the Indian Rights Association, 1887.

Welter, Barbara. "The Cult of True Womanhood, 1820–1860." *American Quarterly* 18 (Summer 1966): 151–74.

White, Joseph M., ed. *The American Catholic Religious Life: Selected Historical Essays*. New York: Garland, 1988.

Willingham, Robert Marion. *Washington, Georgia*. Charleston, S.C.: Arcadia, 2000.

Wilson, Gil. "Letters from St. Augustine." *Ancient City Genealogist*. St. Augustine Genealogical Society, St. Johns County, 4, no. 1 (April 1993): 11–12.

Woodward, C. Van. *Tom Watson: Agrarian Rebel*. 2nd ed. Savannah: Beehive, 1973. Originally published in 1938.

INDEX

active women's religious orders, origins.
See Compagnie de Notre Dame,
Filles de Notre Dame; Compagnie
de Sainte-Ursule (Ursulines);
Daughters of Charity; Sisters of
Mercy; Sisters of St. Joseph; Visitan-
tines (Visitation sisters)

African Methodist Episcopal (AME)
Church. See black denominations

American Missionary Association
(AMA), anti-Catholicism, 77;
establishment of, 71–72; comments
about freed slaves, 83; comments
about poor whites, 83; decline, 84;
Florida and Georgia, work in, 71;
goal of, 72; motivation to teach freed
blacks, 82, 237; rivalry with Catholics,
238; teaching methodology of, 80. See
also Chapter 3, "The Competition for
Black Minds and Souls"

AMA missionary teachers, Auld, 75,
80; Beale, 75; Eveleth, 75, 83; Greely,
72–75; Jocelyn, 74, 75; Wilder, 77;
Williams, 75–76

American Protective Association, 165

American Revolution, Catholic
support for, 10–11; See also Carroll,
Bishop John

"Ancient City." See St. Augustine

anti-Catholicism, generally, 12, 18–19;
presence in colonial America, 164;
in the South, 164, 166–67, 212.
See also Progressive-era war
against Romanism; Chapter 7,
"Politics of Anti-Catholicism and
Racism"

anti-clericalism in France and Ybor City,
Fla., 62–63; 158

anti-Protestant Catholics in St. Augustine, 77, 87–88

Apaches housed as prisoners of war at
Ft. Marion in St. Augustine, 123–28

Arsac, Sister Julie Clotilde (SSJSA),
about suffering, 48; death, 48; founding member SSJSA, 36, 48

Barry, Bishop John (second bishop of the
Diocese of Savannah and portion
of Florida), death, established Barry
male orphan asylum, 194

Barry Male Orphan Asylum, Savannah,
Ga. See St. Joseph's Boys' Orphanage

Barton, Clara. See nurses

Becker, Bishop Thomas (sixth bishop of
Savannah), 220

bishops' authority, 142, 159. See also Cur-
ley, Bishop Michael J.; Gross, Bishop
William; Moore, Bishop John;
Persico, Bishop Ignatius

Black Catholic Congress, 94

black Catholics in St. Augustine, 17, 46,
49, 74, 75, 88, 90–95. See also St. Benedict the Moor Catholic Church

black denominations, generally, 86–90;
SSJSA and AMA discouragement
over growth of black churches, 83–84,
89–90

black women's religious orders, 98–99

Blaine amendment (Article XII, Section
13, Florida state constitution), 165;
citizens' complaint of violation thereof, 171–73, 177–78. See also parochial
school system; "Savannah plan"

Borie, Sister St. Pierre (St. Peter)
(SSJSA, SSJGA), comments about
black children, 47; death, 222;

269

Borie, Sister St. Pierre (*cont.*)
director of orphanage in 1880,
216; founding member SSJSA, 36;
replaced Sister Marie Joseph in
Savannah, 196, 202; superior pro-
tem SSJGA, 209; transferred to
St. Joseph's Academy for Young
Ladies, Washington, Ga., 222–23;
work with orphans, 202–4
brides of Christ. *See* Catholic sisters
Brothers of the Christian Schools (FSC),
arrival in St. Augustine, 23; Civil War
and end of work in St. Augustine,
29fn35; history, 23; recruited by
Verot, 18
Brown, Jeanie Gordon. *See* Brown, Sister
Theresa Joseph
Brown, Sister Theresa Joseph (SSJSA),
133–34
Bureau of Catholic Indian Missions,
125–26

Carroll, Bishop John, American Revolution, role in, 10–11; first Catholic
bishop in America, 11, 193
Catholic Church, emphasis on membership, 9; outlawed by most American
colonies, 10; popular piety, 8–9;
power of liturgy, 70
Catholic lay groups, 244
Catholic schools public funding.
See Blaine amendment
Catholic sisters, brides of Christ, 3,
130–31; development of, 2–6; employment of in public schools, 169;
requirements to become, 12. *See also*
Council of Trent; names of specific
orders
Catholic teaching, enculturation of young
girls, 14–15; goals, 32–33
Chateau Le Vert, Augusta, Ga. *See*
St. Joseph's Academy for Young Girls
Code of canon law, 1917–18 revisions,
241–43
Colored Auxiliary Bureau (CAB). *See*

yellow fever, Jacksonville epidemic
of 1888
Columbus, Ga., during Civil War, 29–30;
Sisters of Mercy's escape to, 29
Compagnie de Notre-Dame (Filles de
Notre-Dame), 4, 14fn22
Compagnie de Sainte-Ursule (Ursuline),
5, 10, 13fn20, 18, 238
comparison of Protestant and Catholic
missionaries, 9–10, 35, 62–63, 69,
76–77, 79–84. *See also* Chapter 3,
"The Competition for Black Souls
and Minds"
convent schools. *See* academies, by name
Cortial, Marie Joseph (SSJSA), death
and funeral, 48–49; founding member of SSJSA, 36, 41
Council of Trent, clarified Catholic
doctrine, 3–4; established official
pietistic practices, 8–9; prohibited
forced professions, 14–15
Counter-Reformation. *See* Council of
Trent
Curley, Bishop Michael J. (fourth bishop
of St. Augustine), appointed archbishop of Baltimore, 191; biographical
sketch, 182; death, 191; progressive
policies of, 242; stands against Florida's anti-Catholic legislation, 190–91;
succeeded Bishop Kenny, 93–95, 182
curricula, of AMA, 80; of Christian
Brothers, 24; of Sisters of Mercy,
21–22, 31; of Sisters of St. Joseph
of St. Augustine, 46–47, 60, 61, 65,
79–80, 126, 136, 144, 235–36, 245

Daughters of Charity, 6
Deleage, Sister Joséphine (SSJSA), death
in France, 155; described Savannah,
195–96; founding member SSJSA,
36; interactions with Mercy sisters,
41; resigned from SSJGA, and returned to St. Augustine, and Le Puy
in 1874, 57; returned to St. Augustine
in 1877, 58, 209; return to Le Puy

Teaching in Black and White: The Sisters of St. Joseph in the American South was designed in Jensen, with Gloucester and Alternate Gothic display type, and composed by Kachergis Book Design of Pittsboro, North Carolina. It was printed on 55-pound Natural Offset and bound by Maple Press of York, Pennsylvania.